The Life and Legend of a Rebel Leader: Wat Tyler

Dedicated to

Sandra Reston

She pushed me to study history, and without her efforts
this book would not have been published.

*   *   *

Now to the purpose – I am He,
Who not for fame competed,
But would have seen my country free
And have her foes defeated:
Mine was a deed the good desired,
The shackled chain was round us;
We rose at once like men inspired,
And burst the links that bound us!

Charles Cole, *The Spirit of Wat Tyler* (1848)

The Life and Legend of a Rebel Leader:
Wat Tyler

Stephen Basdeo

PEN & SWORD
HISTORY

First published in Great Britain in 2018 by
PEN AND SWORD HISTORY
an imprint of
Pen and Sword Books Ltd
47 Church Street
Barnsley
South Yorkshire S70 2AS

ISBN 978 1 52670 979 0

Printed and bound in Great Britain
by TJ International Ltd, Padstow, Cornwall

Typeset in Times New Roman by
CHIC GRAPHICS

Pen & Sword Books Ltd incorporates the imprints of Pen & Sword
Archaeology, Atlas, Aviation, Battleground, Discovery,
Family History, History, Maritime, Military, Naval, Politics, Railways,
Select, Social History, Transport, True Crime, Claymore Press,
Frontline Books, Leo Cooper, Praetorian Press, Remember When,
Seaforth Publishing and Wharncliffe.

For a complete list of Pen and Sword titles please contact
Pen and Sword Books Limited
47 Church Street, Barnsley, South Yorkshire, S70 2AS, England
E-mail: enquiries@pen-and-sword.co.uk
Website: www.pen-and-sword.co.uk

Contents

List of Illustrations

LIST OF ILLUSTRATIONS

Preface

I feel that I should point out, at the very beginning, that this book is not a book about medieval history. There is medieval history in this book, as this work covers the historical events of the so-called 'Peasants' Revolt' of 1381 in the first chapter. But what interests me in this work, rather, is the way that Wat Tyler and the events of the revolt have been reimagined and represented by various authors in subsequent ages. I am interested in his legend. That term is, indeed, the correct term by which we should describe the man, especially if we take it in the way that it is listed in *The Oxford English Dictionary*: 'an extremely famous or notorious person'.[1] Tyler's actions during the revolt certainly made him famous, or notorious, according to those on the side of the establishment. His fame was then kept alive by artists and writers in successive ages. His name could inspire people, such as the Chartists, or it could horrify them. The present study, then, is a work of cultural history which provides a narrative overview of the life, and of the subsequent post-medieval legend of Wat Tyler, the leader of the rebellion, between 1381 and c.1900.

Furthermore, in examining the stories that were written about Wat Tyler in subsequent eras, it is not the intention here to judge whether these writers were historically accurate in their depiction of the rebellion. As we will see, later authors, especially during the early modern period, were rarely concerned with presenting a 'true' picture of the past (assuming any writer, at any period of history, could ever achieve such a thing as historical accuracy). Instead, this book concerns itself with asking what the history of Wat Tyler meant to people who were writing about him hundreds of years after his death. Thus, questions such as the following will be answered: why did the visionary revolutionary thinker, Thomas Paine (1737-1809), invoke Tyler's name in the eighteenth century? Why was he so important to the Chartists during the 1840s? Through studying how Wat Tyler has been represented throughout the ages, we can learn, not only about the medieval period, but also about the early modern period, and the eighteenth and nineteenth centuries.

The first chapter is a concise narrative of the Great Revolt of 1381, one of the most important events in English history. It is a time when people from relatively low stations in life became aware of their own power and importance. Many factors contributed to the outbreak of the revolt. One of them was disease, the Black Death which decimated the population of Europe in the mid-fourteenth century. As tragic as the events of the Black Death must have been for many people, the labouring class of medieval England could, as a result of the decimation of the population, demand more money for their work. The government sought to put a stop to this through the Statute of Labourers (1351), a measure which stoked resentment of the lower orders. Additionally, war with France was eating into the nation's funds, and the people were hit with three poll taxes, in 1377, 1379, and 1380. The final poll tax was the straw that broke the camel's back. Bearing a number of grievances, and fired by the preaching of John Ball, the radical priest, they marched on London to demand redress. They elected Wat Tyler as their leader, who some sources say was a veteran of the Hundred Years War. Wat Tyler's personal motivations for joining in the rebellion are not known, indeed there is much that remains unknown about his life. One of the chronicles, written some time after the rebellion, says that a tax collector visited his home and demanded payment for his daughter. Tyler informed the tax collector that his daughter was underage, and that therefore he was not liable to pay a tax for her. Upon hearing this, the tax collector moved to search his daughter in an indecent manner, whereupon Tyler became enraged and, picking up his hammer, bashed the tax collector's brains out (this apocryphal story became accepted as a historical fact during the seventeenth, eighteenth, and nineteenth centuries, and features in several of the novels written about him in the latter period). The rebels' demands were relatively modest: freedom from serfdom, freedom to buy and sell in the marketplace, and a pardon for all offences committed during the rising. Sadly, the people's grievances would not be remedied at this point, and their leader, Tyler, was murdered by the Lord Mayor of London, William Walworth (d. 1385). It is not the intention here to add anything new to discussions about the historical revolt and its leader. Given that entire books have been written on the subject, hopefully readers will forgive the brevity with which the rising is dealt with in this chapter, it is intended as a preface to the examination of Wat Tyler in post-medieval literature.

The second chapter takes us out of the medieval period and into that era which scholars call early modern. While William Shakespeare (1564-1616) and Christopher Marlowe (1564-93), among others, were authoring their dramatic masterpieces, an interesting, anonymously authored play appeared entitled *The Life and Death of Iacke Strawe* (1593). While chroniclers from the medieval period to the Tudor period depict Wat Tyler as a low-life, drunken, violent brute, the play is interesting in the fact that it sympathises with the rebels. While many people today think that the Elizabethan period was some type of Golden Age, as we will see, this play challenges this idea. It gives voice to contemporary grievances, such as taxes, falling wages, and the high price of food. Approximately half a century after *The Life and Death of Iacke Strawe* was first written, England had its first revolution, between 1642 and 1660. King Charles I (1600-49) went to war with Parliament and he lost. The office of King was dispensed with, and England enjoyed a brief period of republican rule under Oliver Cromwell, which unfortunately degenerated into a mere dictatorship. That the legacy of Wat Tyler and the memory of the events of 1381 should reappear in political pamphlets during this period may come as no surprise. What is interesting about seventeenth century Wat Tyler literature, however, is the fact that he appears, not in writings which support the Parliamentary cause, but in Royalist literature. Wat Tyler's history, and the fact that he was murdered, and his head placed upon a spike in London, was used by Royalists to warn Parliamentarians about the possible consequences of going to war against a king who rules by divine right.

The Stuart dynasty was briefly restored, before another of their line, James II, was also ousted from the throne during the so-called Glorious

Revolution of 1688. In the same year, William of Orange and his wife, Mary, were invited to rule as joint monarchs. After these two passed away, the crown passed to Anne, and then to George of Hanover. The third chapter therefore takes us into the Georgian age. Although by this period Parliament had effectively asserted its sovereignty over the monarchy, very few people had the right to vote. In a country where the vast majority of the population were unenfranchised, there were two main ways in which the common people could express their grievances. If they were educated, they might author a political pamphlet or satire attacking the government. Their other recourse was to riot. The Georgian era, as we will see, was the era in which the elites, while not having to count on people's votes, still had to pay attention to public opinion. It was the era of 'King Mob'. To contemporaries, this term denoted a restless and unruly populace that committed wanton acts of vandalism.[2] Numerous riots occurred throughout the eighteenth century, and when the popular press decided to moralise upon the subject of riots, they often did so with reference to the events of 1381. The rioters were often condemned by moralists as being 'animated with the spirit of Wat Tyler'.

Thus far, Wat Tyler had, with one or two exceptions, been portrayed as the leader of a band of ruffians. But two important events occurred in America and France during the late eighteenth century which led to the gradual rehabilitation of Wat Tyler and his fellow comrades. These events were the American War of Independence (1776-83) and the French Revolution and Napoleonic Wars (1789-1815). Initially, as we will see, the revolutionaries were condemned by writers sympathetic to the establishment as being no better than the traitorous Wat Tyler. But the visionary radical thinker Thomas Paine reassessed Tyler's history, and in his writings portrays him as a man who fought for social justice and political liberty in what was an unjust and oppressive age. Tyler was not the wicked and rebellious leader of a gang of brutish peasants. As Paine argues in his phenomenally successful work *The Rights of Man* (1791), history had been whitewashed in favour of the elites, and Tyler's achievements were set in an unjust light. Wat Tyler was a hero and freedom fighter, according to Paine, and he was deserving of a monument in his honour for his contribution to the advancement of liberty. It did not take long for writers in the popular press to begin comparing Thomas Paine and Wat Tyler, and in some of the popular pamphlets at the time the latter's ghost is depicted in conversation with Paine. In addition to the works of Thomas Paine, also examined in this chapter is Robert Southey's *Wat Tyler: A Dramatic Poem* (1794). Filled with zeal for the principles of the French Revolution, Southey portrays Tyler, like Paine before him, as a freedom fighter. The play remained unpublished, and as time wore on, Southey would most likely have cringed at his juvenile ramblings about equality and fraternity if they should ever come to light. Indeed, by 1817, he was Poet Laureate, a confirmed supporter of the Tory Party, and vehemently opposed to any type of political reform. But *Wat Tyler* did indeed come out of the shadows, for radical publishers decided to embarrass Southey by printing the poem. And he was mocked by his friends and laughed at in the press. People denounced him as a hypocrite, while some politicians declared his writings to be seditious. The reaction to Southey's play illustrates that, even during the eighteenth century, at a distance of over four hundred years from the historical revolt, Wat Tyler was still a divisive figure. Wat Tyler literature from the late eighteenth century, then, is the subject of the fourth chapter.

The fifth chapter examines Wat Tyler's representations in early nineteenth-century radical literature. In the aftermath of the French Revolutionary and Napoleonic Wars, Britain's economy was in crisis and unemployment was on the rise. The majority of people still did not have the vote, and campaigns were mounted by reformers such as Henry Hunt (1773-1835) to secure parliamentary representation for the middle and working classes. Following the precedent set by Thomas Paine, Wat Tyler's name was invoked on a number of occasions after 1815 by Hunt and his fellow radicals, and Tyler is often equated with Hunt in a number of newspapers and satirical writings at this time. While the upper middle classes managed to secure voting rights after the passage of the Great Reform Act (1832), the working classes remained disenfranchised. Consequently, a new working-class political reform movement was formed in the mid-1830s, known as Chartism, and as its members sought historical legitimacy for their actions, they drew upon the memory of 1381. Poems and songs are written about Wat Tyler in Chartist newspapers such as *The Northern Star*, and the rebel leader would receive his greatest literary treatment in Pierce Egan the Younger's penny blood entitled *Wat Tyler; or, The Rebellion of 1381* (1841), which depicts Tyler as a medieval Chartist activist.[3]

The sixth chapter investigates Wat Tyler's appearance in the nineteenth-century historical novel. The first author to give Wat Tyler his 'big break' in this most famous of literary genres was a woman known only as Mrs. O'Neill, who authored *The Bondman* (1833). Scarcely remembered today, the novel is a well-researched, gripping account of the Peasants' Revolt. Essentially it is the story of the growth of a labouring class consciousness among medieval peasants, and their struggle to secure political rights. The novel reflects the political agitation seen in Britain during the lead up to the passage of the Reform Act in 1832. Further novels of varying quality were published throughout the century. There was also an unremarkable, heavily moralistic story authored by the clergyman, William Heygate, entitled *Alice of Fobbing* (1860). It would be a mistake to argue that Heygate's novel was written in response to contemporary events, as it would be with William Harrison Ainsworth's *Merry England; or, Nobles and Serfs* (1874). Ainsworth rarely sought to make a political point in any of his novels, and simply wanted to tell a good story. Sadly, although Ainsworth is one of my favourite nineteenth-century authors, whose works featured prominently during my MA studies, the novel I discuss here is not Ainsworth at his best.[4] *Merry England* was written at a point in his career when his creative powers were in decline, and when he needed money. It is during the late Victorian period that we also see a number of penny dreadfuls featuring Wat Tyler being published. Marketed towards children, magazines such as *The Young Englishman* depict Wat Tyler usually as an outlaw, in a similar manner to Robin Hood, or as a juvenile delinquent in medieval London, getting into scrapes with his comrades and running from the law. The history of the rebellion was appropriated by William Morris in his time travel novella *A Dream of John Ball* (1886). Morris believed that in the teachings of John Ball he could find evidence of proto-socialist thought. While the time traveller tells John Ball that the rebels will ultimately be defeated, he gives the medieval preacher cause for hope: the peasants' rising is a necessary milestone on the road to building a socialist utopia, when all men will live in fellowship.

The final chapter briefly examines some twentieth-century works, but it is a period in which there is no major new literary treatment of the story of the Great Revolt, at least not until Melvyn Bragg's *Now is the Time* (2015). Indeed, Wat Tyler almost disappears from public memory during the 1950s and 1960s (apart from in academia of course). I make the argument that he was not needed during this period as it was the 'never had it so good' era, a time when both Tory and Labour administrations adopted the consensus approach to governing. A planned economy, cooperation between governments and trade unions, along with the establishments of a welfare state, lessened the need for people to adopt Wat Tyler as their hero. This is not to say the 1950s and 1960s were perfect or some sort of golden age, as there certainly were problems during this era. Curiously, however, Wat Tyler only reappears in public consciousness during the 1970s and 1980s when this consensus mode of government begins to break down. Given that one of the main causes of the revolt in 1381 was the imposition of a hated poll tax, it may come as no surprise to anyone that Tyler's name was called upon again between 1989 and 1990, when Margaret Thatcher's government initiated the despised 'Community Charge', a poll tax in all but name. This work then ends with some musings upon what is next for Wat Tyler's post-medieval afterlife.

The above chapter overview provides but a small glimpse of some of the twists and turns which occur in the post-medieval literature of the revolt. The idea to write this book came gradually. Back in September 2016, I was sat in a meeting at Leeds Trinity University with my two PhD thesis supervisors, Professors Paul Hardwick and Rosemary Mitchell. As my thesis on eighteenth- and nineteenth-century literary representations of Robin Hood was nearing completion, towards the end of the meeting, my supervisors asked me if I had any further medievalist projects in mind, perhaps as possible post-doctoral projects. Before the summer, I had been assisting Rosemary with teaching on her undergraduate cultural history module entitled 'Representations of the Middle Ages, c.1750-c.1900'. I remembered how much I enjoyed teaching Southey's *Wat Tyler* to the undergraduates. I had also encountered, in the course of my research upon Robin Hood, a number of Victorian penny dreadfuls which featured Tyler as their hero. So, I answered that I would like to do for Wat Tyler what I was doing for Robin Hood in my thesis: write an account of the post-medieval literary history of the leader of the Great Revolt. My supervisors' answer was to 'Go for it'. Yet as often happens when one has several projects on the go, certain things get shelved to be done 'at a later date', so to speak (I was in the middle of writing an article for *Law, Crime and History* at this point, as well as teaching, and completing my thesis).[5] It was not until I was contacted on Twitter by Jonathan Wright from Pen & Sword Books at the beginning of November 2016 that my idea for a cultural history of post-medieval Wat Tyler literature resurfaced. The book was subsequently contracted and the result is what you are holding in your hand. Although this book is not a formal part of my PhD research, then, my supervisors, Paul and Rosemary, as well as Dr. Alaric Hall from the University of Leeds must be thanked. They have allowed me to develop my interests in medieval history and medievalism beyond the scope of my thesis (on Robin Hood), and their work has informed this book in countless places.

Leeds Trinity is not the first university that I have attended, and so a special note of thanks must go to my former lecturers at Leeds Beckett University. It was at Leeds Beckett that my passion for history was nurtured, and where I began to develop the skills necessary to become a historian through the excellent teaching there. In particular, I must thank my former supervisor, Dr. Heather Shore, who supervised both my BA and MA dissertations. Although Heather did not contribute directly to the writing of this book, her help and encouragement with previous research projects over the years has been invaluable.

I am lucky, furthermore, in that I have always had a strong personal support network to help me while pursuing my interests in history. Debbie and Joseph Basdeo, my parents, have provided emotional (and financial) support. My parents, along with my friend, Hannah-Freya Blake, have proof read the manuscript for this book. A special mention must also go to my sister, Jamila Garrod, her husband, Andrew, and my two wonderful nieces, Mya and Alexa. Finally, my friends, Richard Neesam, Samuel Dowling, and Chris Williams have provided much-needed breaks from time to time.

There are several historians whose research has informed this book, and who must be acknowledged. The first chapter of Antony Taylor's book entitled *London's Burning: Pulp Fiction, the Politics of Terrorism and the Destruction of the Capital in British Popular Culture, 1840-2005* (2012) served as essential background reading for the present study. He gives a general overview of post-medieval Wat Tyler texts in the corpus of British radical writings.[6] As Taylor argues, to later British radicals, the memory of Tyler's actions, as well as those of other medieval peasant leaders such as Jack Cade (c.1420-50), served as important historical examples of Englishmen who were prepared to fight for their political rights.[7] Taylor's work is comprehensive, and the present work does revisit some of the primary sources which he also analyses. However, while Taylor's focus is upon the representation of Wat Tyler in post-medieval radical literature, it is important to remember that it was not *only* by radicals and for radicals that Tyler was appropriated. As the present work reveals, Tyler was also appropriated by conservative authors such as Ainsworth, and was effectively depoliticised in many Victorian penny dreadfuls, being more of a Robin Hood type of figure. Alternatively, he is often cast by later authors as a depraved and drunken brute of a man.

In addition, Juliet Barker, the author of *England Arise: The People, the King, and the Great Revolt of 1381* (2014) deserves a special mention. Her work is a lengthy and well-researched narrative which discusses the origins of the revolt, as well as its legacy. Wat Tyler does not feature greatly in her account of the rebellion, and indeed a discussion of his life and legacy, as well as biographies of Jack Straw and John Ball, are placed in an appendix at the end of the book. This is, of course, due to the fact that very few contemporary documents about the key figures of the rising exist. The relegation of Tyler, Straw, and Ball to supporting roles in Barker's account is further justified by the fact that she examines each of the separate riots that occurred throughout the whole of England. A truly national picture of the revolt of 1381 emerges in her work, and the present study is indebted to Barker's work for providing the essential background reading for chapter one, which recounts the events of the historical revolt. As I stated above, it is not the intention of this book to add anything new to discussions of the historical revolt. The account that is given in the first chapter of this book is more of a *précis* of events than a piece of new research. It is intended to foreground the discussion of Wat Tyler's appearances in literature after the medieval period. Should any readers wish to know more about the events of the historical rebellion, Barker's study of it is highly recommended. Indeed, several histories of the revolt have been written, and the bibliography is not simply a list of works cited in this book but lists many works which I recommend for further reading.

In addition, R.B. Dobson is a historian whose name I have become very familiar with as a result of researching Robin Hood. It was truly a pleasure, therefore, to revisit him in another of his works entitled *The Peasants' Revolt of 1381* (1970). This work is a collection of primary sources relating to the events of 1381. The parts of this work which were particularly useful for the present work were the extracts from medieval chronicles relating to the revolt, such as the *Anonimalle Chronicle*, 'the single most important source for the history of the rising'.[8] Additionally, Dobson has made the writings of Jean Froissart, and other medieval authors such as John Gower (c.1330-1408), Henry Knighton (d. 1396), Thomas Walsingham (d. 1442) easily accessible in his volume.

Another prominent historian of the rising of 1381 is Rodney Hilton. As an English neo-Marxist historian of the late medieval and early modern periods, much of his research focused upon exploring the transition from feudalism to capitalism in England (Marxist historians generally hold to the idea that society progresses in stages according to class struggle and changes in the means of production; society, therefore, transitions from slave societies in the ancient world, in which the two opposing classes are masters and slaves, to feudal societies in the medieval period, in which the classes that oppose each other are the lords and the serfs, to capitalist societies in the early modern and modern periods, which witnesses conflict between bourgeois capitalists and the proletariat). Hilton's major work on Wat Tyler's rebellion is *Bond Men Made Free: Medieval Peasant Movements and the English Rising of 1381* (1973). The idea of class struggle is at the forefront of his work. Hilton argues that, although Tyler's and the rebels' cause failed, their rising was a forerunner of 'European movement[s] in which peasant communities were to be pitted against State, church, and nobility for two or three centuries to come'.[9] Hilton also stresses the importance of the ideological aspects of the revolt, which before him had been considered as secondary to the socio-economic causes of the rising. While there is a sense in academia that things have moved on from the utilisation of social class as a tool of historical analyses, the insights of Marxist historians are still useful.[10] Indeed, it is for this reason that, in my own brief account of the revolt in the first chapter, I have dwelt not only upon the long term social and economic causes of the revolt, but have also given equal importance to the teachings of John Ball. As we will see, authors during the sixteenth, seventeenth, eighteenth, and nineteenth centuries often cited the teachings of John Ball as a major causal factor in the revolt.

At a more general level, much of this research could not have been carried out had not certain resources been available. The researchers who have diligently scanned in old newspapers and periodicals, and the people who maintain databases such as the British Library's Nineteenth-Century Newspapers, ProQuest, Early English Books Online, Eighteenth-Century Collections Online, and Nineteenth-Century Collections Online deserve special thanks here. Many old Wat Tyler poems came to light as I was scouring the library's online archive. With permission from these online archives, I was permitted to publish some of these poems in an appendix for readers' perusal, in addition to the poems I found in physical archives. If these online repositories of primary sources did not exist then this work would have undoubtedly been poorer. This is because, while Tyler is a similar figure to Robin Hood, they were used by people in different ways. Robin Hood is a prominent figure in popular culture, appearing in the novels of Walter Scott (1771-1832), Thomas Love Peacock (1785-1866), as well as in films and television series. But often Tyler is a man whose name is invoked or briefly alluded to by the authors of newspaper articles, or in lengthy footnotes, as he is in Thomas Paine's *The Rights of Man*, rather than having lots of full-length novels written about him.

Finally, I think some recognition should go to the man himself, Wat Tyler. It is true that we know little of his life, but he was one of the first people in England, drawn from society's lower ranks, who mounted a serious challenge to the established order. He sought social justice in what was then an unjust and unequal society. Yet he, along with John Ball, was a man before his time. He would not live to see any of his and the rebels' fairly reasonable demands granted. The historical Tyler appears in the historical records in a flash, and disappears from it almost as quickly, having been treacherously murdered by Walworth. But his legacy lived on. His story, as we will see, has inspired radicals and progressives throughout the ages who fought for social change. Thus, Wat Tyler's life story, and the reactions to it throughout his post-medieval literary history, provides a window through which we can analyse changing responses towards riot, rebellion, radicalism, and revolution.

Notes

1 'Legend', in *The Oxford English Dictionary* (Oxford: Oxford University Press, 2017) [Internet <en.oxforddictionaries.com/definition/legend> Accessed 14 February 2017].

2 David Ashford, *London Underground: A Cultural Geography* (Liverpool: Liverpool University Press, 2013), p. 147.

3 Stephen Basdeo, 'Radical Medievalism: Pierce Egan the Younger's Robin Hood, Wat Tyler, and Adam Bell', in *Leeds Working Papers in Victorian Studies Volume 15: Imagining the Victorians* ed. by Stephen Basdeo and Lauren Padgett (Leeds: LCVS, 2016), pp. 48-64.

4 Stephen Basdeo, 'Dying Speeches, Daring Robbers, and Demon Barbers: The Forms and Functions of Nineteenth-Century Crime Literature, c.1800-c.1868' (Unpublished MA Thesis, Leeds Metropolitan University, 2014).

5 Stephen Basdeo, 'Robin Hood the Brute: Representations of the Outlaw in Eighteenth-Century Criminal Biography', *Law, Crime and History* 6: 2 (2016), pp. 54-70.

6 Antony Taylor, *London's Burning: Pulp Fiction, the Politics of Terrorism and the Destruction of the Capital in British Popular Culture, 1840-2005* (London: Bloomsbury, 2012), pp. 20-45.

7 Taylor, *London's Burning*, p. 20.

8 R.B. Dobson, 'Introduction to "Anonimalle Chronicle"', in *The Peasants' Revolt of 1381* ed. by R.B. Dobson (London: Macmillan, 1970), p. 123.

9 Rodney Hilton, *Bond Men Made Free: Medieval English Peasant Movements and the English Rising of 1381* (New York: Viking, 1973), p. 22.

10 Josh Poklad, 'Signs and Blunders: A Critique of the Current State of Victorian Consumption Studies', in *Leeds Working Papers in Victorian Studies Volume 15: Imagining the Victorians* ed. by Stephen Basdeo and Lauren Padgett (Leeds: LCVS, 2016), pp. 165-179 (p.166).

CHAPTER ONE

The Great Revolt

A great and unexpected calamity not experienced by previous ages.

Thomas Walsingham

They rose and came towards London, to the number of sixty thousand; and they had a captain called Walter Tyler, and with him in company was Jack Straw and John Ball; these three were chief sovereign captains, but the head of all was Walter Tyler; he was indeed a tiler of houses, a man ungracious to his betters.

Jean Froissart

Most of what historians know about the Great Revolt of 1381 comes from chronicles written by men such as Thomas Walsingham, Jean Froissart, Henry Knighton, and an anonymously written source entitled *Anonimalle Chronicle*. None of them are overly sympathetic towards the rebels. The revolt is described by Walsingham as 'a great and unexpected calamity not experienced by previous ages'.[1] There had of course been rebellions in England before this date. In the immediate aftermath of the Norman Conquest in 1066, for instance, there had been groups of people particularly in the north of England who had risen up in order to overthrow the Norman oppressors. The so-called Peasants' Revolt, however, was different. It was not the discontented murmurings of disorganised peasants. They had leaders, they were well-organised and armed. Indeed, it was not simply a peasants' revolt so much as a people's revolt. The rebels were drawn from a range of social classes.

Although Walsingham says that it was 'a great and unexpected calamity', the seeds of the rebellion were being sown earlier in the century. One of the long-term factors contributing to the outbreak of the Great Revolt was disease. The Black Death had ravaged Europe between 1348 and 1353. It was a nasty disease with a mortality rate of fifty per cent, in which the victim suffered swellings, known as buboes, on the neck, thighs, groins, and in the armpits, along with high fevers, until the poor patient died after a week. A more severe variant of the plague, known as pneumonic plague, attacked the lungs, with ninety per cent of patients dying within three days. Contemporaries believed that the plague was a punishment from God. Other people assumed that it was caused by bad air. Modern historians and scientists have surmised that it was a form of *Yersinia pestis*, carried on ships from the Orient. In total, the Black Death is assumed to have killed approximately sixty per cent of the European population during the fourteenth century.

While undoubtedly horrific for its victims, one of the consequences of the high mortality rate was that people from lower down the social scale became aware of their own importance. Some free labourers could now demand higher wages from the lords. Additionally, English society in the fourteenth century was a feudal society. Other labourers, known as villeins, or serfs, were tied to the soil and obliged to work for the nobles essentially for free. They saw the benefits that the free labourers were enjoying and desired to share in the emerging economic and social blessings that free men were enjoying. Consequently, some of the serfs began to demand a wage for the work that they carried out for their lords as well. The government was well aware of the situation as regards to wages and sought to control them. At the height of the plague, Parliament under Edward III (1312-77) passed the Statute of Labourers in 1351 which obliged all labourers to work only for the same amounts that they could command before the pestilence struck. The Act was enforced successfully in some areas, and undoubtedly contributed to discontent among the lower orders, which would eventually spill out into open revolt. As R.B. Dobson notes, 'it can be no coincidence that the risings [of 1381] tended to be most violent in those counties where it is known the labour laws were strictly enforced.'[2] The Black Death did not cause the Great Revolt, but it did bring to the fore certain grievances which, combined with other factors, made for an explosive combination.[3]

Another factor which contributed to the revolt, and one which led to the imposition of the hated poll tax, was the high cost of England's military adventures abroad. This was the period of the Hundred Years War (1337-1453). While the war would witness some decisive and, if war can ever be described in such terms, 'glorious' English victories in the fifteenth century, during the 1370s and 1380s the war was going badly for England. In 1372, for example, the naval Battle of La Rochelle resulted in a French victory, which effectively brought English naval supremacy to an end.[4] Indeed, the entire war at this point is described by one historian as having been 'ill-managed and expensive'.[5] It was so expensive that Parliament in 1377 authorised the first poll tax of four pence per head. At this point, Edward III was still on the throne. He had been a brave and strong king in his youth, and a competent war leader, but by the 1370s old age and infirmity had set in. His son, Edward, the Black Prince, was due to succeed him but he died in 1376. The King's only remaining heir was his young grandson, Richard. In 1377, Edward died and the throne passed to the 10-year-old Richard who was crowned on 16 July 1377. In light of his youth, Parliament decided that a regency should be established. However, they made sure to exclude Richard's uncle, John of Gaunt (1340-99), from having any official role in advising the King. Gaunt was disliked by a large section of both the elites and the people at large. He was the richest man in England and often flaunted his wealth, and had he wanted to, he certainly had the military backing behind him to seize the throne for himself. Yet he did not, which must give pause for thought before we take the words of Walsingham at face value, who declares in his writings that Gaunt was a man who was motivated by 'unbridled malice and greed'.[6] Despite having no official role in the government he still had a lot of influence, and both the people and many members of the elites laid the blame for the nation's military woes and financial ills at his feet. Indeed, it was Gaunt who was one of the main instigators of the poll tax of 1377. While Walsingham's comments regarding Gaunt at this point seem quite bitter (his views towards Gaunt did change somewhat over the course of time), Antonia Gransden remarks that 'there is no reason to suppose that this part of his chronicle is not a fairly accurate reflection of the views of many of his contemporaries.'[7] Indeed, when the common people did revolt in 1381, some of them declared that 'they would be faithful to King Richard and the Commons and that they would accept no King who was called John.'[8]

The original poll tax levied could not meet the needs of the state, and Parliament granted a fresh poll tax in 1379. Although the first two taxes did not elicit any forcible resistance, there was, understandably, considerable and growing discontent among the populace against this measure. Interestingly, one man, a poet named John Gower (c.1330-1408), around the time of the first poll tax in 1377, predicted that the people might rise up due to the growing unhappiness which he observed in the country. In his lengthy poem, *Mirour de l'omme*, Gower warns the ruling classes to be on their guard because if the commoners do rise up, 'they will not be stopped, by either reason or discipline.'[9] The commons' disaffection was no doubt fuelled in some areas of the country by the lay preacher, John Balle (c.1329-81) (hereafter named John Ball for consistency, as this is the way that it is spelt in later works that are cited in this book). Unlike the lazy priest, Sloth, seen in William Langland's *The Vision of Piers Plowman* (c.1377), John Ball was a man whose ideology followed 'in the long tradition of Christian social radicalism which goes back to St. Ambrose of Milan, if not before'.[10] He gave a radical voice to the dire economic and social situation of the commons, highlighting the difference between the 'haves' and 'have-nots' of medieval society.[11] More importantly, John Ball preached equality and common ownership of property. This was revolutionary stuff, especially in a society which, for the most part, believed that people fitted into divinely-ordained estates. There has been some speculation by historians in the past that John Ball was an associate of John Wycliffe (c.1320-84) and his followers the Lollards. Designated as 'The Morning Star of the Reformation' by some nineteenth-century historians, Wycliffe was an early religious reformer who rejected many standard Church practices, such as the sale of indulgences and the practice of private confession. At this time, furthermore, the Church forbade the translation of the Bible into any tongue but Latin, even though the scriptures themselves were originally written in Aramaic and Greek. But Wycliffe believed that all people should be able to read the word of God. Thus he set about translating the Bible into English.[12] This injunction, however, did not preclude preachers from translating the Bible into the vernacular when reading aloud to their congregations. The only source which connects John Ball and John Wycliffe is a confession, supposedly written by Ball shortly before his death, but which scholars today agree is of dubious authenticity.[13]

John Ball appears to have been a constant irritation to the authorities in southern England. King Edward had withdrawn his protection from John Ball in 1364 for 'not prosecuting any business but wanders from country to country preaching articles of faith contrary to the faith of the church to the peril of his soul and the souls of others, especially of laymen'.[14] It was during this period, as Hilton points out, that Ball was first arrested and imprisoned for spreading his radical message.[15] He was soon set at liberty again, however, and Walsingham records that he continued preaching for around twenty years. In April 1381, the Archbishop of Canterbury, Simon Sudbury (1317-81), had decided that enough was enough, and he had Ball arrested and thrown into Maidstone gaol.

Costly military expeditions in France were still eating into the nation's finances. For example, while the graduated tax of 1379 earned £22,000 for the government, the cost of an ill-fated campaign in Breton had cost the government £50,000.[16] The then-Chancellor, Lord Richard Scropes (c.1327-1403), was replaced with Sudbury. It was Sudbury who proposed a fresh poll tax of three groats per head in 1380, which was granted by Parliament in November. Three groats was equal to twelve pennies, or a shilling. This new tax, therefore like the others, disproportionately hit the pockets of the poor. Richard Scropes' salary was six hundred pounds per year, and the tax would have meant nothing to him.[17] In contrast, the average wage for an unskilled labouring man around the year 1380 was three pence per day.[18] The work of collecting the tax started in December, but the government was aware that there was a great deal of tax evasion being committed. Consequently, in March 1381, new measures were put in place to deal with those who refused to pay up. The authority was given to the tax collectors, with the help of local knights, dukes, bailiffs, and mayors, to seize and arrest everyone who opposed the poll tax.[19]

Tax collectors have never been well-liked by the general public, and poll taxes, as Thomas Paine would write in the eighteenth-century, have always been odious. There was considerable resistance to the new tactics employed by the tax collectors, but the first major incident in the Revolt appears to have occurred on 30 May in Brentwood. Thomas de Bamptoun travelled there with two Serjeants-at-Arms in order to find out who in the region was still liable to pay tax. Confusingly, Thomas' Christian name is given as John in some contemporary accounts. In view of the fact that many Georgian and Victorian historians refer to a Thomas de Bamptoun, I have chosen this in order to be consistent throughout this book. But to return to Brentwood in 1381; Bamptoun summoned villagers from the neighbouring areas of Fobbing, Corringham, and Staniforth [Standford-le-Hope] to Brentwood, but one of the people from Fobbing, identified as one Thomas Baker, told him that they refused to pay any more tax because they had already paid up. According to the *Anonimalle Chronicle*, Bamptoun then began to make violent threats against the villagers from Fobbing. The people from Corringham and Staniforth joined with those from Fobbing in refusing to pay any more tax. Bamptoun then ordered his serjeants to arrest the villagers, but the villagers greatly outnumbered Bamptoun and his men. Bamptoun, rather prudently, thought it best to withdraw from the scene, and he and his men fled towards London. After the departure of the tax collectors, some of the villagers took to living in the woods for a short time for fear of reprisals, and thereafter some of them travelled to neighbouring villages encouraging other people to rise up against the tax. Upon learning of the events at Brentwood, Chief Justice Sir Robert Belknap (d. 1401) arrived there bearing a number of indictments with a view to prosecuting those who refused to pay.

By this time, however, the common people would not be cowed. The author of the *Anonimalle Chronicle* records that when the people of Brentwood saw him, they accused him of being a traitor to the king. Moreover, they forced him to tell them the names of a number of jurors that had been appointed to serve in the inquests relating to the revolt. The people of Brentwood, having found out the jurors' names, were subsequently beheaded.[20]

As Bamptoun did before him, Belknap promptly returned to London, and in the meantime the people of Fobbing sent messages to the surrounding towns urging them to join in the rising. While there were evidently some who did not join in the revolt, a great many people did, and in the course of the next few days the mob had swelled to approximately fifty thousand people. On 5 June the rebels from Kent assembled at Dartford and they passed a resolution amongst themselves that 'they would neither suffer nor have any king except King Richard'.[21] It will be noted here that the rebels did not blame the young king for their troubles. Instead, the rebels attributed their woes to the actions of his advisors. The rebels then travelled into Maidstone, where they exhorted their fellow men to join in the rising. All who did not join them in the rebellion had their houses destroyed, and 'one of the best men' of the town was even beheaded for his refusal.[22] The rebels' next act on 6 June was to rescue a serf named Robert Belling from Rochester gaol, who had been imprisoned there at the behest of Sir Simon de Burley, one of the Knights of the King's Household.[23] Although the rebels laid siege to the castle for a day and a half, the constable decided that it would just be easier to set the man free and open the castle. The rebels then entered and freed all of the prisoners. The people pressed forward, but they were largely leaderless at this point. So they, therefore, elected 'Watt Teghler of Maidstone, to maintain and advise them'.[24] Thus it is at this time that our hero himself makes an appearance. There is a possibility that he was a veteran of the Hundred Years War, and that he was chosen because he had military leadership skills. While this is unverifiable, it is not totally outside the bounds of credibility. The story of his alleged military service would, as we will see, be incorporated into the tales of several nineteenth-century novelists. Why Tyler joined the rising nobody knows. The popular story of a tax collector demanding payment for his underage daughter, and then committing attempted rape upon her, and of Tyler's subsequently bashing the tax collector's brains out with a hammer, is an invention of the sixteenth-century chronicler John Stow. Even in Stow's work, the murder of the tax collector is attributed to a John Tiler, not Wat Tyler[25] (John Tiler is also named as the leader of the revolt in Higden's *Polychronicon*).[26]

Under Tyler's leadership, the rebels' next action was to rescue John Ball from Maidstone goal on 7 June and free many of the other prisoners held there as well. Knighton records that the rebels' intention in setting John Ball free from prison was carried out in order that they might elevate him to the archbishopric of Canterbury.[27] After Tyler's rescue of Ball from Maidstone gaol, the rebels began their march on Canterbury on 9 June.[28] Four thousand men entered the city on the following day, and many of them attended Mass at St. Thomas' Mother Church. The castle and the Archbishop of Canterbury's palace were then ransacked. Afterwards, the Mayor, bailiffs, and the common people of the town were assembled before the rebels. Those present were made to swear an oath to be faithful to King Richard and the common people of England.[29] Still the rebels, it will be noted, found no fault with the King. They were resolved instead to rid England of all lords, archbishops, bishops, abbots and priors, monks, and canons.[30] They were, however, not a mindless mob. As we shall see shortly, they had a well-thought-out list of demands. As one of the rebels' demands was an end to serfdom, while the mob was at Canterbury they entered the houses of several local nobles and destroyed any documents that might confirm whether a person was a bondman or not.

The next day, 11 June, Tyler and the people began their march from Canterbury to London. On the way, they came across twelve lawyers and twelve knights, accosting them and forcing them to swear allegiance to their cause upon pain of death. Also along the way, they ransacked the houses of several nobles. The *Anonimalle Chronicle* records that they did the most damage to the house of Thomas de Heseldene, one of Gaunt's men, by burning down his house and stealing his livestock.[31] By this time the King had heard of the uprising, and on their way to London on 11 June the rebels were met by some of the King's messengers. They enquired why the rebels were acting thus, to which they replied that they were rising up to save the king and to destroy all traitors.[32] The King's messengers then informed the rebels that Richard would meet with them and hear their demands. It is also said by Froissart (but *only* by Froissart, it should be noted) that the Queen Mother, Joan of Kent (1328-85), the wife of Edward the Black Prince, was returning from a pilgrimage to Canterbury and ran into the rebels. Froissart records that the insurgents treated her in a very disrespectful manner:

> She was in great jeopardy to have been lost, for these people came to her chare and dealt rudely with her, whereof the good lady was in great doubt lest they would have done some villany to her or to her damosels. Howbeit, God kept her, and she came in one day from Canterbury to London, for she never durst tarry by the way.[33]

I have some reservations about accepting the veracity of this alleged incident. In addition to the fact that the episode is only recorded by Froissart, given that throughout the whole affair the rebels repeatedly emphasised their loyalty to the King, it seems unlikely that they would have 'dealt rudely' with the Queen Mother. The following day, the Kentish rebels arrived at Blackheath, and according to Thomas Walsingham, it is here that John Ball addressed a sermon to the assembled multitude with the famous theme, 'when Adam delved and Eve span, who was then the gentleman?' Meantime, the rebels from Essex made camp at Mile End, while more rebels were arriving from Surrey, Sussex, Norfolk, Cambridgeshire, Buckinghamshire, and Hertfordshire.

At this point, on 13 June, the King, who only had 520 soldiers with him, retreated to the Tower of London along with Sudbury and Robert Hales, the Lord High Treasurer. The high walls and heavy fortifications of the Tower would, of course, have provided some protection against any sudden turn in the rebels' disposition toward him. Upon hearing that the King had retreated to the Tower, Wat Tyler sent a message to the King, asking to meet him at Rotherhithe (unfortunately, this letter allegedly written by Tyler to the King does not survive). The King agreed to this, and by the afternoon he boarded a barge and travelled the short way down the Thames to meet Tyler and the rebels. This was quite a brave act for the young king, as the sight of the rebels lining the banks of the Thames while he was sailing down it to meet with Tyler must have been a daunting one. Accompanying the now 14-year-old king was Sudbury and Hales. It might have been better for the young king to go alone, all things considered, for when the people saw the two hated officials in the barge with Richard the crowd became incensed, calling them traitors. It was these two men, after all, who had first proposed the 1381 poll tax. Perhaps wisely considering the circumstances, Richard decided not to disembark and after ten minutes he decided to return to the Tower.

On the afternoon of the same day, rebels from Kent arrived at the Southwark entrance to London. It is important to note at this point that the rebels enjoyed a significant degree of support from the residents of London. After all, those in London were also liable to pay the poll tax, just as those from the country had been. Thus, some of the rebels' supporters from inside the city lowered the drawbridge and opened the gates to allow them to enter. One of their first acts when they managed to get inside the walls was to rob and then set fire to Gaunt's palace at the Savoy. According to Froissart, the sacking of Gaunt's residence was done under the instruction and supervision of Wat Tyler, John Ball, and Jack Straw.[34] It is more likely, however, that the destruction of Gaunt's palace was carried out at the instigation of John Farringdon, a rebel from Essex. This was the man who, on the same evening, led the rebels into the Hospitallers' Priory at Clerkenwell. There they beheaded the master of the order, and burned the building and several of the surrounding edifices to the ground.[35] Sadly, if Froissart and other chroniclers are to be believed, some of the rebels did turn nasty, for it is reported that some of the rebels went through the street and robbed and killed the Flemings and the Lombards.[36]

THE GREAT REVOLT

Although Tyler had wanted to meet with the King on the same morning, it will be remembered that the young king, perhaps wisely though not very bravely, sped away back to the Tower in his barge. It was not until the following day around eight o'clock in the morning that Tyler came face to face with the boy king at Mile End. Knighton says that most of the King's knights left him to face the mob alone, having been struck by 'womanly fears'.[37] It was here that Wat Tyler put the rebels' reasonable grievances before the King: the end of all feudal services, the freedom to buy and sell goods (serfs at this time could not freely sell the surplus produce of their labour in the marketplace), and a general pardon for all offences that had been committed during the rebellion. Wat Tyler also accused those responsible for the poll tax as being guilty of corruption, and he demanded that they should be executed. The King agreed to the first set of demands by granting a charter confirming them, although whether he ever intended to keep them is open to debate. However, Richard said that his people could be confident that, if any of his advisors were guilty of corruption then they would be punished to the full extent of the law. The granting of the charter, and Richard's assurances, appeared to placate Wat Tyler and the mob for the moment, but as is always the case with statesmen, kings, and politicians, they will often in a heartbeat renege on their pledges when it suits them. Tyler, Straw, Ball and quite a few of the rebels must have suspected this, and while many rebels returned home, Tyler decamped to Smithfield with about 30,000 of his men.

While Tyler was with the King at Mile End, a contingent of rebels remained near the Tower. Led by John Starling, this group gained admittance to the castle, and there they laid hands upon Sudbury. They dragged him to Tower Hill where he was beheaded. His head was then placed upon a spike, and paraded through the city of London. It is here also that Robert Hales, the King's Treasurer, and John Legge (who along with Sudbury was instrumental in bringing about the hated tax) met their ends in a similar manner.

On the following day, the King expressed a desire to meet with Wat Tyler again at Smithfield. The King arrived with a number of armed retainers, and inquired why, when the Charters had been granted, the rebels were still in London. According to the *Eulogium Historiarum*, when the King arrived, Tyler refused to dismount from his horse, or remove his cap, and according to some accounts he spoke to the sovereign in a surly manner.[38] Tyler reiterated his previous demands to the King, as well as adding several new ones, some of which were undoubtedly inspired by the teachings of John Ball: the end of tithes, the abolition of bishops, the redistribution of wealth, equality before the law, and the freedom to kill animals in the forest. At this point, Wat Tyler noticed that one of the King's squires was bearing a dagger, and Tyler demanded that the dagger be given to him. The King ordered his squire to do as Tyler commanded. Tyler then demanded the sword that the squire was carrying. It is at that this point that the villain of the story emerges from the shadows. William Walworth (d. 1385), the Mayor of London, had also arrived at Smithfield with several armed men. Upon seeing that Tyler had not been giving due deference to the King, Walworth began to quarrel with Tyler, at which Walworth called Tyler a 'false stinking knave' for behaving in such a manner towards the King.[39] Walworth then drew forth his dagger and struck Tyler in the neck, causing him to fall from his horse. The next instant, one of the King's squires, John Cavendish (or Ralph Standish in some accounts), alighted from his horse and stabbed Tyler in the stomach.[40] This was the fatal blow, and Tyler did not recover from this murderous act.[41] The rebels grew angry that Walworth had killed their leader and were baying for their enemies' blood. Perhaps sensing a bloodbath, the King addressed the rebels saying, 'Sirs, what aileth you? Ye shall have no captain but me: I am your King: be all in peace.'[42] This appeared to have pacified the rebels for the moment, and the King then turned to his advisors and asked them what should be done with the remaining rebels. Richard was advised to allow them to withdraw by Walworth, with a proviso that they should pursue them afterwards. Afterwards, Tyler's body was decapitated in Smithfield and his head was placed upon a spike, carried through London, and set atop London Bridge as a warning to others who might dare defy the established order.

Predictably, the young royal rescinded all of the charters that he had granted previously. His army pursued some of the rebels on their way out of London, and a battle was fought between the King's soldiers and the Essex men on 28 June. On that day, approximately 500 of the rebels were killed. One by one, former leading figures in the rebellion were hunted down. Thomas Baker and his comrades from Fobbing were executed at Chelmsford. John Ball was arrested in Coventry and taken to St. Albans where he suffered the horrific punishment of being hung, drawn, and quartered on 15 July. The rebel movement without its key central figures effectively collapsed. Further afield in places such as Yorkshire, Lincolnshire, and Suffolk other rebel leaders were hunted down and dealt with in the manner of the times.

Yet the young king would eventually receive his comeuppance. Many nobles were unhappy with the way in which Richard went on to abuse his power later in life, so much so that in 1388 a group of nobles sought to impeach the King's favourite advisors in an attempt to curb what was widely perceived as an increasingly tyrannical reign. The nobles who challenged Richard were led by none other than John of Gaunt's son, Henry Bolingbroke (1367-1413). In response to the nobles' challenging of his power, at a parliament called in Shrewsbury in 1399, Richard effectively declared himself above the law, and placed all parliamentary power into the hands of twelve lords and six commoners who were loyal to him. He was now to all intents and purposes an absolute ruler.

Enough was enough. In 1399, Bolingbroke, whose father's estate had been seized by Richard upon his death earlier in the year, returned to England from France with a view to regaining his lands and titles. Although Bolingbroke insisted that this was all that he wanted to do, the small band of followers that arrived with him when he first landed at Yorkshire soon swelled. Richard at this moment was in Ireland, so as Bolingbroke and his army progressed through England, they encountered little resistance. When Richard returned to England, upon seeing that Bolingbroke had the support of the nobles and that, militarily, he held the upper hand, he surrendered to Henry at Flint

Castle. From there, Richard was taken to Pontefract Castle and imprisoned. The circumstances of his death are unclear, although it appears to be generally agreed amongst historians that Richard simply starved to death in the vaults of the castle.[43]

There are many 'what ifs' in history, and, in spite of Wat Tyler's death, if Richard had kept his word, and not annulled the charters granted to the bondmen, his reign might have gone down as an example of good government. But it was not to be. As we will see, Wat Tyler and the events of 1381 would be remembered throughout succeeding ages. Many times, for the elites, when Tyler's name was invoked by commoners it was usually as a harbinger of radical movements. In the early modern to modern periods, for revolutionaries, Chartists, and socialists, Tyler's name could inspire hope and provide historical legitimacy for their actions.

Notes

1 Thomas Walsingham, 'The Outbreak of the Revolt according to Thomas Walsingham', in *The Peasants' Revolt of 1381* ed. by R.B. Dobson (London: Macmillan, 1970), pp. 131-4 (p.132).

2 R.B. Dobson, 'The Enforcement of the Statute of Labourers', in *The Peasants' Revolt of 1381* ed. by R.B. Dobson (London: Macmillan, 1970), pp. 68-72 (p.68).

3 Philip Ziegler, *The Black Death* (London: Folio Society, 1997), pp. 218-9.

4 L.J. Andrew Villalon and Donald J. Kagay, *The Hundred Years War: a Wider Focus* (Leiden: Brill, 2005), p. 36.

5 Dan Jones, 'The Peasants' Revolt', *History Today* June 2009, pp. 33-9 (p.34).

6 Thomas Walsingham cited in Antonia Gransden, *Historical Writing in England: c.1307 to the Early Sixteenth Century* (London: Routledge, 1996), p. 138.

7 Gransden, *Historical Writing in England*, p. 139.

8 Walsingham, 'The Outbreak of the Revolt according to Thomas Walsingham', p. 133.

9 John Gower, 'John Gower Foresees the Peasants' Revolt', in *The Peasants' Revolt of 1381* ed. by R.B. Dobson (London: Macmillan, 1970), pp. 95-6.

10 Hilton, *Bond Men Made Free*, p. 211.

11 John Ball, 'On the Times', in *Medieval English Political Writings* ed. by

James M. Dean (Kalamazoo, MI: Medieval Institute Publications, 1996), pp. 140-6 (p.141).

12 John Laird Wilson, *John Wycliffe, Patriot and Reformer: The Morning Star of the Reformation* (London: Wagnalls, 1884), p. 12.

13 Margaret Aston, 'Corpus Christi and Corpus Regni: Heresy and the Peasants' Revolt', *Past & Present* No. 143 (1994), pp. 3-47 (p.36).

14 Cited in Juliet Barker, *England Arise: The People, the King, and the Great Revolt of 1381* (London: Abacus, 2014), p.428.

15 Hilton, *Bond Men Made Free*, p. 213.

16 Dobson, *The Peasants' Revolt of 1381*, p. 111.

17 Chris Given-Wilson, *The English Nobility in the Late Middle Ages* (Abingdon: Routledge, 1996), p.157.

18 Christopher Dyer, *Everyday Life in Medieval England* (London: Hambledon, 2000), p.168.

19 'Appointment of Commissioners to Enforce Payment of the Third Poll Tax', in *The Peasants' Revolt of 1381* ed. by R.B. Dobson (London: Macmillan, 1970), pp. 120-2 (p.121).

20 'The Outbreak of the Revolt according to the "Anonimalle Chronicle"', in *The Peasants' Revolt of 1381* ed. by R.B. Dobson (London: Macmillan, 1970), pp. 123-131 (p.124).

21 'The Outbreak of the Revolt according to the "Anonimalle Chronicle"', p. 127.

22 *Ibid.*

23 *Ibid.*, p. 127n: although the *Anonimalle Chronicle* says that Burley was present and took an active part in arresting Belling, he was actually away in France negotiating Richard II's marriage with Anne of Bohemia.

24 'The Outbreak of the Revolt according to the "Anonimalle Chronicle"', p. 127.

25 John Stow, *A Summarie of English Chronicles: Containing the Race of Kings since Brutus the First of this Realm* (London: T. Marshe, 1566), p. 136.

26 'The Peasants' Revolt according to the "Monk of Westminster"', in *The Peasants' Revolt of 1381* ed. by R.B. Dobson (London: Macmillan, 1970), pp. 199-204.

27 Henry Knighton, 'The Outbreak of the Revolt according to Henry Knighton', in *The Peasants' Revolt of 1381* ed. by R.B. Dobson (London: Macmillan, 1970), pp. 135-7 (p.137).

28 Barker, *England Arise*, pp. 212-13: Juliet Barker, however, presents evidence against the established view amongst historians, arguing that Tyler and Ball did not meet at this point. She notes that on 11 June an indictment in Essex was issued against John Bowyers of Pleshey because he broke into

the Bishop of London's gaol at Bishop's Stortford and set free a man called John Ball.

29 In further support of her argument, Barker further highlights the fact that all of John Ball's activities had usually been concentrated in the Bishop of London's diocese, and since the 1330s, the prison at Bishop's Stortford had housed mainly convicted clerics and heretics. Of course, this is not incontrovertible proof against the commonly held view that Ball was rescued by Tyler from Maidstone prison. Barker acknowledges that there are some issues with supposing that Ball had been imprisoned at Bishop's Stortford rather than Maidstone, notably the fact that it would have been 'virtually impossible' for Ball to have travelled from Bishop's Stortford to address the rebels at Blackheath on 12 June.

29 'The Outbreak of the Revolt according to the "Anonimalle Chronicle"', pp. 127-8.

30 *Ibid.*, p. 128.

31 *Ibid.*, p. 128.

32 *Ibid.*, p. 129.

33 Jean Froissart, 'Wat Tyler's Rebellion', in *The Harvard Classics: Chronicle and Romance – Froissart, Malory, Holinshead. With Introductions, Notes, and Illustrations* ed. by Charles W. Elliot (New York: Collier, 1910) [Internet <www.gutenberg.org/files/ 13674/13674-h/13674-h.htm> Accessed 27 March 2017].

34 Jean Froissart, 'The Rebels in London according to Froissart', in *The Peasants' Revolt of 1381* ed. by R.B. Dobson (London: Macmillan, 1970), pp. 187-198 (p.188).

35 Helen Nicholson, 'The Hospitallers and the "Peasants' Revolt" of 1381 Revisited', in *The Military Orders Volume 3: History and Heritage* ed. Victor Mallia Milanes (Aldershot: Ashgate, 2007), pp. 225-233 (p.225).

36 Froissart, 'The Rebels in London according to Froissart', p.189: it is also said at this point that Wat Tyler had a former master of his, one Richard Lyon, killed. That Lyon was killed is evident in other accounts. However, his being a former master of Wat Tyler's is attested by no other source but Froissart's.

37 Henry Knighton, 'The Rebels in London according to Henry Knighton' in *The Peasants' Revolt of 1381* ed. by R.B. Dobson (London: Macmillan, 1970), pp. 181-187 (p.185).

38 'The Peasants' Revolt according to the Continuator of the "Eulogium Historiarum"', in *The Peasants' Revolt of 1381* ed. by R.B. Dobson (London: Macmillan, 1970), pp. 204-8 (p.207).

39 Froissart, 'The Rebels in London according to Froissart', p. 196.

40 *Ibid.*

41 Thomas James Benningfield, *London, 1900–1964: Armorial Bearings and Regalia of the London County Council, the Corporation of London and the Metropolitan Boroughs* (London: J Burrow & Co., 1964). pp. 21-3; throughout the early modern and modern periods, the dagger on the coat of arms of the city of London was said to commemorate the stabbing of Wat Tyler. However, research has shown that the arms were in use before 1381.
42 *Ibid.*
43 Anthony Tuck, 'Richard II (1367–1400)', in *The Oxford Dictionary of National Biography* (Oxford: Oxford University Press, 2004; Online Edn. 2008) [Internet <www.oxforddnb.com> Accessed 12 March 2017].

CHAPTER TWO

The Early Modern Period

I that did act on Smithfield's bloudy stage,
In second Richard's young and tender age;
And there receiv'd from Walworth's fatall hand
The stab of death, which life did countermand...
Which to avoyd let this my ghost intreat,
Yes love your King, feare heaven's tribunall seat;
So shall your soules without disturbance rest,
Till Christ shall come and make you fully blest.

Anon. *The Iust Reward of Rebels* (1642)

Lastly, in our own histories, you shall find that popular insurrections
never raised their ring-leaders above the gallows, as in Jack Straw,
Cade, and Wat Tyler, who was stabbed by the Maior of London, in the
height of his jollity, and in the head of twenty thousand rabble,
without the least hurt and injury to any of the contrary side.

Anon. *A Letter to Lieutenant Collonel John Lilburne,*
Now Prisoner in the Tower (1653)

As we have seen, most of what we know of the historical Wat Tyler's life appears in chronicles written by medieval clerics and scholars. Most of these accounts are predominantly negative towards the rebels. With little nuance, they portray Tyler and his army as ungodly wretches seeking to overthrow the divinely established social and political order. In the succeeding centuries, their view of Tyler and his fellow insurgents was largely the norm. Let us now leave the medieval period and enter what scholars call the early modern era, specifically the late sixteenth and seventeenth centuries.

THE EARLY MODERN PERIOD

The first major reincarnation of Wat Tyler and Jack Straw in popular culture came in an anonymously authored play entitled *The Life and Death of Iacke Straw, A Notable Rebel in England* (1593).[1] The play was written during the Golden Age of English theatre, when playwrights such as Christopher Marlowe (1564-93), William Shakespeare (1564-1616), and Anthony Munday (c.1560-1633) flourished. Many playwrights at this time used medieval settings in their works. Marlowe authored *The Troublesome Reigne and Lamentable Death of Edward the Second, King of England* (1593). Shakespeare's medieval plays include *King John, Richard III*, and *Macbeth*. He also authored *Richard II*, based upon the story of the boy king that has figured previously in this history (the play does not feature Wat Tyler or any of the other rebels, but instead focuses on the last two years of Richard's life). It is in early modern plays that some medieval figures acquire, for better or for worse, the reputations that would stick with them throughout the whole of their literary afterlives. For example, Shakespeare is responsible in large part for popularising the image of Richard III as a cruel and deformed tyrant. It is also in this period that Robin Hood is first elevated to the peerage, having been portrayed as a dispossessed nobleman for the first time in two plays, authored by Munday, entitled *The Downfall of Robert Earle of Huntington*, and *The Death of Robert, Earle of Huntingdon* (1597-8).[2]

Unlike Robin Hood, who in this period is appropriated by conservative authors, Tyler defies any such co-option by the establishment. As its title suggests, Jack Straw is the principal protagonist in *The Life and Death of Iacke Strawe*.[3] Straw is also named 'the Tyler', even though, puzzlingly, there is a separate character in the work called Wat Tyler. A possible source of this confusion may have been Geoffrey Chaucer's fourteenth-century *Nun's Priest's Tale*, in which the leader of the revolt is said to be Jack Straw instead of Wat Tyler.[4] Evidently drawing upon John Stow's chronicle, the play begins with the tax collector visiting Straw's home and enquiring as to the age of his daughter, upon which Straw vents his frustration at the government:

Collector. Now such a murmuring to rise upon so trifling a thing,
In all my life neuer saw I before:
And yet I haue beene Officer this seuen yeare and more,
The Tyler and his wife are in a great rage,
Affirming their Daughter to be vnder age.
Iacke Strawe. Art thou the Collector of the Kings taske?
Collector. I am Tyler why dost thou aske?
Iacke Strawe. Because thou goest beyond the Commission of the King,
We graunt to his Highnes pleasure in euery thing;
Thou hast thy taske money for all that be heere,
My daughter is not fourteene yeares olde, therefore shee goes cleare.[5]

The tax collector is unconvinced and attempts to indecently examine Straw's daughter. Enraged, Straw strikes the tax collector upon the head. Immediately afterwards, John Ball, Wat Tyler, Nobs, and Tom Miller enter, and Ball tells Straw that 'thou hast done a good seruice to thy country'.[6] As a result of the tax collector's assault upon Straw's daughter, the men begin plotting the rebellion.

It is tempting to believe that the Elizabethan era was some sort of 'golden age', during which a largely benevolent monarch presided over an era of economic prosperity and a flourishing of the arts. Certainly there were advancements in these areas, but the idea that the period was any kind of golden age, especially in the latter period, is far from the reality of the situation. It was a period of increasing crime, war, famine, and courtly intrigues. Most importantly for our purposes here, it was an era that was marked by a number of popular disturbances.[7] Many of these small-scale riots were caused by low wages and the high price of food, and hardships were felt particularly by apprentices.[8] Matters became bad enough for Queen Elizabeth I to issue a Royal Proclamation in 1590 against unruly apprentices and 'masterless men' who might be tempted to publicly express their discontent by rioting. The provisions of the proclamation ordered that such men be confined in their houses after nine o'clock on an evening upon pain of imprisonment.[9]

The description of the apprentices as 'masterless men' and 'vagabonds' here is quite telling as to how the political elites view those who participated in popular disturbances. The apprentices are not men who have been driven to riot as a result of want and penury. They are instead depicted as criminals, on a par with the rogues that flourished in Tudor England, and who were similarly described as 'masterless men and vagabonds'. In such a context, it was quite daring for the author of *The Life and Death of Iacke Strawe* to paint the doctrines of John Ball in a positive light, much less to show any sort of sympathy with the rebels. This is the impassioned speech which Ball gives to those assembled after the slaying of the tax collector. It is a damning indictment on the state of England which undoubtedly had resonance for those who saw it performed:

> *Parson Ball.* Neighbours, neighbours, the weakest now a
> dayes goes to the wall,
> But marke my words, and follow the counsell of *Iohn Ball.*
> England is growne to such a passe of late,
> That rich men triumph to see the poore beg at their gate.
> But I am able by good scripture before you to proue,
> That God doth not this dealing allow nor loue.
> But when Adam delued and Eue span,
> Who was then a Gentleman.[10]

Having appropriated and adapted the historical John Ball's famous sermon, the Ball of the play preaches further egalitarian principles and advocates the equal division of wealth and land among the people, to be achieved, if necessary, through force of arms:

> The rich haue all, the poor liue in miseries,
> But follow the counsell of *Iohn Ball,*
> I promise I loue yee all:
> And make diuision equally,
> Of each mans goods indifferently,

And rightly may you follow Armes,
To rid you from these ciuil harmes.[11]

Later on, Tyler speaks of 'communalitie', and what the conspiring rebels propose – the redistribution of wealth and lands equally – is akin to a type of proto-communism.

While Ball and Straw are the brains of the rebellion, Tyler and Tom Millar are its brawn:

Wat Tyler. I Iacke Strawe, or else Ile bide many a fowle
blow.
It shall bee no other but hee,
That thus favours this Communalitie,
Stay wee no longer prating here,
But let vs roundly to this geare,
Tis more than time that we were gone,
We be Lords and Maisters eueryone.
Tom Millar. And I my Maisters will make one,
To fight when all our foes be gone.
Well shall they see before wele lacke,
Wele stuffe the Gallowes till it cracke.[12]

The execution of noblemen, an egalitarian ideology, and the advocating of a redistribution of wealth and property make this play revolutionary for its time. Later in the play, when the rebels send a messenger to the royal household, even the King admits that he has some slight sympathy with those who feel they have had no choice but to rebel:

King. Admit him neere, for wee will heare him speake,
Tis hard when twixt the people and the King,
Such termes of threats and parlies must be had,
Would any Gentleman of worth,
Be seene in such a cause without offence,
Both to his God, his countrie and his Prince,
Except he were inforced thereunto?[13]

Later on, when the rebellion is at its height, the King, seemingly in good faith, offers all of the rebels a pardon, but this is rejected by Jack Straw with scorn, who intimates that the words of kings and noblemen can never be trusted:

> *Iacke Straw.* The King and his Nobles thinke they may sleep in quiet,
> Now they have given us a little holy water at the Court,
> But there's no such matter, we be no such fooles,
> To be bobd out with words and after come to hanging.[14]

Matters come to a head at Smithfield, and as the King and Straw are negotiating terms, Walworth stabs the latter:

> *Maior* ... Villaine I doe arrest thee in my Princes name,
> Proud rebel as thou art take that withal, (*here he stabs him*)
> Learne thou and all posteritie after thee,
> What tis a seruile slaue, to braue a King.
> Pardon my Gratious Lord for this my fact,
> In seruice done to God and to your selfe.[15]

Walworth is subsequently knighted for his heroism in slaying the leader of the revolt. Despite the sympathy allotted to the rebels throughout the play, it ends in moralistic fashion with an injunction to always obey the King who rules by divine right.

The play is something of a mystery to scholars. Besides the debates surrounding its authorship, critics are not even sure whether the play was performed or not.[16] Leonard R.N. Ashley suggests that if it was, then it would have been part of 'low' street entertainment culture, most likely presented as a morality play at a city pageant.[17] W.J. Lawrence downgrades the play's status even further, suggesting that it was probably intended as an inn-yard production.[18] If it was performed in either of the contexts that Ashley and Lawrence suggest, it was most likely abbreviated. The text would have served as a loose guide to what the performers should say, rather than being prescriptive. Furthermore, researchers are not agreed as to how the play was received during the period, although Stephen Schillinger suggests that the play 'gives voice to the period's most radical ideas about popular revolt and protest, suggesting how public theatre could reflect a sense of political unrest in the city'.[19] While the sentiments expressed by the play's leading protagonists seem at first glance to be subversive, the anti-establishment tone of the play is of course nicely contained. At the end, the rebels meet with justice at the hands of Walworth. There is only ever one outcome for rebels who betray their King. Schillinger further notes that in editions of the play that were printed after 1593, much of the radicalism was edited out of it.[20] This suggests that the publishers of the play, at least, were conscious of the implications of the original text's effect upon the minds of audiences.

Shortly after this play was published, Wat Tyler appears in a ballad entitled *The Rebellion of Wat Tyler, Jack Straw and Others against King Richard the Second* which, as far as I can ascertain, was first published in *The Garland of Delight* (1612).[21] Ballads have a long history in English culture. We know from William Langland's *Piers Plowman* (c.1377) that the first stories of Robin Hood circulated orally as ballads. With the arrival of the printing press, some medieval ballads such as *A Gest of Robyn Hode* (c.1450) began to be published in the early sixteenth century. By the seventeenth century, new songs were published as broadsides. These were single sheets of paper containing song lyrics which were then sold for a penny or even less by itinerant street-sellers. The trade in broadside ballads would last until the nineteenth century.[22] In the early modern period, the lyrics of various broadside ballads were then often reprinted in 'garlands', which contained numerous songs arranged around a theme (if we can make a modern analogy, we might say that broadsides were the singles and garlands were the albums). Collections of Robin Hood ballads entitled *Robin Hood's Garland*, for example, flourished in the latter part of the seventeenth century. Although no broadside version of *The Rebellion of Wat Tyler, Jack Straw, and Others* survives, it is likely that it was published in such a format before appearing in *The Garland of Delight*.[23]

THE EARLY MODERN PERIOD

While *The Life and Death of Iacke Straw* elicits a limited degree of sympathy with the rebels, in the ballad we see a return to the negative portrayals of Tyler and his men which we find in medieval chronicles. With a great multitude of 100,000 men following them, Wat Tyler, Jack Straw, Hob Carter, and Jack Shepheard march to London to wage war 'upon our noble King'.[24] Obviously the rebels have become semi-revolutionary here, for it will be recalled that at no point did the historical rebels wish to wage war upon the King. The ballad, therefore, anticipates some of the portrayals of Wat Tyler during the English Revolution of the mid-seventeenth century, which we shall examine momentarily. Numerous atrocities are attributed to the rebels, and their violence is portrayed as mindless:

> And then they marched with one consent
> Through London with a rude intent;
> And to fulfil their leud desire,
> They set the Savoy all on fire:
> And for the hate they did bear
> Unto the Duke of Lancashire,
> Therefore his house they burned quite,
> Through envy, malice and despite.
> Then to the Temple did they turn,
> The lawyers books eke did they burn,
> And spoil'd their lodgings one by one,
> And all they laid their hands upon.[25]

The nobility of the King is repeatedly emphasised. At Smithfield, despite the King and the courtiers having dealt fairly with the rebels, Walworth, unable to tolerate Tyler's 'villainy' any longer, slays him. The ballad then ends by saying, 'Thus did the proud rebellion cease, and after followed joyful peace.'[26]

Scholars can never be sure as to the exact date when a ballad was first written or published, and this makes any historicist interpretation of the lyrics difficult. We will never truly know why Tyler is portrayed negatively here. If, as seems likely, it is the text of a ballad which was in circulation before it was first printed in *The Garland of Delight* in 1612, we might say that it reflects a condemnation of the various riots that occurred towards the end of the sixteenth and the beginning of the seventeenth century, which were alluded to in the discussion of *The Life and Death of Iacke Strawe*. However, we can only speculate this matter.

Wat Tyler does briefly appear in another seventeenth-century broadside ballad entitled *The Wandering Jew's Chronicle; or, A Brief History of the Remarkable Passages from William the Conqueror to this Present Reign*. As with *The Rebellion of Wat Tyler, Jack Straw, and Others*, this ballad cannot be dated with any accuracy (the Bodleian Library lists a date range of between 1623 and 1660 for its publication).[27] Unusually for a broadside, scholars do know who the author was: the famous ballad writer Martin Parker who died in 1656. Therefore, the ballad must have been written before that date. The Wandering Jew is a European folk legend. He is said to have been one of the Jews who taunted Jesus on the cross, and was subsequently cursed to walk the earth until the Second Coming. He is referenced in numerous historical and literary works throughout the medieval and early modern periods, such as the thirteenth-century *Flores Historiarum*. The Wandering Jew received his most famous literary treatment in Eugene Sue's novel entitled *The Wandering Jew* (1844). In the ballad, as a man who has observed the whole of human history, the Wandering Jew is present when Tyler is murdered at Smithfield:

> I knew Wat Tyler and Jack Straw,
> And I the mayor of London saw,
> In Smithfield with him slew.
> I was at Pomfret-castle, when
> The Second Richard there was slain,
> Whose death eer since I rue.[28]

The Wandering Jew is not the only medieval legend to have been forgotten by modern-day audiences: Adam Bell, Clim of the Clough, William of Cloudeslie, Guy of Warwick, and the story of *The Wise*

Men of Gotham are stories, all of which were told through ballads, which were once familiar to early modern audiences but have been almost entirely forgotten in public memory.[29]

It is tempting to believe that old ballads were the songs of the common people, sung in taverns and in the fields as they toiled away for a pittance. That is a romanticised view of plebeian culture during the early modern period, and it is a view that was held by Victorian and Edwardian folk song historians such as Cecil Sharpe (1859-1924).[30] The common people certainly did sing ballads, but the truth is that early modern popular songs were not *only* the songs of the plebeian classes. In keeping with Peter Burke's theories relating to sixteenth- and seventeenth-century entertainment, ballads were part of a popular culture which people from all classes enjoyed. The appeal of ballads to the elites can be seen when we examine the provenance of those which survive. For example, the famous diarist Samuel Pepys (1633-1703) was one notable collector of street songs. The seventeenth-century civil servant had a passion for collecting books and manuscripts, and he collected nearly two thousand broadside ballads, which now form the 'Pepys Ballads Collection', housed at Magdalen College, Oxford. Similarly, a large part of the surviving corpus of ballads known as the Roxburghe Collection, currently held in the British Library, was initially assembled by Robert Harley, 1st Earl of Oxford (1661-1724), and later added to by John Ker, 3rd Duke of Roxburghe (1740-1804). Further evidence that ballads were not the sole preserve of the plebeian classes comes from the Augustan author, Joseph Addison (1676-1719). In the 7 June 1711 issue of *The Spectator,* he writes that the ballad of *The Two Children in the Wood* 'has been the delight of *most* Englishmen in some part of their age' (emphasis added).[31] Addison also devotes the entire 21 May 1711 issue of *The Spectator* to a discussion of the 'folk' ballad of *Chevy Chase.*[32] Thus, broadside ballads were indeed the songs 'of the people', but they were songs enjoyed by *all* people, that is to say, people from all classes of society.

While it has been theorised that *The Life and Death of Iacke Strawe* gave expression to contemporary political grievances, during the

Tudor and Jacobean periods there were no *serious* challenges to monarchical power (that is to say, that none of the movements against the authorities aimed to do away with the institution of the monarchy).[33] Wat Tyler's fame, or infamy, however, would reach new heights later in the seventeenth century, particularly during the English Revolution which began in 1642, when King Charles I went to war against his own subjects. It is necessary to give a very brief overview of the events leading up to the war between the King and Parliament in order to contextualise the literary representations of Wat Tyler that appeared during this period. The nation's coffers were empty after the reigns of Elizabeth (1533-1603) and the extravagant rule of James I (1566-1625). But it was Parliament that controlled the nation's finances. Arrogant and conceited, and knowing that the Commons would likely raise objections to his demands, Charles decided to govern without Parliament, and began a period of personal rule in 1629. Just as the imposition of unpopular taxes caused the great disturbance in 1381, so taxes would be one of the main causes of opposition to Charles's rule. In 1635, Charles, with the aid of the hated Court of the Star Chamber, ruled that everyone in the country should be liable to pay Ship Money, which historically was an ancient levy that had been raised only from the inhabitants of coastal towns. Further complications between Charles and the ruling elite followed, and in 1642, Charles raised his military standard against Parliament. The nation was now in the midst of a civil war. Ultimately, Charles and the Royalists lost the war that he had started. At the behest of Oliver Cromwell (1599-1698) and some members of the Rump Parliament, Charles was tried for treason and found guilty. The King was subsequently executed on 30 January 1649. The office of monarch was then formally abolished in England a couple of months later on 17 March.[34] Two days later, an act abolishing the House of Lords was brought to Parliament.[35] A Council of State was established, with Cromwell as its first chairman, and England was declared to be 'governed as a Commonwealth and Free State by the supreme authority of this nation, the representatives of the people in Parliament … without any King or House of Lords'.[36] Cromwell's power and influence subsequently grew, and by 1653, he was installed as the Lord Protector of the Commonwealth of England, Scotland, and Ireland.

Propagandists, particularly on the Royalist side of the conflict, appropriated Wat Tyler's history in order to highlight the moral dangers of fighting against a king who had a divine right to rule. Thanks to advances in printing, there was now a perfect medium for people to voice their support for each cause: the political pamphlet. These publications permeated early modern political culture (the Newberry Library in Chicago, for example, holds over two thousand such pamphlets), and sought to shape people's opinions upon contemporary issues. Strangely, it appears that Wat Tyler's story was never used to any great degree by the Parliamentarian forces. Perhaps he was too radical, even for regicides. After all, in histories written up to the seventeenth century, Wat Tyler and John Ball were represented as men who wished to completely overturn the social order, dispensing with the nobles and having the King only as their ruler. Furthermore, the Parliamentarians, and Cromwell himself, did not hold to an egalitarian ideology of the type preached by John Ball.[37]

The first notable appropriation of Tyler during the English Revolution is *The Iust Reward of Rebels; or, The Life and Death of Iack Straw, and Wat Tyler* (1642). The author looks back to the events of 1381 and uses the rebels' stories as a warning of what happens to revolt leaders when they oppose their King. As in the medieval chronicles, the rebels are depicted as mindless brutes, 'all of them of that dissolute and desperate condition'.[38] The story of the tax collector indecently assaulting Tyler's daughter is present, although, in spite of the monarchical support in the text, the actions of the tax collector are justly condemned.[39] It is in this text that we see one of the first clear identifications in the English language of the rebels as peasants. Tyler, Straw, and Ball, along with the army they led into London are called 'peasantly rustics void of all manners or humanity',[40] a passage no doubt inspired by the descriptions of the rebels as *rustici* in Latin chronicles.[41] The description of those who participated in the revolt as peasants, of course, is one that would continue in scholarship throughout the succeeding centuries, with the events of 1381 gaining the name of 'The Peasants' Revolt' during the Victorian period, in spite of the fact that, as we have seen, the rebels of 1381 were drawn from a diverse range of social classes. It is in *The Iust Reward of Rebels* that we also first see subtle hints of republicanism in Wat Tyler's post-medieval literary history, as he is described as a man who wished to install himself as ruler and 'to change the Monarchy into anarchy'.[42] Of course, we know, from the historical records, that Tyler and his fellow comrades never wished to get rid of the King, merely his evil advisors.

A similar work appeared a few years later entitled *The Idol of the Clovvnes, or, the Insurrection of Wat the Tyler with his Priests Baal and Straw* (1653). The work was written by the staunch Royalist poet, John Cleveland (1613-58), who was, according to Jason McElligott, 'the most famous poet of his day'.[43] Upon several occasions he mocked Cromwell in his writings, as in *The Character of a London Diurnall* (1645), where the future Lord Protector is portrayed as an absurd, comic figure.[44] The misspelling of John Ball's name as 'Baal' in the subtitle of *The Idol of the Clovvnes* is likely to be deliberate, evoking images of the heathen god of the Canaanites, Ba'al, in the Old Testament. Ba'al is also said to have been one of the principal Kings of Hell in a contemporary work of demonology entitled *The Lesser Key of Solomon* (this work is currently undated by scholars, but perhaps the reference to Ba'al in *The Idol of Clovvnes* suggests that it was known about when Cleveland published his work). Indeed, the events of the revolt of 1381 are presented as a battle of Biblical proportions. The false 'idol' of the clowns, Wat Tyler, is said to have been struck down like Dagon before the forces of truth and right (in the Bible, at 1 Samuel 5: 2-7, the Philistines capture the Ark of the Covenant and place it inside the temple of their false god, Dagon, but in the morning the Philistines awake to find the statue of Dagon prostrate before the Ark).[45] The Biblical allusions serve to give a very dramatic air to the text, although in its basic substance Cleveland's account is a fairly standard narrative of the historical revolt which builds upon some of the earlier chronicles we have already encountered, with the bulk of the information taken from Froissart.[46]

Unsurprisingly, Wat Tyler and the rebels receive censure in this work. And the criticism is vitriolic, with the protestors described as 'the dregs and off-scum of the Commons'.[47] One of the reasons that Tyler is wicked, among the many that Cleveland gives, is because he set himself up as 'Lord Paramount' of the rebels.[48] This is a reference to Cromwell, who was on occasion referred to as 'Lord Paramount'. Even Cromwell's son, Henry, in a letter dated November 1642, describes his father as a man who '[although] in appearance a zealous republican, yet in his heart he would not be sorry to be a Lord; not of Charles's making, but lord paramount over his delightful republic, upon which he broods continually'.[49] Another contemporary observer, speaking of Cromwell's plans for America, Ireland, and Scotland, wrote that it appeared as though Cromwell aimed to 'make himself Lord Paramount, King or Emperor over the whole, and the succession of his heirs'.[50] The clear message of *The Idol of the Clovvnes*, then, is that 'the world cannot subsist without order and subjection, men cannot be freed from lawes: if they were, there could be no society, no civility, anywhere.'[51] Men such as Wat Tyler and Oliver Cromwell, who seek to overturn existing hierarchies, are like demons from Hell.

Cleveland certainly found himself on the wrong side of the law under the Cromwellian Commonwealth. He was arrested in Great Yarmouth in 1655 and imprisoned there for three months, although it is not known for what charge he was incarcerated. But perhaps Cromwell, whom Cleveland alludes to in *The Idol of the Clovvnes*, and criticises in several of his other works, was not so bad after all? While in gaol, Cleveland appealed directly to Cromwell in a letter, who released him forthwith. After this, it appears as though Cleveland subsequently lived out the remaining three years of his life in relative peace in London, and his subsequent writings do not appear to have honed in on Cromwell.

Cromwell died in 1658, and the title of Lord Protector passed to his weak and ineffectual son, Richard. The latter did not enjoy the confidence of either Parliament or the army. Finally, it was decided by Parliament that Charles I's son, the future Charles II (1630-85), should be invited to rule England.[52] This does not mean that the people and Parliament alike were completely enamoured with the restored Stuart dynasty. In 1688, Parliament deemed it expedient that another Stuart King, James II (1633-1701), should be ousted from the English throne. England by 1688 was a Protestant nation, having been through the Reformation in the sixteenth century. The Catholic James II, with his absolutist tendencies, represented, it was feared, a style of government that was incompatible with liberty-loving Englishmen. Consequently, William of Orange (1650-1702) and his wife Mary (1662-94) were invited to rule England as joint monarchs instead. As part of their 'contract' with Parliament, which at this point was gradually asserting its sovereignty over the figure of the monarch, William and Mary had to make certain promises such as not to infringe upon the liberties of the subject. Of course, when the elites spoke of the liberties of the subject in this period, by and large, it did not include the plebeian classes. Politics in late seventeenth- and eighteenth-century England was dominated by an aristocratic oligarchy. People who owned property worth less than forty shillings did not have the right to vote. This often meant that the primary means through which commoners might vent their political grievances was through rioting. Let us take a look at Wat Tyler's literary afterlife in the era of King Mob.

Notes

1 There have been various attributions to contemporary authors by scholars for this play, including George Peele and even Shakespeare. For a critique of these theories see Irving Ribner, *The English History Play in the Age of Shakespeare* (Princeton, NJ: Princeton University Press, 1957; repr. Abingdon: Routledge, 2005), pp. 72-3.

2 It is Munday's portrayal of Robin Hood as a dispossessed earl that has persisted in modern portrayals of the Robin Hood story.

3 By far the best analysis of *The Life and Death of Iacke Strawe* is carried out by Stephen Schillinger in the following article: Stephen Schillinger, 'Begging at the Gate: Jack Straw and the Acting Out of Popular Rebellion', *Medieval & Renaissance Drama in England* 21 (2008), pp. 87-127.

4 R.B. Dobson, 'Introduction: Geoffrey Chaucer and the Peasants' Revolt' in

The Peasants' Revolt of 1381 ed. by R.B. Dobson (London: Macmillan, 1970), p. 387.

5 *The Life and Death of Iacke Strawe, A Notable Rebel in England: Who was Kild in Smithfield by the Lord Maior of London* (Printed at London by Iohn Danter, and are to be Solde by William Barley at his Shop in Gratious-Street ouer against Leaden-Hall, 1593), [p. 3]. The original edition has neither lines nor page numbers, but I have inserted page references.

6 *The Life and Death of Iacke Strawe*, [p. 4].

7 Curtis C. Breight, *Surveillance, Militarism and Drama in the Elizabethan Era* (Basingstoke: Palgrave Macmillan, 1996), p. 88.

8 For more information about the disturbances and riots of the late Elizabethan period see Ian W. Archer, *The Pursuit of Stability: Social Relations in Elizabethan London* (Cambridge: Cambridge University Press, 1991).

9 'Enforcing Curfews for Apprentices', in *Tudor Royal Proclamations* ed. by Paul L. Hughes and James F. Larkin 3 Vols. (New Haven: Yale University Press, 1969), 3: 42 cited in Mihoko Suzuki, 'The London Apprentice Riots of the 1590s and the Fiction of Thomas Deloney' *Criticism* 38: 2 (1996), pp. 181-217 (pp.181-2).

10 *The Life and Death of Iacke Strawe*, [p. 5].

11 *Ibid.*, [p. 6].

12 *Ibid.*, [pp. 6-7].

13 *The Life and Death of Iack Strawe,* [p. 14].

14 *Ibid.*, [p. 31].

15 *Ibid.*, [p. 34].

16 Schillinger, 'Begging at the Gate', p. 87.

17 Leonard R. Ashley, *Authorship and Evidence: A Study of Attribution and the Renaissance Drama Illustrated by the Case of George Peele (1556-1596)* (Geneva: Libraire Droz, 1968), p. 83.

18 W.J. Lawrence, *Pre-Restoration Stage Studies* (Cambridge, MA: Harvard University Press, 1927), p. 27

19 Schillinger, 'Begging at the Gate', p. 87.

20 Schillinger, 'Begging at the Gate', p. 87.

21 Roy Lamson, 'English Broadside Ballad Tunes of the 16th and 17th Centuries', *Papers Read by Members of the American Musicological Society at the Annual Meeting* (11-16 September 1939), pp. 112-121 (p.120): Lamson dates *The Garland of Delight* to 1612.

22 Henry Mayhew, *London Labour and the London Poor* ed. by Robert Douglas-Fairhurst (Oxford: Oxford University Press, 2010), pp. 74-104: Mayhew goes into great detail discussing 'Street-Sellers of Stationary, Literature and the Fine Arts'.

23 There are a great many folk song singers and scholars who hold that these

seventeenth-century broadside ballads existed as part of an oral tradition first, and were then set down in writing and/or published. This is perhaps true of very early ballads such as *A Gest of Robyn Hode* (c.1450). But generally speaking, the ballads of the seventeenth and eighteenth centuries were usually printed first and subsequently disseminated orally. In the case of *The Rebellion of Wat Tyler*, there is no evidence to suggest that it was originally part of an oral tradition.

24 'The Rebellion of Wat Tyler, Jack Straw and Others Against King Richard the Second; how Sir William Walworth, lord Mayor of London, stabbed Tyler in Smithfield, for which the King knighted Sir William, with Five Aldermen More, Causing a Dagger to be Added in the Shield of the City Arms', in *Old Ballads, Historical and Narrative, with Some of Modern Date* ed. by Thomas Evans 2 Vols. (London: T. Evans, 1777); 1: 280-4.

25 'The Rebellion of Wat Tyler, Jack Straw and Others against King Richard the Second', p. 281.

26 Ibid., p. 284.

27 Martin Parker, *The Wandering Jew's Chronicle: or, The Old Historian, His Brief Declaration, Made in a Mad Fashion, of each Coronation, that Past in this Nation, Since William's Invasion, For no Great Occasion, But Meer [sic] Recreation, To Put Off Vexation* ([n.p.] [n.pub.] [n.d.]) Bodleian Library Broadside Ballads Wood 401(121) RoudV13587 [Internet <ballads.bodleian._ox.ac.uk> Accessed 11 February 2017].

28 *Ibid.*

29 The name 'Gotham' from *The Wise Men of Gotham* will of course conjure images of Gotham City in the *Batman* series of comics and films to modern readers. The story runs thus: in the 1200s, the villagers of Gotham, Nottinghamshire learnt that King John was due to pass through their small village; John, perhaps more than any other English King, was almost universally detested; all of the villagers thus feigned madness in an attempt to stop the King from visiting as insanity was presumed to be infectious. The plan worked and the King chose to travel by a different route. In the early nineteenth century, the American author Washington Irving, noting the villagers' seeming madness, became the first to equate New Yorkers with the people of medieval Gotham. Bob Kane then chose the name of Gotham for the city where Batman lives.

30 Cecil J. Sharp, *English Folk Song: Some Conclusions* (London: Simpkin & Novello, 1907), p. 3.

31 Joseph Addison and Richard Steele, *The Spectator* ed. by Henry Morley (London: G. Routledge [n.d.] c.1880), pp. 136-8 (p.136).

32 Addison, *The Spectator*, pp. 113-5.

33 The Pilgrimage of Grace between 1536 and 1537, led by Robert Aske, had

at its heart religious grievances, as did the so-called Prayer Book Rebellion of 1549. The Northern Rising of 1569 merely sought to place Mary, Queen of Scots upon the throne, thus replacing one queen with one another. Again, the Babington Plot of 1586 merely sought to replace Elizabeth I with Mary. The London Food Riots in 1595 were centred upon localised economic and social woes. But none of the main players in these revolts and rebellions ever imagined life without a monarchy.

34 'The Act for Abolishing the Office of King', in *Constitutional Documents of the Puritan Revolution* ed. by Samuel Rawson Gardiner 2nd Edn. (Oxford: Clarendon Press, 1899), pp. 384-7.

35 'An Act for Abolishing the House of Lords', in *Constitutional Documents of the Puritan Revolution* ed. by Samuel Rawson Gardiner 2nd Edn. (Oxford: Clarendon Press, 1899), pp. 387-8.

36 'An Act Declaring England to be a Commonwealth', in *Constitutional Documents of the Puritan Revolution* ed. by Samuel Rawson Gardiner 2nd Edn. (Oxford: Clarendon Press, 1899), p. 388.

37 R.B. Dobson, 'Interpretations of the Peasants' Revolt', in *The Peasants' Revolt of 1381* ed. by R.B. Dobson (London: Macmillan, 1970), pp. 351-6 (p.355).

38 *The Iust Reward of Rebels; or, The Life and Death of Iack Straw, and Wat Tyler, who for their Rebellion and Disobedience to their King and Country, were Suddenly Slaine, and all their Tumultuous Rout Overcome and Put to Flight. Whereunto is added the Ghost of Iack Straw, as he lately appeared to the Rebels in Ireland, wishing them to Forbeare and Repent of their Divellish and Inhumane Actions against their lawful King and Country* (London: Printed for F. Couls, I. Wright, T. Banks, and T. Bates, 1642), p. 3.

39 *The Iust Reward of Rebels*, p. 3.

40 *The Iust Reward of Rebels*, p. 7.

41 Barker, *England Arise*, p. xv.

42 *The Iust Reward of Rebels*, p. 10.

43 Jason McElligot, *Royalism, Print and Censorship in Revolutionary England* (Woodbridge: Boydell, 2007), p. 94. For a full biography see L.A. Jacobus, *John Cleveland* (Boston: Twayne, 1975).

44 Laura Lunger Knoppers, *Constructing Cromwell: Ceremony, Portrait, and Print 1645-1661* (Cambridge: Cambridge University Press, 2000), pp. 11-12.

45 John Cleveland, *The Idol of the Clovvnes, or, Insurrection of Wat the Tyler with his Priests Baal and Straw together with his Fellow Kings of the Commons against the English Church, the King, the Laws, Nobility and Royal Family and Gentry, in the Fourth Year of King Richard the 2d, An. 1381* (London: [n.pub.] 1653), p. 61.

46 Cleveland, *The Idol of the Clovvnes*, p. vii.

47 Cleveland, *The Idol of the Clovvnes*, p. 1.

48 Cleveland, *The Idol of the Clovvnes*, p. 12.

49 Henry Cromwell, 'Letter II: To Lord Wentworth, November 1642' in *Memoirs of Oliver Cromwell and His Children* 3 Vols. (London: Chapple, 1816), 1: 185.

50 Cited in Abigail L. Swingen, *Competing Visions of Empire: Labor, Slavery, and the Origins of the British Atlantic Empire* (New Haven: Yale University Press, 2015), p. 52.

51 Cleveland, *The Idol of the Clovvnes*, p. 65.

52 *The Character of a Leading Petitioner* (London: W. Davis, 1681), pp. 1-2; Jack Straw is briefly mentioned in this pamphlet, which is essentially a tirade of abuse from a Tory to an unnamed Whig: 'He is an incest produc'd by the carrion of a commonwealth ... He's unmannerly, mean, senceless [sic], and impertinent ... He has the wit of a dame, the truth of a Frenchman, and the conscience of a grand jury man ... he is that unnatural greensickness of the body politic ... He is that troublesome vapour that breaks out of the earth to make a wind ... He is the cruder humors and itch of a kingdom, and not only tickels [sic] himself into torment, but revengefully infects his neighbour ... HE is the epitome of all sorts of villainies and compriseth in his own peculiar nutshell the bold contrivances and ridiculous attempts of Jack Straw and his successless gang.'

CHAPTER THREE

The Eighteenth Century

*If they had succeeded, their intention was, to murder the king,
to extirpate the nobility and clergy, excepting only the
mendicant friars, to divide England into several kingdoms, to
make Wat Tyler king of Kent, and to abolish all the ancient
laws and make new ones. By these two instances only, it will
be easily perceived, of what absolute necessity it is for the
nation to be provided with such laws, as may prevent even the
first steps and approaches towards any riotous and disorderly
meetings of the people; for, when once a mob are collected
together, and they have done one act of violence, they soon
proceed to another, till they perpetrate the most extravagant
enormities, and the most horrid cruelties ... that may shake
the foundation of a government.*

The Weekly Magazine; or, Edinburgh Amusement (1769)

Thus far we have seen how Wat Tyler has been predominantly
portrayed by elite writers as the traitorous leader of a riotous mob, who
disgraced the laws of England and dared to oppose his King. During
the eighteenth century, this interpretation of Tyler's life and deeds
continued. For example, an anonymous journalist in *The Weekly
Magazine* on 30 November 1769 wrote that 'whoever has read the
history of our country has seen what terrible convulsions in the state
have been occasioned by very small and insignificant accidents.'[1] 'The
insurrection of Wat Tyler,' the same author continues, 'is a memorable
instance of this kind ... it will be easily perceived, of what absolute
necessity it is for the nation to be provided with such laws, as may

prevent even the first steps and approaches towards any riotous and disorderly meetings of the people.'[2] Most likely the writing of this article came as a result of the author having heard of, or maybe even having been witness to, the spate of recent riots at Spitalfields in London that occurred between 1765 and 1769. Alternatively, it may have been occasioned by news from across the Atlantic of the Stamp Act Riots in the American Colonies. Perhaps it was the St. George's Fields Riots in 1768. In truth, there were many events in recent memory that could have prompted the author to write the article in question.

As I pointed out previously, it is important to remember that only a small section of society had the vote at this point. There were very few ways that people could express their political grievances. One relatively safe way to express them was through the publishing of political satires, a genre that flourished during the eighteenth century. However, an author could not go too far, for Daniel Defoe was sentenced to a spell in the pillory for publishing a supposedly seditious work entitled *The Shortest Way with Dissenters* (1702).

Alternatively, if certain government policies became unbearable, the populace might appeal to King Mob. That is to say that the people might riot. As Dorothy George says in *Hacks and Dunces* (1972), the eighteenth-century authorities were in constant fear that 'King Mob might at any time resume his reign after the briefest interregnum'.[3] And people might riot over the smallest reasons, even over the price of gin as they did in 1743. Let us take a look at how Tyler and his associates were represented during the era of King Mob.[4]

The first work we will examine is *The History of All the Mobs, Tumults, and Insurrections in Great Britain* (1715). The text was written in response to the Jacobite Rising which occurred in the year that it was published. After the deaths of William and Mary, the throne passed to Mary's sister, Anne (r. 1702-14). However, Anne died childless and the throne of the newly united Kingdom of Great Britain passed to the Protestant Prince George of Hanover. Consequently, in 1715, forces loyal to the Catholic James Francis Edward Stuart, or 'the Pretender', as he would be called by his Hanoverian detractors, invaded England in an attempt to regain the thrones of England, Scotland, and Ireland from the Hanoverian dynasty. Although the rebellion was ultimately unsuccessful, a number of leading Scottish and English politicians defected to the Pretender, and the Hanoverian government grew so concerned that it suspended *habeas corpus*. Reflecting the establishment's paranoia about the possibility of the invasion being successful, the reader of *The History of All the Mobs* is first greeted with a reprint of the government's Proclamation against Rebels:

> That whereas of late some people have been stirred to riots and tumults, and the same are now carried into open rebellion, and a levying of war against his Majesty and his Royal authority ... It is therefore thought fit to issue a proclamation, declaring; that all officers civil and military, are by their duty obliged to use their utmost endeavours, by force of arms, to suppress all such traitorous rebellions.[5]

It was, therefore, a citizen's patriotic duty to assist in suppressing rebels. *The History of the Mobs* would go on to recount all manner of instances in which rioters had attempted to challenge the government, but who had met with an untimely end.

The History of All the Mobs is essentially a compendium of the lives of various figures who had challenged their governments. The way that work is structured, as well as its sensationalised content, bears many similarities to another genre of literature which flourished during the same period, the criminal biography. Examples of criminal biographies include Captain Alexander Smith's *A Complete History of the Lives and Robberies of the Most Notorious Highwaymen, Footpads, Shoplifts and Cheats* (1714), and Charles Johnson's *A General and True History of the Robberies and Murders of the Most Notorious Pyrates* (1724), as well as Johnson's *Lives of the Most Remarkable Criminals* (1735). As the titles of Smith and Johnson's works suggest, they are compendia of the lives of notorious criminals, much like *The History of all the Mobs* is a compendium of short biographies of mob leaders. Another manner in which *The History of All the Mobs* resembles a criminal biography is in the fact that it is a moralist text. In the preface the reader is told that,

> In all our histories of Great Britain and Ireland, we meet with nothing more frequent than mobs and insurrections, which tho' they have always terminated in the destruction of the ring leaders and the principal abettors, yet we still find that the madness of the people has fatally spread itself from one age to another, and is become even at this day, no less dangerous and infectious than it was at the very beginning. Upon this account it is, this short History is attempted, that it may be a standing caution to the common people, for whose use 'tis chiefly intended, against plunging themselves into such unhappy circumstances, by which they are rendered not only enemies to the publick peace and welfare of their country, but likewise to themselves, and obnoxious to all good men.[6]

Moreover, *The History of All the Mobs* was not a piece of trashy literature. The title page lists a retail price of six shillings which would have made it relatively expensive for a poorer reader. During the late seventeenth, and into the nineteenth century, the sale and distribution of books was different to the way that it is today. The block of text was usually sold by the publisher in cheap paper boards. If the purchaser wished, they could then take the text block to a bindery where it would be bound according to the author's specification, usually in expensive leather covers. This would have raised the total cost of the product significantly. *The History of all the Mobs*, therefore, is a work for the middle and upper classes, and a subtle elite class consciousness is evident in the preface, which speaks disparagingly of 'the common people'.[7]

Another way that *The History of All the Mobs* resembles eighteenth-century criminal biography is in its free use of facts, for rarely did the writers of such works strive for historical veracity. For example, in speaking of Tyler's rebellion, the reader is told that it occurred in the year 1383. John Ball, instead of being imprisoned in Maidstone gaol at the beginning of the revolt, is present when Wat Tyler strikes the tax collector:

> In the year 1383 being the 6th year of the reign of Richard the Second, there happen'd a very dangerous insurrection in Kent ... A collector of the pole, coming into the house of one Tyler to demand the money for her daughter's head, the woman answer'd that her daughter was not yet of age. The fellow told her he would soon satisfy himself whether she was or not, and offering some rudeness to the girl, the mother cry'd out, which brought her husband to their assistance, who with a lathing staff gave the collector a blow on the head, of which he dyed immediately. Tyler making heavy complaint of this to his neighbours, and being seconded by one John Ball a seditious clergy-man, who represented to them the mismanagements of the government, and the infringement of their liberties, and the people grew so incens'd, that they assemble themselves into a body.[8]

Tyler and the rebels make their way to London to see the King and demand redress. One of the first things that Tyler does when in London is to send for his master, 'a sober honest citizen, and cut off his head'.[9] This story is based upon an account in Froissart's Chronicles which probably never occurred. This little incident is most likely inserted into the narrative because the author wishes to portray Tyler as some sort of bitter and vengeful Hogarthian idle apprentice. The rebels then make their progress through London, burning and pillaging, and rebels from other areas soon join them in committing 'murder and cruelty'.[10] The King does not actually meet with Tyler in this account, instead he simply sends Walworth to Smithfield where Walworth hits him over the head. After this, Walworth's men begin 'to stab [Tyler] in several places, of which wounds he dyed upon the spot'.[11]

Tyler's followers are then all arrested, including John Ball. We have seen how closely this account of the rebellion resembles eighteenth-century criminal biography with its moralist undertones. Another manner in which *The History of all the Mobs* resembles the genre is in the fact that it includes a copy of a supposed confession written by Jack Straw when he was in his cell in Newgate. 'Last Dying Speeches' broadsides, as well as lengthier criminal narratives such as Smith's *History of the Highwaymen*, often included a made-up copy of a letter that was supposedly written by a felon in gaol, or the text of a speech delivered by the condemned at the gallows. Straw's last confession in *The History of all the Mobs* is a hackneyed version of the supposed confession which appears in Thomas Walsingham's fourteenth-century account of the revolt, at a point in Walsingham's narrative when 'he gladly relieves himself of facts and gives free rein to his powerful imagination'.[12] Had the rebels succeeded, the fictional confession implies that the consequences would have been horrifying for the establishment:

> When we were assembled, says he, upon Black Heath, and had sent the King to come to us, our purpose was to have slain all knights and gentlemen that should be about him; and as for the King, we would have kept him among us, to the end the people might more boldly have repaired to us; and when we had gotten power enough, we would have slain all Noblemen, especially the knights of Rhodes, and lastly would have killed the King and all men of possessions, with bishops, monks, parsons of churches, only fryars mendicant would have been spared, for administration of the sacraments. Then we would have devised laws according to which the people should have liv'd, for which we would have created Kings; as Wat Tyler in Kent, and others in other counties: And in the same night that Wat Tyler was kill'd, we intended to have set fire to the city in four corners, and to have divided the spoil amongst us. And this was our purpose as God may help me now at last.[13]

The confession is included in order to highlight to readers 'how fit an orator [John Ball] was for a mob, and what strength of perswasion

[sic] there is in nonsense and enthusiasm'.[14] The account then abruptly ends and goes on to give the story of Owen Glendow of Wales (d. 1416) who raised an army against Edward IV, before turning to that other famous medieval rebel, Jack Cade.

As we have seen, *The History of All the Mobs* was an expensive and predominantly middle-class work of literature. But there was a thriving trade in chapbooks during the eighteenth century as well. These were small pamphlets that numbered between eight and twelve pages and, like broadside ballads, were sold for a penny or less by itinerant salesmen in the streets of the towns as well as in rural areas. The sale and distribution of chapbooks continued into the Victorian era when it was largely superseded by the penny blood and penny dreadful publishing industry. Numerous chapbooks detailing Tyler's life were published throughout the century, and given their ephemeral nature it is difficult to date the first appearance of any chapbook with precision. The chapbook of *The History of Wat Tyler and Jack Straw* was printed, as it happens, in Smithfield where Tyler met his doom. And the narrative is firmly on the side of the authorities. As with *The History of All the Mobs*, there is little attempt in this chapbook to provide a true and faithful account of the revolt, and John Ball's name is even mistakenly changed to John Wall. According to the anonymous author (chapbook authors were usually anonymous) Wat Tyler was 'a restless spirited man'.[15] He is elsewhere described as 'a lewd bold fellow'.[16] The account of the attempted rape upon his daughter is absent, and how Tyler comes to be involved in the revolt at all is rather unclear. Not that it mattered to hack writers in the eighteenth century, for as in *The History of All the Mobs*, facts are freely invented. For example, the reader is told that Wat Tyler was a tailor, and not a blacksmith or a tiler, as it was commonly accepted in the eighteenth century.[17] While the poll tax is mentioned in this account, the main cause of the revolt is said to be the seditious teachings of John Wall:

> One John Wall, a seditious priest, perceiving that the common sort of people exceedingly grudged and murmured at the payment of the Taxes, took that advantage to stir them up to

rebellion, by preaching up and informing the baser sort, who were pinched with want and penury, that all men by parentage and descent from Adam were of one condition and of equal worth, and that the laws of the kingdom were injurious and unjust, which set so great a difference between man and man, by making some lords and potentates, and by giving others large authority and command in enlarging of great possessions, thereby make the rest beggars, enduring misery and poverty.[18]

This doctrine of equality, described here as 'this treacherous and leud [sic] doctrine' deceives more rebels and then they march on London. The reader is never told what the rebels' specific demands are.[19] It is much better for the author to paint Tyler and his men as a mindless mob, or, 'brainsick people'.[20] Tyler and his fellow insurgents are seen committing heinous acts of vandalism, 'beating down, firing and plundering the houses of such as were professors of the law, or were against their rebellious proceedings, compelling all knights and gentlemen either to fly or to take part in their uproar'.[21] They plunder and burn down the Savoy, killing all the people they find therein.[22] It was noted in the first chapter, furthermore, that Froissart records in his chronicle that the rebels were rude to the Queen Mother. I also pointed out that this episode is of dubious authenticity. Yet in this chapbook the rebels treat the Queen Mother even more cruelly than they are portrayed as doing in Froissart's chronicle: '[Wat Tyler] broke her head that the blood ran down about her ears, saying, he would teach such saucy housewives to learn who they spoke to.'[23] In contrast to Tyler and the insurgents, who are really just brutes in the work, there is the noble young king, described as 'gallant and resolute'.[24] When the two meet, Wat Tyler 'deeply swore desperate oaths [to the King]' and commands his followers to cut off the King's head.[25] It is then that Walworth strikes Tyler on the head with a mace, not a dagger, and he is then stabbed repeatedly by Walworth's men.

Other chapbooks telling a slightly different story were printed during the century such as the similarly titled *The History of Wat Tyler and Jack Straw*. The same attitude towards Tyler and the mob that is found in *The History of All the Mobs* and the earlier chapbook is evident here also, although at least this author manages to spell John Ball's name correctly. He is described as 'a factious clergyman, a scholar of Whickliffe'.[26] It is the preacher's teachings that are given as the main cause of the revolt. John Ball's phrase, 'when Adam delved and Eve span, who was then the gentleman' may not appear to be controversial in modern times, given the fact that most of the western world today holds to the theory of equality before the law, in theory if not always in practice. But in the eighteenth century Britain was not an egalitarian society, and the elites certainly thought of themselves as 'better' than their plebeian counterparts. It is with 'such seditious and traitorous persuasions' that John Ball convinces the populace to rise up against their superiors.[27]

Wat Tyler is not mentioned until the revolt reaches London and, as in the earlier chapbook, the reader is told nothing of his motivations for joining the revolt. Tyler physically and verbally assaults the Queen Mother.[28] He and the mob then travel to John of Gaunt's house where they burn his house down, and murder Gaunt and all of his servants.[29] Of course, John of Gaunt was never murdered by the rebels, and he was far from London at the time of the revolt in 1381. The murder of Gaunt in this account is illustrative of the extent to which chapbook writers were unconcerned with presenting a 'true' account of the past. When Tyler finally meets the King, his demands are painted in as unreasonable light as possible:

> The King ... was rather unwilling to provoke a mad dog, and with fair speeches and a pleasing countenance, he began to expostulate with Tyler, and was willing to condescend to come to dishonourable submissions (betwixt sovereign and subject) to content him; but the more [Tyler] found the King pliable, the more unreasonable were his demands, and insolent his behaviour. Among many other villainous as well as unreasonable demands, the following was one, viz. To have all law abolished; affirming with an execrable oath, before night

all laws of England should pass through the strait, clapping his hands to his mouth.[30]

As expected, Walworth kills Tyler, and John Ball is imprisoned. The chapbook then ends with a statement that is highly supportive of the status quo: 'thus ended this monstrous rebellion, which tended to and must have accomplished the destruction of the Kingdom, had it not been for the gallant behaviour of its citizens.'[31]

The portrayal of Tyler found in books such as *The History of All the Mobs* and the two chapbooks we have discussed are also replicated in multi-volume history books. In G.F. Raymond's *A New, Universal, and Impartial History of England* (1790), Tyler and the rebels are said to have been 'of a more ferocious disposition ... determined to revenge themselves upon the heads of the nation'.[32] In Oliver Goldsmith's *A History of England from the Earliest Times to the Present* (1790), Tyler's insurrectionary force is described with terms such as 'rabble', 'murderers', and 'insurgents'.[33]

A more comic representation of Tyler's life is to be found in a play entitled *Wat Tyler and Jack Straw; or, The Mob Reformers* (1730), performed in London at the St. Bartholomew's Fair celebrations. The Bartholomew Fair began during the twelfth century. Henry I issued a Royal Charter to Prior Rahere to hold a celebration at Smithfield to raise money for the newly-established Bartholomew Hospital. Local tradesmen were invited to sell their wares at the event, and entertainments were permitted. This is the description of the event from the nineteenth-century antiquary John Timbs:

The Prior ... looked to temporal as well as spiritual aid for his [hospital]; and, therefore, obtained a royal charter to hold a fair annually at Bartholomewtide, for three days – on the eve, the fete-day of the saint, and the day after; 'firm peace,' being granted to all persons frequenting the fair of St. Bartholomew. This brought traders from all parts to Smithfield; thither resorted clothiers and drapers, not merely of England, but of all countries, who exposed their goods for sale. The stalls or booths were erected within the walls of the priory churchyard, and a watch was set in order to protect the various wares.[34]

Soon the Fair became more of a carnival than a business and fundraising function, and by 1604 the Lord Mayor of London had taken over the running of the event, instead of the hospital authorities.[35] It also became a bawdy and rowdy event by the early modern period. By the eighteenth century, the event was described by one city official as being full of 'obscene, lascivious, and scandalous plays, comedies, and farces, unlawful games and interludes, drunkenness'.[36] No doubt *Wat Tyler and Jack Straw* would have been considered as one of those 'scandalous plays'. In the play, there is no account of the attempted rape upon Wat Tyler's daughter and neither does John Ball make an appearance. Instead, the play opens with Tyler leading the rebels to London, addressing four characters each named Mob who want to install Tyler as King:

> *Mob.* Huzzah! Long live Wat the first –
> *Mob.* Tyler the great!
> *Mob.* The Prince of popular Princes!
> *Mob.* The Mighty head of us, the quarters of rebellion!
> *Tyl.* You all then swear to follow and pursue these heels and feet, that have resolved to kick the tyrant Dick, and lay him sprawling down?
> *All.* We do, we do![37]

Interspersed throughout the play are farcical scenes involving Tyler's wife and daughter, as well as scenes in Richard II's household in which the servants are poked fun at. Although not hinted at in the text, one can quite easily imagine that this was the type of play in which there was a high degree of audience participation. Like the sixteenth-century *Life and Death of Iacke Strawe*, the script may have been intended to serve as a loose guide for the actors, who would then be free to improvise at random in response to their audiences' reaction. It was, after all, a piece of street entertainment and the audiences were not obliged to pay.[38] Sometimes, if an audience did not like a particular ending, they could demand it be changed to something more acceptable. That such practices existed is suggested in the finale to John Gay's *The Beggar's Opera* (1728). Essentially a play within a play, as the hero, the highwayman Captain Macheath, is about to be hanged one of the players turns to the playwright and says, 'but, honest friend, I hope you don't intend that Macheath shall really be executed.'[39] The playwright agrees, and decrees that the highwayman must receive a reprieve, 'to comply with the taste of the town'.[40]

When the rebels reach London and Wat Tyler meets with the King at Smithfield, Tyler has nothing but contempt for the King:

> *King.* Yes, with amazement, and with aking hearts we see the tumults, murthers, and disorders which your mistaken frenzy has committed. Where are your wrongs? And what should we redress?
>
> *Tyl.* Nothing – we'll do it all ourselves. –
>
> Where are our wrongs! And what should you redress! Why, the laws wrong us, and the Parliament; you wrong us, everybody wrongs us, and in short we'll bear it no longer.
>
> *Mob.* Let Wat alone, Scythe, I'll warrant he's fit to talk to an Emperor.
>
> *King.* Blindly you argue, and wou'd blindly lead these poor unthinking wretches to destruction. Accept our gracious pardon for all past, disperse your numbers, and we love you still.
>
> *Tyl.* Ay, pr'ythee, who is fool then? – No, you insignificant prig, I won't disband even a taylor, or the ninth part of a man. – but if you please you may hear our conditions: pull from that sawcy, lousy head the crown, and put it where it should be – upon mine. As for your carcass, take it where you please. To France or to the Devil, as you please.[41]

At first glance, it might appear that this play is almost revolutionary in its tone, with its talk of installing Wat Tyler as king and righting the people's wrongs. After all, there was certainly no great love for the early Georgian kings amongst Britons in the early eighteenth century. It was only really in 1745 with the second Jacobite rebellion that the British people found themselves forced to decide between loyalty to the Stuarts or the Hanoverian George II.[42] It was also an era in which, as we have seen, the elites feared the appearance of King Mob, and the play was performed at an event which the authorities in London were already becoming concerned about. However, while it is tempting to read this as a play with subversive sentiments, ideas about the carnivalesque are useful here (and indeed are useful in part for studying the aforementioned *Life and Death of Iacke Strawe*). The theory of the carnivalesque is based upon a study of the medieval carnival, in which peasants swapped their social positions with the lord, and where Church and State were openly mocked, which allegedly functioned as a safety valve which cemented the status quo. In a world turned upside down, it supposedly gave people an outlet for enjoyment and an opportunity to thumb their noses at their superiors. At the end of the festival the social order was restored. These harmless celebrations supposedly kept the people from spilling out into open revolt.[43] It is such an opportunity to laugh at their superiors, perhaps, which *Wat Tyler and Jack Straw* presented to its audiences at the rowdy Bartholomew Fair. Any potentially subversive elements in the play remain nicely contained: Walworth stabs Tyler, who is not a good leader in the play but is in reality a bit of a brute, and the mob in the play is graciously pardoned by Richard II. The mob then sees the folly of their ways:

> *King.* Be not dismay'd, my countrymen and friends, you are all safe, and have our royal pardon; only repent, and you are still good subjects.
> *All Mob.* Long live King Richard the Second! Huzza! Huzza! Huzza![44]

Then it turns out that the mob never wanted to follow Tyler all along. They had been duped by their wicked captain. Thereafter, due to the good King's grace all of the rebels are pardoned. Thus, any subversive feelings aroused in the watching of the play had been neutered. Of course, there can be a tendency to take ideas about the carnivalesque too far, as Natalie Zemon Davis points out in *Society and Culture in Early Modern France* (1965). In spite of plays such as *Wat Tyler and Jack Straw*, which, if we apply the theory of the carnivalesque in full, supposedly contained people's inclinations to revolt, they do not appear particularly effective at stemming revolts, for people often did riot during the eighteenth century.

Tyler's name continued to be invoked in the press throughout the century, especially at times of riots. We have seen how King Mob was an ever-present threat to the ruling classes during the eighteenth century. One of the most notorious riots to have ever occurred in England was the Gordon Riots in 1780. For one week during June of that year, London was under mob rule. The protest began as a reaction to the implementation of the Papists Act of 1778 which was intended to reduce discrimination against Catholics in civic and political life.[45] One man who objected to this was the Scottish aristocrat, Lord George Gordon, the head of the Protestant Association. Gordon stirred the populace with fears of a prospective return to Catholic absolutism, which the British thought they had finally gotten rid of after the Glorious Revolution of 1688. Totally groundless were Gordon's claims, but they were enough to incite a crowd of around fifty thousand people, headed by Gordon himself, to march on Parliament on 2 June and deliver a petition to the government protesting against the passage of the Act. The petition was rejected by the House of Commons, and the mob assembled outside was ordered to disperse. The crowd did indeed disappear when ordered to but that was not the end of the matter. That night the people began to attack the embassies of Catholic countries, as well as the homes of the poor Irish Catholics in Moorfields. Although the riots started out as anti-Catholic, they soon switched their attention to all symbols of authority. Newgate gaol was attacked, and the Bank of England and the Fleet Prison were also raided. Eventually the riots calmed down and Gordon was indicted for high treason, although he was found not guilty.

It is unsurprising that in the wake of the Gordon Riots there was a lot of chatter in the press about Wat Tyler. After the riots, *The Gazetteer and New Daily Advertiser* published an account of Tyler's insurrection, which also was reprinted in several other newspapers. Although the riots of 1780 were horrible indeed, the anonymous author says, at least it was led by somebody 'of higher quality' than the rebellion of 1381.[46] Tyler's insurrection, in contrast, was a fearsome revolt of the common people. Luckily for the authorities in Britain, the riots of the eighteenth century never spilt out into open revolution. But there were developments in America and France that would have a profound influence on Wat Tyler's literary afterlife, and these are the subject of the next chapter.

Notes

1 'Of Mobs and Riots; with an Account of Wat Tyler's Insurrection', *The Weekly Magazine, or, Edinburgh Amusement* 30 November 1769, pp. 266-8 (p.266).

2 'Of Mobs and Riots', p. 266 and p. 268.

3 Dorothy George, *Grub Street: Studies in a Subculture* (London: Methuen, 1972; repr. Abingdon: Routledge, 2014), p. 4.

4 *British Mercury* 12 May 1714, p. 2.

5 *The History of all the Mobs, Tumults, and Insurrections in Great Britain, from William the Conqueror to the Present Time. To Which is Added, The Act of Parliament and Proclamation Lately Publish'd for Punishing Rioters* (London: Printed for J. Moore near St. Paul's, 1715), p. i.

6 *The History of all the Mobs*, pp. 1-2.

7 *Ibid.*, p. 2.

8 *The History of All the Mobs*, p. 8.

9 *Ibid.*, p. 8.

10 *Ibid.*, p. 9.

11 *Ibid.*, p. 10.

12 Dobson, *The Peasants' Revolt of 1381*, p. 363.

13 *The History of All the Mobs*, p. 13.

14 *Ibid.*, p. 12.

15 *The History of Wat Tyler and Jack Straw. Being a Relation of their Notorious Rebellion, Which Begun in the Fourth Year of King Richard the Second's Reign, how it was Carried on and Ended in the Death of Wat Tyler, who was Slain by Sir Will. Walworth, Lord Mayor of London, in West*

Smithfield: with their Villainous Mad Pranks they Plaid and the Mischief they did before they were Dispersed (London: Printed and Sold by Edw. Midwinter, at the Star in Pye Corner, near West Smithfield [n.d.]), p. 2. Referred to hereafter as *The History of Wat Tyler and Jack Straw* (a).

16 *The History of Wat Tyler and Jack Straw* (a), p. 2.

17 *The History of Wat Tyler and Jack Straw* (a), p. 7.

18 *The History of Wat Tyler and Jack Straw* (a), p. 3.

19 *The History of Wat Tyler and Jack Straw* (a), p. 3.

20 *The History of Wat Tyler and Jack Straw* (a), p. 3.

21 *The History of Wat Tyler and Jack Straw* (a), p. 4.

22 *The History of Wat Tyler and Jack Straw* (a), p. 7.

23 *The History of Wat Tyler and Jack Straw* (a), p. 8.

24 *The History of Wat Tyler and Jack Straw* (a), p. 9.

25 *The History of Wat Tyler and Jack Straw* (a), p. 9.

26 *The History of Wat Tyler and Jack Straw* (London: [n. pub.], 1788), p. 6. Referred to hereafter as *The History of Wat Tyler and Jack Straw* (b).

27 *The History of Wat Tyler and Jack Straw* (b), pp. 7-8.

28 *The History of Wat Tyler and Jack Straw* (b), p. 11.

29 *The History of Wat Tyler and Jack Straw* (b), p. 11.

30 *The History of Wat Tyler and Jack Straw* (b), p. 13.

31 *The History of Wat Tyler and Jack Straw* (b), p. 23.

32 G.F. Raymond, *A New, Universal, and Impartial History of England, From the Earliest Authentic Records, and Most Genuine Historical Evidence, to the End of the Present Year. Containing an Authentic, Candid, and Circumstantial Account of Every Memorable Transaction, Interesting Event, and Remarkable Occurrence, Recorded in the Annals of Great Britain* (London: C. Cooke, 1790), p. 206.

33 Oliver Goldsmith, *The History of England, From the Earliest Times to the Death of George II* (4 Vols. London: T. Davies, 1771; repr. 2 Vols. Boston: Chester Stebbins, 1814), 2: 267-8.

34 John Timbs, *The Romance of London: Strange Stories, Scenes, and Remarkable Persons of the Great Town* 2 Vols. (London: F. Warne [n.d.]), 2: 191-2.

35 Richard Cavendish, 'London's Last Bartholomew Fair' *History Today* 55: 9 (2005) [Internet <www.historytoday.com/richard-cavendish/londons-last-bartholomew-fair> Accessed 26 November 2016].

36 Henry Morley, *Memoirs of Bartholomew Fair* (London: Chapman & Hall, 1859), p. 336.

37 *Wat Tyler and Jack Straw; or, The Mob Reformers. A Dramatick Entertainment as it is Performed at Pinkethman's and Gifford's Great Theatrical Booth in Bartholomew Fair* (London: J. Roberts, 1730), p. 5.

38 Richard Butsch, 'Crowds, Publics and Consumers: Representing English
   Theatre Audiences from the Globe to the OP Riots', *Participations: Journal
   of Audience and Reception Studies* 7: 1 (2010), pp. 31-48 (p.34).
39 John Gay, *The Beggar's Opera* 3rd Edn. (London: John Watts, 1729), p.59.
40 Gay, *The Beggar's Opera*, p.60.
41 *Wat Tyler and Jack Straw; or, The Mob Reformers*, p. 30.
42 Dustin Griffin, *Patriotism and Poetry in Eighteenth-Century Britain*
   (Cambridge: Cambridge University Press, 2002), pp. 10-11.
43 For a discussion of the carnivalesque, and a critique of the theory, see
   Mikhail Bakhtin, *Rabelais and His World.* Trans. by Helene Iswolsky
   (Bloomington: Indiana University Press, 1984).
44 *Wat Tyler and Jack Straw; or, The Mob Reformers*, p. 32.
45 The following are just some of the sanctions which Roman Catholics faced:
   exclusion from holding public office; unable to marry a protestant; unable
   to bear arms or join the army; excluded from voting.
46 *The Gazetteer and New Daily Advertiser* 12 June 1780, p. 1.

CHAPTER FOUR

Romanticism and Revolution

Now it is well known, that those peasants were in a state of actual slavery, denominated villeinage; whereas the present reformers pique themselves upon being free-born Englishmen: but like their predecessors, they are headed by their Wat Tyler and Jack Straw, and animated by a reverend apostle of equal virtue and capacity with the celebrated John Ball, the honest priest of those days, who acted as principal incendiary, spiriting up the multitude to mischief and rebellion by inflammatory sermons, quaint rhimes, and treasonable papers, dispersed among the leaders of the people. What a loss it was to mankind, and a disgrace to the government of England, that this worthy reformer in canonicals, should have been hanged as a sower of sedition!

Anon. *The Briton* (1762)

*Why give to your Alfred the laurel of fame,
When Wat Tyler deserves a much nobler name?
That Alfred, they say, made some good wholesome laws,
But Wat Tyler lost life in the Levelling cause.*

William Thomas Fitzgerald, *The Sturdy Reformer* (1791)

Notwithstanding the sycophancy of historians, and men like Mr. Burke, who seek to gloss over a base action of the court by traducing Tyler, his fame will outlive their falsehood. If the Barons merited a monument to be erected in Runnymede, Tyler merits one in Smithfield.

Thomas Paine, *The Rights of Man* (1791)

ROMANTICISM AND REVOLUTION

Why could'st not thou, Wat Tyler, rest
Within the confines of thy peaceful chest?
With Joan of Arc thy still reposing sister,
Why rise, thy poor poetic sire to pester?
See, how thy presence cuts him to the core;
Bob is not what he was in days of yore;
O! for another Walworth with a thwack,
To lay, thee blacksmith, flat upon thy back.

Anon. *Wat Tyler* (1817)

In the first half of the eighteenth century, whenever authors and artists wished to represent the medieval period, they often did so with reference to antiquity and the culture of Ancient Greece and Rome.[1] This classicising of the past came about as a result of increased access to the classical works, as well as a desire on the part of the elites to adapt ancient manners and models of government to modern life.[2] This is why we see, in the 1731 edition of John Dryden's and Henry Purcell's opera *King Arthur; or, The British Worthy* (1691) a frontispiece depicting King Arthur dressed in the habit of a Roman centurion. England's medieval heritage needed to be refined for a polite eighteenth-century audience. As Joseph Addison muses in *An Account of the Greatest English Poets* (1694), medieval poets such as Chaucer should be respected for their achievements, but their works in their original form were not polished enough for an enlightened age:

Long had our dull forefathers slept supine,
Nor felt the raptures of the tuneful nine,
Till Chaucer first, a merry bard arose,
And many a story told in rhyme and prose,
But age has rusted what the poet writ,
Worn out his language, and obscur'd his wit:
In vain he jests in his unpolish'd strain,
And tries to make the reader laugh in vain.[3]

The medieval period was rusty, and it needed refining, much as Dryden himself had done to Chaucer with his 'translations' of *The Canterbury Tales* into heroic couplets. Around the middle of the century, however, there was a gradual rediscovery of and appreciation for England's ancient medieval past. Neoclassicism as the dominant artistic mode would eventually give way to the Gothic in art, architecture, and literature. The owners of England's medieval ruins made them more accessible while keeping them in a suitably ruined state to enable them to be appreciated by poets and artists for picturesque value.[4] Historical English literary works began to be seen as classics and enjoyed for their own sake. Amateur scholars and antiquaries such as Thomas Percy (1729-1811) began to turn their attention to the recovery, editing, and publishing of medieval romances and ballads. Percy's *Reliques of Ancient English Poetry* (1765) was the first significant piece of scholarship upon medieval romances such as the fifteenth-century poem *Robin Hood and Guy of Gisborne*, as well as later traditional poems such as *The Ballad of Chevy Chase.* Its aim was to show 'the gradual improvement of the English language and poetry from its earliest ages down to the present'.[5] Other notable scholars include Joseph Ritson, whose two-volume work entitled *Robin Hood: A Collection of all the Ancient Poems, Songs, and Ballads* (1795) is the single most important work in the entire Robin Hood tradition. Both the *Reliques* and Ritson's *Robin Hood*, as well as Ritson's other works such as *Ancient English Metrical Romances* (1802), were anthologies of popular poems and songs. Ritson was a vehement radical who refashioned Robin Hood into a quasi-medieval revolutionary, 'a man who, in a barbarous age and under a complicated tyranny, displayed a spirit of freedom and independence'.[6]

'Radical' is a term which we will encounter frequently from here on, so it is best that I define what I mean by it. While there were many strains of radical thought during the late eighteenth and early nineteenth century (Painites, English Jacobins, etc.), Michael J. Turner points out that there are common traits to these disparate movements. Radicals placed great emphasis upon natural rights and the sovereignty of the people. They sought fundamental improvements in society. They placed the blame for all of the nation's political, social, and economic woes firmly with the operations of a corrupt state, its abuses of authority, and the selfish motivations behind the elites' passage of oppressive legislation. But it was not enough for these writers simply to complain about the political class, they had to offer a vision of a better society as well.[7] Hence many radicals looked back to the medieval past, to the actions of men such as Robin Hood to find solutions to the social and economic problems of the present.

Given his republicanism, Ritson never chose to write anything significant upon Wat Tyler. The only ballad anthology from this era that includes any Wat Tyler poems is Thomas Evans' *Old Ballads, Historical and Narrative* (1777).[8] Evans was a bookseller and antiquary whose volumes were not particularly innovative in their content, for most of the songs he published were available from broadside street vendors, but he does include in his collection the ballad *The Rebellion of Wat Tyler, Jack Straw and Others against Richard the Second*. While the content of the ballad *The Rebellion of Wat Tyler* was considered in a previous chapter, its inclusion in Evans' ballad anthology is significant because along with Percy's *Reliques* a nascent British nationalism can be detected. Evans' aim in putting the collection together was a patriotic one.[9] What Percy and Evans were doing, in accordance with Benedict Anderson's ideas of an 'imagined national community', was constructing a national English past, composed of, as Evans intimates, the deeds of kings, knights-errant, and gallant outlaws:[10]

Many of the ancient ballads have been transmitted to the present times, and in them the character of the nation displays itself in striking colours. The boastful history of her victories, the prowess of her favourite kings and captains, the wonderful adventures of the legendary saint and knight-errant, are the topics of rough rhyme and unadorned narration.[11]

Although Tyler receives a predominantly negative portrayal in the text of the ballad, his story was still part of this idea of a truly national past that began to be constructed around mid-century. The ballad's praise of Richard II also fits with Evan's patriotic, nationalist agenda. As the eighteenth century progressed, however, the uses to which various parts of England's national past would be put would vary considerably.[12] There would be new developments in Wat Tyler's literary afterlife, for after the writings of Thomas Paine, Tyler's story would be appropriated by radical thinkers to highlight political and social injustices, and alternatively appropriated by conservatives as a means of highlighting the immorality and dangers of revolution.

But let us first briefly examine Wat Tyler's appearance in the visual culture of the period. James Northcote's painting *The Death of Wat Tyler* (1787) is one of the most interesting pictorial representations of Tyler that emerged during the eighteenth century. Northcote (1746-1831) was born in Plymouth and maintained an interest in artistic pursuits throughout his youth. In October 1771 he enrolled as a student at the Royal Academy. After some adverse turns in business during the late 1770s he managed to secure a contract with the publisher and engraver John Boydell to produce a series of historical paintings to be housed in the Royal Academy's Shakespeare Gallery. The gallery was designed with the aim of trying to create a specialist school of British historical painting similar to that which existed on the continent.

The painting strikes an almost Biblical tone: Tyler is upside down, much like depictions of the death of Saint Peter who is said to have been crucified in the same position. Walworth is half-hidden behind the young king, and has emerged only to stab Tyler, sneakily and underhandedly. Tyler is a martyr to the cause of political liberty here. Moreover, the young king's effeminate and youthful looks are suggestive of the pampered luxury of the eighteenth-century aristocracy.[13] The representation of Richard II as effeminate is criticised in a contemporary report in *The Times*, where it is said that 'the greatest fault of Northcote's painting is that the young Richard is represented as one of our modern smock-faced effeminate youths, while the other characters bear the true resemblance of those times.'[14] With its portrayal of an effeminate young king, it recalls the anti-

Royalist undercurrent of the national history paintings produced by the Society of Arts in the 1760s.[15]

Jean Francis Rigaud's painting entitled *Wat Tyler Killing the Tax Collector* (1798) depicts the incident with the tax collector in Tyler's home. Rigaud (1742-1800) was born in Turin and, having exhibited artistic skill from an early age, was apprenticed to Chevalier Beaumont, the King of Sardinia's official painter (Italy was not, at this point in time, a single unified state but a collection of petty kingdoms).[16] He arrived in London in 1771 and in the following year was elected as an associate to the Royal Academy. According to *The Oxford Dictionary of National Biography*, Rigaud's historical paintings were not well-received, and the majority of his income appears to have come from the works that he produced for the country houses of the aristocracy.[17]

However, although it might not have been well received at the time, likely as a result of the paranoia of revolution among the elites due to the French Revolution and the war with Napoleon, his painting of *Wat Tyler killing the Tax Collector* is breathtaking. All of Rigaud's paintings were produced in the Italian style, and with his dark curled hair Wat Tyler looks Italian. He is most definitely a member of the plebeian classes, as the only clothes that he is wearing hang from the waist down, which is how seamen and boxers were usually portrayed during the eighteenth century.[18] Also, Tyler is very muscular, and looks Herculean, poised with a hammer ready to strike down the tax collector who has laid hands on his daughter. The famous Romantic poet and illustrator William Blake, in the same year as Rigaud's painting, also produced an engraving of Wat Tyler killing the tax collector for Charles Allen's *A New and Improved History of England* (1798). In this picture, a muscular Tyler stands poised over the body of the dead tax gatherer. During the eighteenth century, the muscular male arm connoted the capacity to both smite and protect.[19] Tyler's killing the tax man after the attempted rape upon his daughter fits this eighteenth-century trope perfectly.

Furthermore, in much eighteenth-century art the labouring man's body is depicted as strong and tough. This may seem strange, given that a majority of art during the period was produced either by the elites and/or for the elites. But Joanne Begiato notes that the muscular and stout bodies of labouring men were idealised 'as symbols, progenitors, and defenders of gender, society, and nation in the eighteenth and nineteenth centuries'.[20] This trend is evident, Begiato notes, in depictions of late eighteenth- and nineteenth-century portrayals of seamen who were vital to the Napoleonic war effort. The upper classes may have ruled and provided the 'brains' of the country and the nascent empire, but it was the labouring men – descendants of men such as Tyler – who provided the 'brawn' of the country.

The late eighteenth century, most importantly for our purposes here, was the era of two major revolutions: one in America and the other in France. A key thinker in both revolutions was Thomas Paine (1736-1809) who, as we will see, appropriated Tyler as the symbol of a man who fought for rights and political liberty. Thomas Paine was also equated with Wat Tyler by his enemies in the press. Although Paine was born in England, he emigrated to America in 1774, just before the American Revolution (1776-83). During his time in America, Paine authored the pamphlet *Common Sense* (1776), which argues that 'mankind [were] originally equals in the order of creation'.[21] Paine argues further that there is no natural or religious reason as to why mankind should be divided into that of king and subject.[22] This was revolutionary thinking, although the term 'revolution' had a somewhat more nuanced meaning than it does today. In modern times, people usually think of revolutions as being large-scale rebellions against the state, and this is often the case, as with the recent revolution in Egypt in 2011. But to have a 'revolution' in the eighteenth century meant trying to 'return to the beginning'. What was needed was a revolution, a return to the beginning, when all men were 'equals in the order of creation'. Of course, by the late eighteenth century, it seemed to be the case that one could only achieve a return to these egalitarian origins through a violent overthrow of the existing political establishment.

Unsurprisingly, Thomas Paine's pamphlet was a boon to those who advocated for American independence, although the British establishment, unsurprisingly, did not look favourably upon either Paine's work or the actions of the American rebels. Jonathan Boucher's *A View of the Causes and Consequences of the American Revolution* (1797) states that the breakaway from Britain was an act of insanity, madness on a par with that which possessed the rebels back in 1381:

> Where is the man, who, having read the history of mankind with all proper care, will take upon him to affirm that nations, as well as individuals, are not liable to paroxysms of insanity or phrensy [sic]; and that the revolt of America may not as fairly be ascribed to a strong spirit of delusion on the subject of politics, as the rebellion of 1641 was to a similar spirit upon the subject of religion? ... and what more could be said of the celebrated knight of La Mancha; or what less of Wat Tyler, Tom Paine, or any other fanatical reformer of States?[23]

The result of the American War of Independence from Britain is well-known, with the Thirteen Colonies breaking away from British rule and forming the United States of America. By 1787, Thomas Paine was back in London. But in 1789, another revolution would erupt across the Channel after King Louis XVI of France convened the Estates-General on 5 May 1789 (this was a convention of the clergy, aristocracy, and the commons) in order to address the grievances of his people and remedy the financial crisis which the country faced. Much of the fiscal crisis that the French government faced was the result of having aided America in its war of independence against Britain. From there events snowballed: the representatives of the commons formed their own National Constituent Assembly, after having realised that they had been locked out of the proceedings of the Estates-General; shortly afterwards there was the Storming of the Bastille, a prison which housed mainly political prisoners, which occurred on 14 July 1789. Finally, the Declaration of the Rights of Man and Citizen was adopted by the National Constituent Assembly on 26 August 1789, a document which emphasised the rights and sovereignty of the people. The buzzwords of the Revolution were 'rights', 'liberties', and 'equality', and of course 'fraternity'. Although the initial feeling amongst the elites in Britain was that this was a well-overdue and much-needed development for the Kingdom of France, opinions towards the revolution soon soured. With reference to Wat Tyler, *The Times* in September 1789 stated that

> The Parisian insurgents are exactly in that same habit of mind which possessed Wat Tyler and his levelling companions, and carrying the idea of liberty into licentiousness, they must in the end be completely overthrown.[24]

The British establishment's souring opinion towards the French Revolution was summed up by the Whig MP, Edmund Burke, in his *Reflections on the Revolution in France* (1790). One of Burke's arguments in the *Reflections* is that an unwritten constitution such as Britain had, which had been tried and tested over time, was preferable to a complete overthrow of the existing order, as the French revolutionaries were doing. Interspersed among Burke's writings is a reverence for historical institutions such as the monarchy, which supposedly contributed to a well-ordered and stable society. The English people did not like sudden change, as the rebels of 1381 tried to effect, but preferred gradual reform.

Burke's writings drew a response in Thomas Paine's *The Rights of Man*. Paine was aware of several comparisons between the French revolutionaries and Wat Tyler made in the British press. It is in *The Rights of Man* (1791) that we first see Wat Tyler's legacy rehabilitated:

> Several of the court newspapers have of late made frequent mention of Wat Tyler. That his memory should be traduced by court sycophants, and all those who live on the spoil of a public, is not to be wondered at. He was, however, the means of checking the rage and injustice of taxation in his time, and the nation owed much to his valour. The history is concisely this:-

In the time of Richard the second, a poll-tax was levied, of one shilling per head, upon every person in the nation, of whatever estate or condition, on poor as well as rich, above the age of fifteen years. If any favour was shown, it was to the rich rather than to the poor ... Poll-taxes had always been odious; but this being oppressive and unjust, it excited, as it naturally must, universal detestation amongst the poor and middle classes. The person known by the name of Wat Tyler, whose proper name was Walter, and a tyler [sic] by trade, lived at Deptford. The gatherer of the poll-tax, on coming to his house, demanded tax for one of his daughters, whom Tyler declared was under the age of fifteen. The tax-gatherer insisted on satisfying himself, and began an indecent examination of the girl, which enraging the father, he struck him with a hammer, that brought him to the ground, and was the cause of his death.

This circumstance served to bring the discontents to an issue. The inhabitants of the neighbourhood espoused the cause of Tyler, who, in a few days was joined, according to some histories, by upwards of fifty thousand men, and chosen their chief. With this force he marched to London, to demand an abolition of the tax, and a redress of other grievances. The court, finding itself in a forlorn condition, and unable to make resistance, agreed, with Richard at its head, to hold a conference with Tyler in Smithfield, making many fair professions, courtier like, of its disposition to redress the oppressions. While Richard and Tyler were in conversation on these matters, each being on horseback, Walworth, then mayor of London, and one of the creatures of the court, watched for an opportunity, and like a cowardly assassin, stabbed Tyler with a dagger ... Tyler appears to have been an intrepid and disinterested man, with respect to himself. All his proposals made to Richard, were on a more just and public ground, than those which had been made to John by the Barons; and notwithstanding the sycophancy of historians, and men like Mr. Burke, who seek to gloss over a base action of the court by traducing Tyler, his fame will outlive their falsehood. If the Barons merited a monument to be erected in Runnymede, Tyler merits one in Smithfield.[25]

To Thomas Paine, the events of 1381 are as important as that of the signing of Magna Carta in 1215. The idea that sycophantic historians had whitewashed history and skewed it in favour of the elites, while the heroes of the people were painted as villains was a recurring one in eighteenth- and nineteenth-century radical thought (a mode of thinking not unlike those who denounce the 'mainstream media' as favouring the political establishment today). According to Joseph Ritson, whom we have already encountered, the only reason that Robin Hood is viewed as a criminal is because of 'the malicious endeavours of pitiful monks, by whom history was consecrated to the crimes and follies of titled ruffians and sainted idiots, to suppress all record of [Robin Hood's] patriotic exertions and virtuous acts'.[26] Similar sentiments are expressed in the nineteenth century in the radical *Reynolds's Newspaper*:

> Servile historians have depicted as robbers, rascals, and freebooters men who were in reality doing their utmost to save themselves and posterity from being plundered by the ancestors of those coroneted robbers who now hold possession of a large portion of English soil.[27]

Throughout the Georgian and Victorian periods, radicals saw the oppressive aristocracy and monarchy as the real villains of history, rather than men such as Robin Hood or Wat Tyler.[28]

When it was first published, Thomas Paine's *The Rights of Man* became a sensation, and sold over 200,000 copies. As Eric Hobsbawm notes, this sales figure is impressive at a time when the whole population of Britain was less than that of London today.[29] Burke was also quick to respond to Paine in *An Appeal from the New to the Old Whigs* (1791). Beginning in quite a sarcastic manner, Burke addresses Paine's points about Wat Tyler, and says that, 'little as I respect the memory of Wat Tyler, yet justice may, perhaps, require that I should apologise for degrading him by an indirect kind of comparison with

one so infinitely beneath him in every respect as Tom Pain.'[30] Burke
then goes on to critique Paine's arguments about Tyler on a point by
point basis in the format set out below (Burke was petty, and
deliberately misspelled Paine's name as 'Pain' in an attempt to cause
him offence, although there is no evidence that Paine was ever
mortally offended by this).

Pain and Falsehood

The court, finding itself in a forlorn condition, and unable to
make resistance, agreed, with Richard at its head, to hold a
conference with Tyler in Smithfield, making many fair
professions, courtier like, of its dispositions to redress the
oppressions. While Richard and Tyler were in conversation on
these matters, each being on horse-back, Walworth, then mayor
of London, and one of the creatures of the court, watched for
an opportunity, and like a cowardly assassin, stabbed Tyler
with a dagger; and two or three others falling upon him, he was
instantly sacrificed.

History and Truth

During these transactions, another body of the insurgents had
forced the gates of the tower, where they *murdered* Simon
Sudbury, archbishop of Canterbury, the Chancellor; and Sir
Robert Hales, the treasurer, with some other persons of
distinction; and then extended their ravages into the city, which
it was the intention of their desperate leader, Wat Tyler, to
reduce to ashes, after seizing the person of the King, and
putting all nobles to death ... On the fifteenth of June, 1381, as
the King was passing through Smithfield, with a slender train
of sixty horse, he met Wat Tyler at the head of twenty thousand
of his followers. The insolent demagogue no sooner perceived
his sovereign, than he set spurs to his horse, and entered into a
conference with him; having previously ordered his company
to keep still till he should give them a signal, at which they
were to advance, murder all the attendants of Richard, and take

the King himself prisoner. But the extreme insolence of Tyler prevented the execution of his plan, by provoking Walworth, then mayor of London, who was present, to strike him a violent blow with his mace, which felled the ruffian to the ground, when Philpot put an end to his existence, by thrusting his sword through his body!![31]

Thomas Paine and Wat Tyler, moreover, became synonymous in some works, such as William Thomas Fitzgerald's *The Sturdy Reformer: A Song, Exemplifying the Doctrines of the 'Rights of Man'* (1791). At first glance, it appears as though Fitzgerald might support the egalitarian ideology expressed in Paine's *The Rights of Man*:

Why give to your ALFRED the laurel of fame,
When WAT TYLER deserves a much nobler name?
That ALFRED, they say, made some good wholesome laws,
But WAT TYLER lost life in the LEVELLING CAUSE
Sing Balliomona, oro, &c.
The Levelling System for me![32]

Fitzgerald then goes on to mention another medieval rebel, Jack Cade, who led a revolt against the government of King Henry VI in 1450, before progressing onto Paine:

Shall JACK CADE be forgot when an Hero I sing,
Who detests proud Nobility, Clergy, and King?
We Moderns such shameful ingratitude spurn,
For we honour his dust, and his doctrines we learn.
Sing Balliomona – JACK CADE and WAT TYLER for me!

TOM PAINE, a Republican Wight [mighty] of renown,
His right foot on the Mitre, his left on the Crown!
Bellows out Reformation to every degree,
And shews all (*gratis*) the way to be free.
Sing, &c. &c. – A French Revolution for me![33]

The line 'shews all (*gratis*)' refers to the fact that Paine ensured his writings were published and sold as cheaply as possible. Lest readers are concerned about where his sympathies lay, however, Fitzgerald at the end of the poem denounces all of these so-called reformers throughout history as 'wolves in sheep's clothing'.[34]

The pamphlet *A Dialogue between Wat Tyler, Mischievous Tom, and an English Farmer* (1793) is similarly critical of both Tyler and Paine, with the 'Mischievous Tom' being a soubriquet for the author of *The Rights of Man*. In the pamphlet, Tyler speaks to Paine from beyond the grave, opening with the lines, 'well, Tom, I am glad to see thee, though thou hast stolen my tricks.'[35] The 'tricks' of course refer to stirring up anti-monarchical sentiment. Paine praises Tyler by saying, 'thanks, my good brother! I give thee the kiss of fraternity. O! Citizen Tyler, if I could but raise such a mob as thou didst at Greenwich!'[36] Despite being a rebel, the French-inspired salutation is too much for the Englishman Tyler:

> *Wat T.* Off, Frenchman! No kiss or fraternity – no French manners – no French mobs for me; thou hast but little chance of success if thou canst not mislead the people of England without French help. But where are thy friends, where are thy assistants? As for thee, I believe thee, without compliment, equal to any devil sedition ever produced. But where is thy Straw? Where is thy Dr. Ball to back thee? Every age does not produce such heroes.[37]

Wat then issues a challenge to Mischievous Tom:

> *Wat T.* Success attend you – but let's see how thou wilt manage this English farmer, who is coming to join us – of all the animals of creation one is most tempted to deceive a simple English farmer, and yet one never finds any great success in the attempt.[38]

The hardy English farmer comes along. Like eighteenth-century portrayals of John Bull, the farmer is a rustic, no-nonsense type of fellow. Tom salutes the farmer and asks, 'what did your hat cost you?'

> *English Farmer.* What's that to you? It's paid for, which is more than you can say of what you buy, though not perhaps of what you either fell or give; but it cost me twelve shillings, and what of that?
> *Tom.* Twelve shillings! That's the King's fault, and the gentry's fault; if thou hadst no King, you'd have half that expence [sic]; and if there was no gentry, and all property was equal, you'd have the rest, and so have thy hat for nothing.
> *English Farmer.* That's a lie; if there was no gentry, and property equal, there would be no trades, and consequently no hatters, and I should have no hat at all; and if there was no King, perhaps, I should have no head to want one, under your government.[39]

The farmer then argues that inequality is good for society before going on to criticise Englishmen who go abroad to learn of foreign 'experiments'. Tyler then scoffs at Tom for being unable to convince an English farmer about the benefits of revolutionary ideals.

It might be tempting to read the appearance of this and other pamphlets as the confident expression of British patriotism against perfidious French Revolutionary ideals. But that was far from being the case in Britain. Indeed, the fact that certain authors feel moved to publicly pronounce against revolutionary sentiments should be telling. Just as the Jacobin clubs were some of the main engines behind the revolution in Paris, so there were Jacobin clubs in England who thought they too could engineer a revolution. The government was paranoid of anything that smacked of rebellion. Relatively harmless dramatic works which told the story of the Great Revolt were censored. The playwright Richard Cumberland submitted a play to the Lord Chamberlain entitled *Richard the Second* (1792). (All dramatic works had to be submitted to the Lord Chamberlain for review prior to being staged, a practice which lasted until the 1960s.) Although it was not intended to be politically radical, it was deemed to be potentially inflammatory at a time of revolution in France. The Lord Chamberlain, therefore, returned the manuscript asking for revisions, with the end result that the blacksmith's murder of the tax collector happens because the collector is a procurer and attempts to carry off his daughter to be sold for sex. Thus, Tyler smiting the tax collector is not an act of aggression against the establishment, but rather the natural reaction of a father wanting to protect his daughter.[40] Cumberland was not impressed with how the play appeared in the end, and in his lengthy autobiography he writes only a few lines upon it, saying that he was 'not surprised that the public was not greatly edified by what was left'.[41]

At the time, many of the leading lights of the late eighteenth-century Romantic movement, such as Samuel Taylor Coleridge (1772-1834), William Wordsworth (1770-1850), and William Hazlitt (1778-1830) were firm proponents of revolutionary ideology.[42] Along with Coleridge and Wordsworth, there was another young man who shared in this enthusiasm for all things revolutionary, Robert Southey (1774-1843). He was a pioneering medievalist, who authored the first Robin Hood novel, *Harold; or, The Castle of Morford* (1791), in which the famous outlaw is portrayed as a revolutionary freedom fighter (at present the novel remains unpublished).[43] Southey was born in Bristol and lived with his aunt until the age of seven. She appears to have had a profound effect upon the young aspiring poet, for it was she who encouraged his cultural pursuits from a young age. In November 1792, he was enrolled at Balliol College, Oxford. It was here that his fondness for the works of Thomas Paine and the ideals of the French Revolution found expression. Imbued with revolutionary zeal, in 1794, Southey began authoring *Wat Tyler; a Dramatic Poem in Three Acts*.

The poem, written like a play and divided into Acts with stage directions, opens in Tyler's blacksmith shop. Tyler 'lays down his hammer, and sits mournfully before his door,' when along comes his friend Hob Carter:

Tyler. Have I not been a staid, hardworking man?
Up with the lark at labour – sober – honest –
Of an unblemish'd character.

Hob. Who doubts it.
There's never a man in Essex bears a better.

Tyler. And shall not these, though young, and hale and happy,
Look on with sorrow at a future hour?
Shall not reflection poison all their pleasures?
When I – the honest, staid, hardworking Tyler,
Toil thro' the long course of a summer's day,
Still toiling, yet still poor! When with hard labour,
Scarce can I furnish out my daily food …
I have only six groats in the world,
And they must soon by law be taken from me.

Hob. Curse on these taxes – one succeeds another –
Our ministers, panders of a King's will –
Drain all our wealth away – waste it in revels –
And lure, or force away our boys, who should be,
The props of our old age! – To fill their armies
And feed the crows of France! Year follows year,
And still we madly prosecute the war –
Draining our wealth – distressing our poor peasants –
Slaughtering our youths – and all to crown our chiefs.[44]

This is an indictment of British society in the late eighteenth-century.
Tyler is the epitome of the industrious and hard-working labourer who
suffers under a corrupt political system. Yet the fruits of Tyler's labour
are sucked dry by the state to pay not only for the various foreign wars
which the government is involved in but also to keep the monarchy
and the nobility maintained in their extravagant lifestyle. The whole
system needs changing, and the political situation that Tyler describes
looks a lot like Old Corruption:

Tyler. What matters me who wears the crown of France?
Whether a Richard or a Charles possess it?
They reap the glory – they enjoy the spoil –
We pay – we bleed! – The sun would shine as cheerly,
The rains of heaven as seasonably fall,
Tho' neither of these Royal pests existed ...
Oh! 'Tis of vast importance who should pay for
The luxuries and riots of the court?
Who should support the flaunting courtier's pride,
Pay for their midnight revels, their rich garments.[45]

'Old Corruption' is a term which will be encountered in the succeeding chapter as well, so it is useful for us to dwell briefly upon what the term meant to contemporaries. It was an idea that flourished between c.1780 and c.1860 among reform-minded members of the middle and working classes, and is best defined by the historian W.D. Rubenstein, who says that

> The common or narrow meaning of 'Old Corruption' is fairly plain. It is the widespread use of pensions, sinecures, and gratuitous emoluments granted to persons whom the British government, between the earlier eighteenth century and the Age of Reform, wished to bribe, reward, or buy.[46]

Thus a government composed mainly of aristocratic and propertied elites made sure they looked after other landed elites when it was in their interests, and vice versa, all to the detriment of the disenfranchised common people.

The reference to 'the luxuries and riots of the court' is a further allusion to the alleged depravity and debauchery of the eighteenth-century aristocracy. Members of the nobility are often portrayed in contemporary literature as immoral, often by middle-class writers. Daniel Defoe in *Robinson Crusoe* (1719) speaks of how the middle classes of society are industrious and not addicted to vice and luxury like their upper-class counterparts, saying that 'the middle state, or

91

what might be called the upper station of low life […is] the best state in the world'.[47] In Samuel Richardson's *Pamela, or, Virtue Rewarded* (1740) there is the degenerate and voyeuristic Mr. B., an aristocrat who attempts to rape the eponymous servant girl (until so impressed with the girl's virtue that he marries her in the end instead). Similarly, in Henry Fielding's *Joseph Andrews* (1742) it is Lady Booby who attempts to seduce the innocent young footman, Joseph. In contrast to the idle and depraved aristocracy, Tyler is industrious, sober, honest, 'and of an unblemish'd character'.[48]

Much of the first act of the play/poem is taken up with airing grievances about the poll tax, which, as we have seen, serves as a front for Southey to air grievances about his own day. The eighteenth-century authorities' virtual paranoia of anything which had a whiff of reform about it is also alluded to in Southey's poem, for this was a time when freedom of speech was being curtailed by the government. Tyler, therefore, points out to his daughter, Alice, the fact that good men such as John Ball can often find themselves victims of government oppression for airing radical views:

Alice. My father, wherefore was John Ball imprisoned?
Was he not charitable, good, and pious?
I have heard him say that all mankind are brethren,
And the like brethren they should love each other;
Was not that doctrine pious?

Tyler. Rank, sedition –
High treason, every syllable my child!
The priests cry out on him for heresy,
The nobles detest him as a rebel,
And this good man, this minister of Christ,
This man, the friend and brother of mankind,
Lingers in the dark dungeon![49]

Thomas Paine had already been tried *in absentia* for the publication of *The Rights of Man*; he did not attend as he had fled to France. After all, there was no point in attending when the guilty verdict was a foregone conclusion. Between 1792 and 1794, over thirty radicals found themselves in gaol charged with sedition. The most notorious cases were those of Thomas Hardy (1752-1832), John Horne Tooke (1736-1812), and John Thelwall (1764-1834). All of these men were members of the London Corresponding Society whose demands for reform were quite modest: universal male suffrage and annual parliamentary elections (both demands would be incorporated into the People's Charter during the Victorian era). The government, however, deemed their actions and their association to be seditious. All three men were arrested and charged with high treason, with the specific accusation being that they were plotting to overthrow the government and assassinate George III. Luckily, the jurors in their trials were a bit more balanced and realised that this was nothing more than a trumped-up charge and all three men were acquitted. The authorities might not win every case, but at the time reformers and radicals were conscious that they were being watched. Joseph Ritson believed that he too was being watched by government spies.[50] And reformers had good reason to be worried, for in 1794, the year that Southey authored *Wat Tyler*, the government suspended *habeas corpus* for those accused of high treason.[51] Just as the Committee of Public Safety in France unleashed a reign of terror upon its citizens, so radicals and reformers in Britain believed that they were living under 'Pitt's Terror', named after the then Prime Minister, William Pitt the Younger (1759-1806).

The tax collector then enters Tyler's dwelling and demands money for the 'glorious war'. Not being satisfied as to Alice's age, he demands a tax be paid for her too. The tax gatherer then lays hands upon Alice at which point 'Tyler knocks out the Tax-gatherer's brains'.[52] A mob then gathers outside Tyler's door shouting 'Liberty! – Liberty! – No Poll Tax! – No War!'[53] It is Tyler's friend, Hob Carter, who is leading the mob. News of Tyler's actions have spread through the town, for in Southey's medieval world it seems that news travels at lightning fast speed. Hob then says,

We have broke our chains – we will arise in anger –
The mighty multitude shall trample down
The handful that oppress them.
…
Of your vengeance.
Piers ran through the village – told the news –
Cried out, to arms! – arm, arm for liberty!
For liberty and justice.[54]

Events then move at a fast pace. The mob travels to London crying
John Ball's famous refrain, 'When Adam delved and Eve span, who
then was the gentleman?'[55] Jack Straw, Hob, and Tom Miller survey
the London crowd:

Jack Straw. The mob are up in London – the proud courtiers
Begin to tremble.

Tom Miller. Aye, aye, 'Tis time to tremble;
Who'll plow their fields, who'll do their drudgery now?
And work like horses, to give them the harvest?

Jack Straw. I only wonder we lay quiet so long.
We had always the same strength, and we deserved
The ills we met with for using it.

Hob. Why do we fear those animals called lords?
What is there in the name to frighten us?
Is not my arm as mighty as a Baron's?[56]

Tyler and Straw then lead the mob to Smithfield to address the King.
The King comes forth and asks Tyler why he has brought the mob to
him:

Tyler. Because they were oppressed.
King. Was this the way
To remedy the ill? – you should have tried,

ROMANTICISM AND REVOLUTION

By milder means – petition'd at the throne –
The throne will always listen to petitions.
Tyler. King of England,
Petitioning for pity is most weak.
The sovereign people ought to demand justice.
I killed your officer [the tax collector], for his lewd hand
Insulted a maid's modesty: your subjects
I lead to rebel against the Lord's anointed,
Because his ministers have made him odious …
The hour of retribution is at hand,
And tyrants tremble – mark me, King of England.[57]

It is when Tyler speaks those last two lines that Walworth appears and
stabs Tyler in the back. Hob then cries 'Seize the King' but Richard II
says,

My friends and loving subjects,
I will grant all that you ask: you shall be free –
The tax shall be repeal'd – all, all you wish.
Your leader menaced me, he deserv'd his fate.
Quiet your angers; on my royal word
Your grievances shall all be done away.
Your vasalage abolish'd. – A free pardon
Allow'd to all: so help me God it shall be.[58]

But of course Richard II is not to be trusted. John Ball is dragged away
to prison after the tumult and is ordered to suffer a traitor's death:

John Ball, whereas you are accused before us
Of stirring up the people to rebellion,
And preaching to them strange and dangerous doctrines …
I condemn you
To death; you shall be hanged by the neck,
But not till you are dead – your bowels opened –
Your heart torn out and burnt before your face –
Your traitorous head be sever'd from your body –

95

> Your body quartered, and exposed upon
> The city gates – a terrible example –
> And the Lord God have mercy on your soul.[59]

Richard then turns to his soldiers and says, 'let the blood-reeking sword of war be sheathed, That the law may take vengeance on the rebels.'[60]

However, Southey leaves his readers with a glimmer of hope. Despite the oppression faced by the peasants of fourteenth-century England,

> The distant hour must come,
> When it shall blaze with sun-surpassing splendour,
> And the dark mists of prejudice and falsehood
> Fade in its strong effulgence. Flattery's incense
> No more shall shadow round the gore-dyed throne;
> The altar of oppression fed with rites,
> More savage than the priests of Moloch taught,
> Shall be consum'd amid the fire of justice;
> The ray of truth shall emanate around,
> And the whole world will be lighted.[61]

By the time that Southey was writing, the 'light' of revolution had already shined in America and in France. Soon it would shine in Britain too, so Southey thought in his youth at least.

The story of what happened next with Southey's play is quite amusing. He never actually published it in 1794, but left the manuscript in the hands of his brother-in-law. He instructed his relative to give the poem to the radical publisher, Samuel Ridgeway. But Ridgeway in 1794 was in Newgate gaol on charges of sedition. Although he eventually received the manuscript, for whatever reason Ridgeway decided not to publish it. What happened to the manuscript in the decade or so afterward scholars are not quite sure. But by the 1810s Southey was a changed man, for as time wore on he became ever more conservative, and the older Southey gave his wholehearted support to the Tory party who opposed any form of political reform or extension of voting rights. This is a trend which other Romantic radicals followed such as Wordsworth and Coleridge. In 1813, Southey was even appointed as the Prince Regent's Poet Laureate. The position of Poet Laureate means that its incumbent has to shower the monarchy and the ruling classes with praise. So the former radical poet, Southey, was now an establishment stooge, with a job for life and a pension (Southey only got the job of Poet Laureate because Walter Scott refused).

What would Southey's former radical friends say about him? Would it not be embarrassing for the Poet Laureate if his play was leaked to the press? Well, that is exactly what happened. Southey had probably forgotten about the manuscript entirely, and what is more, given that he never registered the poem with the official Stationers back in 1794, the work was technically out-of-copyright. Radical publishers, therefore, decided to embarrass Southey by printing *Wat Tyler*. The play's publication was in response to an article by Southey that appeared in *The Quarterly Review* in 1817, in which he vehemently criticised parliamentary reform. Reformers and radical activists were aghast that a man who so zealously upheld the ideals of *liberté, égalité*, and *fraternité* in his youth could be so anti-reform. Thus, within days of the publication of Southey's article in *The Quarterly Review* his old play was available for purchase, having been printed by William Hone (1780-1842) and John Fairburn (1789-1854).[62] Hone made sure to include the following snipe at Southey on the title page to his edition:

Come, listen to a TALE OF TIMES OF OLD! —
Come, for ye know me – I am he who sung
The 'MAID OF ARC,' and I am he who fram'd
Of 'THALABA' the wild and wondrous song.
SOUTHEY!
And I was once like this!
Twenty years
Have wrought strange alteration.
SOUTHEY![63]

Twenty years had indeed 'wrought strange alteration' in Southey's political outlook. And Southey was laughed at in the public arena. The following is typical of several satirical poems published in contemporary newspapers at the time:

Why could'st not thou, Wat Tyler, rest
Within the confines of thy peaceful chest?
With Joan of Arc thy still reposing sister,
Why rise, thy poor poetic sire to pester?
See, how thy presence cuts him to the core;
Bob is not what he was in days of yore;
O! for another Walworth with a thwack,
To lay, thee blacksmith, flat upon thy back.
…

Robert, *adieu*, for all our laughter,
Do not discard thy Muses' new found daughter,
With all defects, she's something pretty rather,
At least she's prettier than her *present* father.
Her errors were not of the heart, but head,
A troubled stream from a pure fountain fed;
No hireling then, no *pensioner* to *praise*,
Nor envying Pye, his sherry and his bays.[64]

A reviewer in *The Monthly Review* argued that while no one can be faulted for changing their political opinions as they progress through life, Southey's vehement anti-reform stance, and criticism of many of his former colleagues, simply makes him a hypocrite:

At the same time, [Southey] must equally admit the privilege of others to judge of the wisdom of his change; and of the motives which, as far as the world can perceive them, may have operated to produce it. In spite, also, of the almost universality of the fact that proselytes are intemperate defenders of their new faith, and illiberal antagonists of any who hold that which they have forsaken, the calm and candid spectator will not fail to censure this intemperance, and to denounce his illiberality.[65]

ROMANTICISM AND REVOLUTION

The opposition Whig MP William Smith took a slightly more serious tone. Reading out excerpts from *Wat Tyler* and *The Quarterly Review* in Parliament, he branded Southey a shameless renegade, and said that the play was seditious.[66] Southey responded with an open letter which was published in a variety of newspapers. He denied that *Wat Tyler* was in any way seditious and that furthermore,

> The piece was written under the influence of opinions which I have long since outgrown, and repeatedly disclaimed, but for which I have never affected to feel either shame or contrition; they were taken up conscientiously in early youth, they were acted upon in disregard of all worldly considerations, and they were left behind in the same straightforward course.[67]

In his letter, Southey further argues that when one reads *Wat Tyler* the most 'seditious' sentiments in it are 'an enthusiastic love of liberty, a detestation of tyranny wherever it exists'.[68] In fairness to Southey, these were not particularly seditious sentiments at the time. Most English people living in the late eighteenth and early nineteenth centuries would have argued that they too prized the idea of political liberty. A love of freedom, to take one example, is the very reason why England had opposed the establishment of a police force during the eighteenth century (organised systems of law enforcement were viewed as something that the absolute monarchies of Europe had to keep their subjects in line, and the idea of a police force was viewed as being totally incompatible with the political ideology of freedom-loving Englishmen). In his *Apology*, Southey also warns that one of the root causes of any seditious activity in the country is the political elites' insensitivity to the needs of the poor:

> Let us not deceive ourselves. We are far from that state in which anything resembling equality would be possible; but we are arrived at that state in which the extremes of inequality are become intolerable. They are too dangerous,

as well as too monstrous, to be borne much longer. Plans, which would have led to the utmost horrors of insurrection, have been prevented by the Government, and by the enactment of strong but necessary laws. Let it not, however, be supposed that the disease is healed, because the ulcer may skin over ... The government must better the condition of the populace; and the first thing necessary is to prevent it from being worsened.[69]

Southey may have discarded the revolutionary ideals of his youth, but this does not mean that he thought that nothing should be done to better the condition of the poor. As part of a discussion that will be more fully illuminated in the next chapter, the end of the Napoleonic Wars brought a trade depression and unemployment. The price of food was also kept artificially high by the Corn Laws. In consequence of this, there were several riots. As Southey points out, the government had bigger problems than the publication of his juvenile republican musings, and there were certainly more firebrand revolutionary writings widely available during the nineteenth century due to the government's seemingly relaxed attitude to the press. In actual fact, the government was not relaxed about the free press at all and attempted to suppress the radical press on a number of occasions throughout the early nineteenth century. The suppression of the radical press by the government was noted by the author William Hone in *The Political House that Jack Built* (1819). Hone refers to the situation in his pamphlet, speaking of the printing press and the many 'attempts to restrain it, by soldiers or tax'.[70] The artist George Cruikshank in a widely-sold print depicted 'the Freeborn Englishman' with a padlock through his mouth, his hands and feet chained, and an axe lying over the Bill of Rights and Magna Carta.[71]

Had Southey's play been published when it was first written back in 1794, it is likely that it would not have had the same impact. There were literally hundreds of pro-revolutionary writings written in England during the early years of the French Revolution, and it would have likely faded into obscurity.[72] As we have seen in this chapter, it was during the late eighteenth century when Wat Tyler gets rehabilitated in public memory as a result of the writings of Thomas Paine and Robert Southey. Having been depicted predominantly as the depraved leader of a mindless and brutish mob in previous centuries, to reformers in this period Tyler became the symbol of a man who stood up to tyranny and fought for political rights. As a result of Paine and Southey's writings, going forward, radicals knew that the invocation of Wat Tyler's name would spook the authorities into paying attention to them, if not always granting their demands. Let us look at the purposes for which Wat Tyler's ghost is resurrected at various points throughout the early nineteenth century in the next chapter.

Notes

1. Rosemary Mitchell, *Picturing the Past: English History in Text and Image, 1830-1870* (Oxford: Oxford University Press, 2000), p. 9.
2. Joseph M. Levine, 'Why Neoclassicism? Politics and Culture in Eighteenth-Century England' *Journal for Eighteenth-Century Studies* 25: 1 (2002), pp. 75-101
3. Joseph Addison, 'An Account of the Greatest English Poets', in *The Works of the English Poets, with Prefaces, Biographical and Critical* ed. by Samuel Johnson 75 Vols. (London: A. Strachan, 1790), 30: 34-9 (p.34).
4. John Brewer, *The Pleasures of the Imagination: English Culture in the Eighteenth Century* 2nd Edn. (Abingdon: Routledge, 2013), p. 460.
5. *Reliques of Ancient English Poetry* ed. by Thomas Percy 3 Vols. (London: J. Dodsley, 1765), p. x.
6. Joseph Ritson (ed.), *Robin Hood: A Collection of All the Ancient Poems, Songs, and Ballads Now Extant, Relative to that Celebrated English Outlaw* ed. by Joseph Ritson 2 Vols. (London: T. Egerton, 1795), 1: xi.
7. Michael J. Turner, *Independent Radicalism in Early Victorian Britain* (Westport, CT: Praegar, 2004), pp. 2-4.
8. For information on Thomas Evans see Stephen Knight, *Robin Hood: A Mythic Biography* (Ithaca: Cornell University Press, 2003), pp. 92-3.
9. Nick Groom, 'The Purest English: Ballads and the English Literary Dialect', *The Eighteenth Century* 47: 2/3 (2006), pp. 179-202 (p.181).

10. See Benedict Anderson, *Imagined Communities: Reflections on the Origin and Spread of Nationalism* 3rd Edn. (London: Verso, 2006).
11. Evans, *Old Ballads, Historical and Narrative*, 1: i.
12. Operas such as Thomas Arne's *Alfred* (1740) sought to use the medieval period to inspire patriotism and nationalist feeling. Indeed, from this opera comes the now-famous song *Rule Britannia*. On the other hand, radical authors such as Joseph Ritson, for example, used the story of Robin Hood to espouse support for the ideals of Thomas Paine and the French Revolution.
13. Martin Myrone, *Bodybuilding: Reforming Masculinities in British Art 1750-1810* (New Haven: Yale University Press, 2005), p. 248.
14. *The Times* 7 May 1787, p. 3
15. Myrone, *Bodybuilding: Reforming Masculinities in British Art 1750-1810*, p. 248
16. For more information on the history of Italy in the 18th and 19th centuries, see Christopher Duggan, *A Concise History of Italy* (Cambridge: Cambridge University Press, 1994).
17. L.H. Cust, 'Rigaud, John Francis (1742–1810)' rev. Martin Myrone in *The Oxford Dictionary of National Biography* (Oxford: Oxford University Press, 2004; Online Edn. 2008) [Internet <www.oxforddnb.com/view/article/23639> Accessed 11 Nov 2016].
18. Joanne Begiato, 'Between Poise and Power: Embodied Manliness in Eighteenth- and Nineteenth-Century British Culture', *Transactions of the Royal Historical Society* Vol. 26 (2016), pp. 125-47 (p.142).
19. *Ibid.*, p. 142.
20. Joanne Begiato, 'Manly Bodies in Eighteenth- and Nineteenth-Century England', Royal Historical Society Conference: Masculinity and the Body in England, 1500-1900. University of Northampton, July 2015 [Internet <royalhistsoc.org/joanne-bailey-manly-bodies-in-eighteenth-and-nineteenth-century-england/> Accessed 11 November 2016].
21. Thomas Paine, 'Common Sense', in *The Constitution of the United States of America and Selected Writings of the Founding Fathers* (New York: Barnes & Noble, 2012), pp. 127-72 (p.134).
22. Paine, 'Common Sense', p. 134.
23. Jonathan Boucher, *A View of the Causes and Consequences of the American Revolution* (London, 1797), pp. i-ii.
24. Anon. 'The Parisian Insurgents', *The Times* 4 September 1789, p. 3.
25. Thomas Paine, *The Rights of Man* ed. by G. Vale (New York: G. Vale, 1848), p. 157-8.
26. Ritson, *Robin Hood*, 1: xii.

27. 'The Robbery of the Land by the Aristocracy' *Reynolds' Newspaper* 10 January 1869, p. 5.
28. Hobsbawm, *Uncommon People*, p.4; As radical as Thomas Paine was in his writings, however, he did not share the extremist views of Robespierre and the Jacobins in France who initiated the Reign of Terror. Having emigrated to France, he joined the Girondins party and was elected to the French National Convention. Although he was one of the first people in the Convention to call for a republic, he campaigned against executing the King in 1792.
29. Eric Hobsbawm, *Uncommon People: Resistance, Rebellion, and Jazz* (London: Abacus, 1998), p. 3.
30. Edmund Burke, *An Appeal from the New to the Old Whigs* 3rd Edn. (London: J. Dodsley, 1791), p. 7.
31. Burke, *An Appeal from the New to the Old Whigs,* pp. 7-8.
32. 'The Sturdy Reformer: A Song, Exemplifying the Doctrines of "The Rights of Man" Published in 1792' *The Morning Post* 9 January 1817, p. 3.
33. 'The Sturdy Reformer', p. 3.
34. *Ibid.*, p. 3.
35. *A Dialogue between Wat Tyler, Mischievous Tom, and an English Farmer* (London: J. Stockdale, 1793), p. 1.
36. *Ibid.,* p. 4.
37. *Ibid.*, p. 5.
38. *A Dialogue between Wat Tyler, Mischievous Tom, and an English Farmer*, pp. 5-6.
39. *Ibid.*, pp. 6-7.
40. *The Encyclopaedia of Romantic Literature* ed. by Frederick Burwick 3 Vols. (Chichester: John Wiley & Sons, 2012), p. 1046.
41. Richard Cumberland, *The Memoirs of Richard Cumberland Written by Himself* (London: Lackington, 1806), p. 513.
42. See Carl B. Cone*, The English Jacobins: Reformers in Late 18th Century England* (New Brunswick: Transaction, 1968).
43. Robert Southey, *Harold; or, The Castle of Morford* (1791). Bodleian MS. Eng. Misc. e. 21 (Summary Catalogue 31777); this Robin Hood novel currently remains unpublished. It bears all the hallmarks of Southey's early radicalism; Robin Hood is a revolutionary freedom fighter; Richard I is a reformist king who detests the Catholic Church.
44. Robert Southey, 'Wat Tyler; A Dramatic Poem in Three Acts' *Sherwin's Weekly Political Register* (London: T. Sherwin [n.d.] c.1817), pp. 2-3.
45. *Ibid.*, p. 3.

46. W.D. Rubenstein, 'The End of Old Corruption in Britain, 1780-1860' *Past and Present*, No. 101 (1983), pp. 55-86.

47. Daniel Defoe, 'The Life and Strange Surprising Adventures of Robinson Crusoe' in *The Works of Daniel Defoe* ed. by J.S. Keltie (Edinburgh: W. P. Nimmo, 1869), pp.31-208 (p.35).

48. Southey, 'Wat Tyler', p.3.

49. *Ibid.*, p. 4.

50. Joseph Ritson, 'Letter CXXV: To Mr. Laing, 5 March 1794', in *The Letters of Joseph Ritson, Esq. Edited Chiefly from Originals in the Possession of his Nephew* ed. by Nicholas Harris 2 Vols. (London: William Pickering, 1833), 2: 47; whether he was truly being watched is difficult to say. He did suffer from a number of mental health problems, and most people just viewed him as a harmless old eccentric.

51. E.N. Williams, *The Eighteenth-Century Constitution, 1688-1815* (Cambridge: Cambridge University Press, 1960), pp. 424-5.

52. Southey, 'Wat Tyler', p. 5.

53. *Ibid.*, p. 6.

54. *Ibid.*, p. 6.

55. *Ibid.*, p. 7.

56. *Ibid.*, p. 7.

57. *Ibid.*, pp.10-11.

58. *Ibid.*, p.11.

59. *Ibid.*, p.11.

60. *Ibid.*, p. 11.

61. *Ibid.*, p. 11.

62. An excellent history of the publication of Southey's *Wat Tyler* is given on the following website: Matthew Hill and Neil Fraistat, *Romantic Circles: A Refereed Scholarly Website Devoted to the Study of Romantic-Period Literature and Culture*, University of Maryland [Internet <www.rc.umd.edu/editions/wattyler/> Accessed 3 November 2016].

63. Robert Southey, *Wat Tyler; a Dramatic Poem in Three Acts* (London: W. Hone, 1817), p. 1.

64. 'Wat Tyler' in *The Bury and Norwich Post: Or, Suffolk, Norfolk, Essex, Cambridge, and Ely Advertiser* 9 April 1817, p. 1.

65. 'Art. X: Wat Tyler', *The Monthly Review, or, Literary Journal* March 1817, pp. 313-17 (p.314).

66. Jean Raimond, 'Southey's Early Writings and the Revolution', *The Yearbook of English Studies: The French Revolution in English* Vol. 19 (1989), pp. 181-96 (p.181).

67. Robert Southey, 'Mr. Southey's Apology for his "Wat Tyler"', *The Gentleman's Magazine and Historical Chronicle* May 1817, p. 389.
68. Southey, 'Mr. Southey's Apology for his 'Wat Tyler'', p. 389.
69. *Ibid.*, p. 390.
70. William Hone, *The Political House that Jack Built* (London: Printed for W. Hone, 1819), p. 7.
71. George Cruikshank, *A Free Born Englishman! The Admiration of the World!!! And the Envy of Surrounding Nations!!!!!* (London [n.pub.] 1819) London, British Museum BM Satires 1865,1111.2136.
72. Raimond, 'Southey's Early Writings and the Revolution', p. 181.

CHAPTER FIVE

Radicalism and Chartism

As to the motives that have always actuated REFORMERS and LEVELLERS; (for the words are, with very few exceptions, synonymous) – whether Wat Tyler, Jack Cade, Kit the Tanner, Tom Paine, or the Spa Fields Orators – Reformation is the specious pretext, but REVOLUTION and PLUNDER the real object and end!

Anon. *The Morning Post* (1817)

This man was much in advance of his period; he was well-informed and well-intentioned; he was a radical of a nature that astounded 'the powers that were' – an aristocracy so very high in Toryism, they could believe no improvement in the people's condition less than a crime, for which there was no punishment bad enough. All who attempted to show that the people's necks were bowed down, trodden on, and they were fools to submit to it, were stigmatised as 'scandalous and wicked traytours'; and the idea of abolishing villeinage was greeted with a shout of scornful laughter.

Pierce Egan the Younger, *Wat Tyler; or, The Rebellion of 1381* (1841)

Up! Up! Ye English peasantry, for whom Wat Tyler bled;
Up! Cited serfs, whose sturdy sires Cade and Archamber led;
Up! Up! For equal rights and laws: your cause is all as good
As when in the presence of the Smith a traitor monarch stood.

Anon. *A Song for the Next Rebellion* (1841)

RADICALISM AND CHARTISM

We have seen how Wat Tyler was radicalised during the late eighteenth century when he was appropriated by authors such as Thomas Paine and Robert Southey. Radical appropriations of Wat Tyler continue during the early-to-mid nineteenth century at precisely the same moment that political reform movements burst onto the political scene. Radical orators invoke Wat Tyler's name at mass meetings. Radical poets call on Tyler's spirit to rouse the working classes into action. Tyler's name was particularly important to members of the working-class Chartist movement, which existed between 1838 and 1858. Chartist poets would sing Tyler's praises. Novelists portray Tyler as a proto-Chartist, notably Pierce Egan the Younger, whose novel *Wat Tyler, or, The Rebellion of 1381* (1841) was a huge bestseller. Various branches of the Chartist movement named themselves the Wat Tyler Brigade or the Wat Tyler League.[1] Let us now examine representations of Tyler between c.1800 and c.1840.

Let it be remembered that, during the early nineteenth century, by and large, neither the middle classes nor the working classes had the vote. A man had to own over forty shillings in freehold property to be eligible to vote. The property qualification for the vote, having been established during the fifteenth century, was clearly inadequate for the nineteenth century. Moreover, the constituency map was outdated. Important 'new' towns such as Manchester and Leeds, which had grown in size and economic importance, returned no MPs, while places like Old Sarum in Wiltshire which was nothing but a field by the 1830s, returned two MPs. The practice of voting itself was open to corruption. Voting was not via secret ballot as it is today but done in public. Voters were often either bribed or 'persuaded' to vote a particular way. The system simply could not meet the needs of a modern industrial society. Yet still, the government was wary of any reforms to the political system, having just fought the long-running French Revolutionary and Napoleonic Wars.

What emerged after the wars, then, was a political reform movement that was composed of an alliance of both the working and middle classes. It was not simply a reform of the political system that these men and women required, however, for there were other grievances that they had, notably the Corn Laws. These were enacted immediately following the Napoleonic Wars and imposed tariffs upon imported grain. This form of protectionism was a boon to domestic producers of food because it kept the price of food high, but at the same time hurt the pockets of the poor who were already experiencing the effects of an economic depression. This was at a time of high unemployment due to the fact that the labour market had been flooded with soldiers returning home from the wars.

But the government still resisted any movements towards reform. There were several riots during the period, such as the one which occurred at Spa Fields in 1816.[2] There were two gatherings held at Spa Fields in this year. The first meeting on 15 November was a peaceful demonstration attended by approximately ten thousand protesters. A petition was drawn up for King George IV demanding universal male suffrage, annual general elections, and a secret ballot. The person invited to speak was none other than the famous radical orator Henry Hunt (1773-1835). He was a celebrity who built up his popularity speaking at many public gatherings on the issue of parliamentary reform.[3] He was known as 'the protector of the poor' and was an early advocate for votes for women as well.[4] Yet when Hunt attempted to deliver the petition to the King a few days later, he was refused admission. A second public meeting was held at Spa Fields on 2 December, and Hunt again addressed the protestors:

> I am sorry to tell you that our supplication to the Prince has failed. He, the father of the people, answered – 'My family have never attended to Petitions but from Oxford and Cambridge, and the City of London.' And is this man the father of the people? No. Has he listened to your petition? No. We must do more than words. We have been oppressed for 800 years, since the Norman Conquest. If they would give a hod, a shovel, a spade, and a hoe, your mother earth will supply you. Countrymen, if you will have your wrongs redressed, follow me. – *(We will!)* Wat Tyler would have succeeded had he not been basely murdered by a Lord Mayor ... Have the Parliament done their duty? – *(No)* – Has the Regent done his duty? – *(No, no!)*[5]

In the speech, Hunt draws upon the idea of the Norman Yoke. According to this idea, before William of Normandy's invasion of England in 1066, the Anglo-Saxons enjoyed a degree of political freedom. This changed when a foreign king imposed a continental form of feudalism upon the liberty-loving Saxons. What followed was eight hundred years of political oppression, punctuated by various attempts by common Englishmen to regain their liberties.[6] Hunt singles out Tyler as an exemplar of a brave man who was 'basely murdered'. While Hunt never claimed to be a revolutionary, unbeknownst to him a small revolutionary faction was present at the gathering. They were led by one Doctor Watson, and his son Arthur. After Hunt had finished speaking, Watson and his son hoisted the French tricolour and incited some of those present to riot. A gunsmith was robbed, and a bystander was killed as the protestors made their way to the Royal Exchange. This was to be a failed revolt, however, for by nightfall the protestors had been arrested and order was quickly restored in the city. Due to the similarity of their names, Watson was easily equated with Wat Tyler, as the pair are in a satirical print depicting the meeting entitled *And this is Wat's Son, 'all Tattered and Torn'* (1817), where he is described as 'the Spawn of Wat Tyler'.[7]

Hunt said that he would have not attended had he known that extremist factions of revolutionaries would be present. It did not matter what he said really, and the riots generated heated debates on both sides of the political spectrum. Wat Tyler's history at this period continued to be appropriated by writers with radical sympathies to condemn the nineteenth-century authorities, who were denounced as 'brutes in human form':

> It is the fashion to condemn the people of that era as if they were
> so sunk in ignorance, poverty, and slavery that in manners and
> intellect they were little better than brutes ... It is through the
> pages of such writers that the name of Wat Tyler is become a
> term of opprobrium; although it belonged to a man who, if he
> wanted the courtly obsequiousness of modern times, possessed
> a just sense of moral and manly decency, and knew how to

vindicate a daughter from the brutality of a tax gatherer. There were brutes in the human form, in that time, as well as at the present; but at all times those brutes are to be found on the side of tyranny and corruption.[8]

But for every journalist who wrote in support of reform in the national press, there were probably two who were ready to denounce them. Fitzgerald's poem was reprinted in an 1817 issue of *The Morning Post*, and there it is prefaced with the following remarks on contemporary reformers:

[As to] the motives that have always actuated REFORMERS and LEVELLERS; (for the words are, with very few exceptions, synonymous) – whether WAT TYLER, JACK CADE, KIT THE TANNER, TOM PAINE, or the SPA FIELDS ORATORS – Reformation is the specious pretext, but REVOLUTION and PLUNDER the real object and end!'[9]

At this time, another writer for *The Weekly Entertainer* felt the need to moralise upon the subject of popular revolts. Although they do not mention the Spa Fields Riots by name, it would probably have been obvious to readers that the article is referencing the events of 1816:

There are often great riots in England, which are sometimes very dangerous, for when mobs assemble, nobody knows what such a great crowd of foolish ignorant people may do: but one time, about four hundred years ago, there happened the most dangerous riots that ever were known, for all the country armed themselves with clubs and staves, and scythes, and pitchforks, and they drove away all the King's soldiers and got possession of London. The chief leaders of this mob were not gentlemen nor soldiers, but common peasants and tradesmen, who were called after by the names of their trades, Wat Tyler, Hob Carter, and Tom Miller; and as these fellows could neither read nor write, and were poor ignorant wretches, they took a great hatred to all gentlemen.[10]

There is a great deal of snobbery in that article. Wat Tyler and his associates were not respectable gentlemen but uncouth and base characters. Rebelling against the king is wrong, and the article makes sure to point out that Tyler was *justly* punished, having 'well deserved his fate for his rebellion against the king, and for all the mischief and murders that his rebellion had occasioned'.[11]

Further riots followed, notably the Pentrich Rising on 9 and 10 June 1817.[12] During this rebellion, a few hundred men armed with guns and pikes led by Jeremiah Brandreth marched on Nottingham. Their expectation was that the populace would rise with them and that there would be a revolution. It was not to be, however, for among their number was a government spy, and the principal rebels were arrested by the army, brought to trial and hanged for their actions on 7 November 1817 outside Derby Gaol.[13] Hunt took no part in the Pentrich Rising, but on 22 July 1819, he held a mass meeting in Smithfield, London which was attended by forty to fifty thousand people. It was at Smithfield, of course, that the historic Wat Tyler met his death. As he did in his speech at Spa Fields, Hunt made further reference to the rebel leader on this occasion.[14] The peasants may not yet have been revolting, but the demand for change was in the air. The history of the fourteenth-century rebellion was evidently providing nineteenth-century reformers with a sense of historical legitimacy for their actions.

Sadly, the authorities' paranoia and suspicion of any political reform movement as a result of the French Revolution would have deadly consequences. On 16 August 1819, a crowd of between sixty and eighty thousand peaceful protesters gathered in Peter's Fields, Manchester to hear Henry Hunt speaking again upon the issue of parliamentary reform. It has to be remembered at this point that there was no professional police force. Robert Peel's establishment of the Metropolitan Police Force was still ten years off, and Manchester would not see a police force established until 1839. The little law enforcement that existed was conducted by part-time, unpaid constables and watchmen. In 1819, the policing of large public gatherings such as the one at Peter's Fields was delegated to the local militia or yeomanry. William Hulton (1787-1864) was the chairman of the board of magistrates at the time of the mass meeting. Despite the fact that the protest was a peaceful one, the magistrates grew nervous and summoned the Manchester and Salford Yeomanry. The Riot Act was read and the crowd were commanded to disperse, but obviously at a gathering of between sixty and eighty thousand people, very few are going to hear the declaration being read aloud. Then the cavalry, some of whom were drunk, charged at the protesters killing fifteen people and injuring seven hundred more. The event was christened 'Peterloo' in an ironic reference to the Battle of Waterloo four years earlier, for some of the protestors who were injured were veterans of the Napoleonic war and had fought to defend their country.

Peterloo did not immediately lead the government to contemplate reforming parliament, but in fact led to further suppression in the form of the Six Acts. These were a series of Bills that went through Parliament rapidly with the intention of suppressing mass meetings. As the next decade progressed, however, there was a feeling amongst some people in the political classes that parliamentary reform was necessary. The campaign for reform then received a major boost in 1830 when the Whigs under Earl Grey won the election.[15] Grey had been advocating parliamentary reform as early as 1792, when he was part of the Society of the Friends of the People. Grey's government attempted to pass two reform Bills in the early part of its administration. The intention was to extend the franchise and to redraw constituency boundaries. But both of these Bills were rejected by Tory peers in the House of Lords, who dominated the second chamber at this point. At this time, unelected peers could veto any law sent up to the House of Commons, and this undemocratic practice was only put an end to when David Lloyd George's Liberal Party passed the Parliament Act in 1911. Nowadays, peers can only suggest amendments and delay the passage of an Act of Parliament for a maximum of two years. Grey's next thought, then, was to simply raise a number of pro-reform men to the peerage, but William IV was apprehensive of doing this, and so Grey and his government resigned. The King then invited the Tory Duke of Wellington to form the next government. But Wellington had a hard time rallying support,

John Ball preaching to the commons at Blackheath, from Froissart's Chronicles.

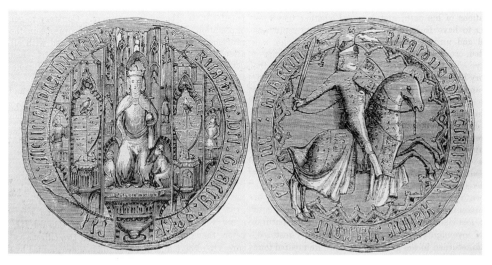

Great Seal of Richard II.

Richard II in his barge meeting the rebels, from Froissart's Chronicles.

The murder of the archbishop, Simon Sudbury, from Froissart's Chronicles.

The death of Wat Tyler, from Froissart's Chronicles.

Portrait of Richard II.

Portrait of John of Gaunt.

Joan of Kent appealing to Wat Tyler for protection from the mob.

Portrait of John Wycliffe.

The surrender of Richard II to Henry Bolingbroke at Flint Castle.

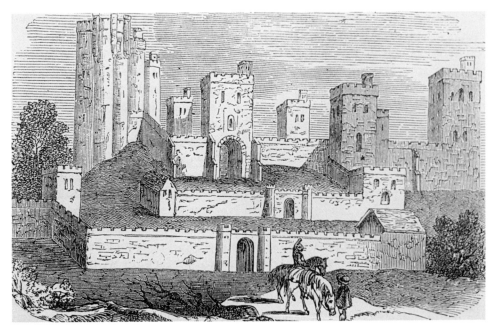

Pontefract Castle in the time of Richard II.

Facsimile of the first chapter of the Gospel of John in Wycliffe's New Testament.

Portrait of Geoffrey Chaucer.

Fourteenth-century illustration of a blacksmith.

RICHARD II *appeases the* REBELS *on the* Death *of* Wat Tyler *in* The Year 1380.

Richard II appeases the rebels on the death of Wat Tyler.

Wale delin.

Walker sculp.

The BURNING of St. JOHN's MONASTERY in Smithfield,
by WAT TYLER and his RABBLE

The burning of St. John's Monastery in Smthfield, c.1784.

Wat Tyler killing the poll tax collector by J. Rigaud, 1798.

The death of Wat Tyler by James Northcote, 1777.

Frontispiece to Thomas Evans' *Old Ballads, Historical and Narrative* (1777).

Joan of Kent by A. Penley, 1837.

Portrait of Robert Southey (1774-1843).

Portrait of Pierce Egan the Younger (1814-1880).

Portrait of William Harrison Ainsworth (1805-1882).

Frontispiece to Pierce Egan the Younger's *Wat Tyler; or, The Rebellion of 1381* (1841).

Wat Tyler addressing the rebels at Smithfield, from Pierce Egan's *Wat Tyler; or, the Rebellion of 1381* (1841).

Frontispiece to William
Morris's *A Dream of
John Ball* (1888).

WHEN ADAM DELVED AND EVE SPAN,
WHO WAS THEN THE GENTLEMAN?

The death of William
Langland, as imagined in
Florence Converse's *Long
Will* (1902).

and the country certainly was not behind him. Political agitation during May of 1832 was reaching fever pitch, with some protesters advocating tax evasion, a run on the banks, and even the abolition of the monarchy. Wellington soon resigned and Grey and the Whigs were invited back by the King to form the next government. Wisely, Wellington counselled Tory peers in the Lords not to oppose the passage of the Reform Bill when it was sent up for another reading. The Bill passed and the so-called Great Reform Act received Royal Assent on 7 June 1832.

But from the standpoint of the working classes, the Act was not 'great' in any sense. It did indeed extend the franchise and give political representation to the new towns. However, the Reform Act gave the vote to *some* men only, namely those who owned over ten pounds of freehold property and tenants paying fifty pounds or more per annum. In what became known as 'the Great Betrayal', the upper middle classes of society, who were now happy with their lot, having gained the right to vote, abandoned any further attempts at political reform. As if to add insult to injury, the Whig government appeared to be passing punitive laws deliberately designed to hurt the poor. One of these was the Poor Law Amendment Act, passed in 1834, which established a national system of workhouses, replacing the rather disorganised system of poor relief that existed prior to the nineteenth century.[16] With reference to the Reform Act and the New Poor Law, an article written by James 'Bronterre' O'Brien entitled 'Who are Our Real Foes and Oppressors?' appeared in *Bronterre's National Reformer* in 1837. In the article, Bronterre draws upon the events of 1381. He uses the incident at Smithfield to vent his anger towards the middle classes who had abandoned their former working-class comrades:

Another instance of the baseness of the ruling class occurred in the reign of Richard II, on the occasion of the insurrection of Wat Tyler. Though slavery had been nominally abolished by Act of Parliament two centuries before, yet had the slave owners, by the introduction of a cunning clause, about 'openly in the market,' managed to make that act (as usual) a mere instrument for promoting their own interests ... The object, therefore, of [Tyler's] insurgents was to obtain a real emancipation from personal slavery, freedom of trade in market-towns, and a fixed rent on lands. These demands were so just and moderate, that they were granted at once by the young King Richard. Now mark the villainy of the ruling classes. In the first place, Walworth, a London shopocrat, murdered Tyler, according to the lying middle-class histories, though it don't appear that the King took any offence at the extraordinary and noble bearing of Tyler. Even the court sycophants, being of more gentle blood, had imbibed some respect, some regard for a manly and honest deportment. The confidence, too, which Tyler had reposed in their honour, in coming alone amongst them, was with them a guarantee of his safety. 'Twas otherwise, however, with the base and bloody-minded middle-man, Walworth.[17]

Whereas in Southey's account, the blame for Wat Tyler's death is placed firmly with the King and the aristocratic classes, Bronterre now lays the blame for Tyler's death at the feet of the middle classes, the betrayers. His reference to 'lying middle-class histories', furthermore, is another example of radicals believing that the true history of the nation had been modified in order to favour the elites. The same article goes on to argue that the labouring classes suffer in workhouses because the middle classes coerced Whig and Tory politicians, both of which parties at this point were composed of many members of the aristocracy, to bend to their will and to punish the poor:

And to the English operatives, that other 'large instalment,' the New Poor Law! Much has been said, much has been written upon this subject; the Whigs have been abused as the authors of that atrocious measure, while the Tories have gone scot-free; but the fact is, that this is another true middle-class measure, and your Whig and Tory rulers are but instruments in their hands. The very classes who obtained power under the Reform Act forced this measure upon the government. Under the Tory or borough-mongering Parliament, the ruling classes were neither numerous nor powerful enough to carry such a measure through.[18]

Bronterre is angry, and with good reason. According to Bronterre, the middle classes of society cannot be trusted. This was as true with Walworth and Wat Tyler as it was with the nineteenth-century middle classes, the Whigs, and the Poor Law Amendment Act.

Subsequently, a number of working-class reform movements were established during the 1830s, such as the London Working Men's Association, the National Political Union, and the Manchester Political Union. The leaders of these working-class organisations believed that if they could replicate the political agitation seen in the run up to 1832 then their own demands would similarly be met. The working classes did still have a few friends in Parliament, and in 1837 six MPs and six educated working men drafted the People's Charter which, in its final form, would include six demands: the vote for *all* men over the age of twenty-one; vote by secret ballot; equally-sized electoral districts; the abolition of property qualifications to become an MP; payment of MPs, and annual elections.

It is here that I must challenge R.B. Dobson's assertion that 'the legacy of the Peasants' Revolt to the nineteenth-century working class was rarely relevant and often ambiguous.'[19] Leading members of the historical revolt were on occasion equated with the Chartists. John Ball, for example, is described in Cassell's *Illustrated History of England* (1865) as 'a thorough democrat or Chartist of his day, drawing his opinions from the literal declarations of the gospel that God is no respecter of persons'.[20] And Wat Tyler's history was appropriated by many Chartist writers during this period. Indeed, while Tyler's name appears as a spectre in radical literature between the 1790s and the 1830s, it is really with the emergence of the Chartist movement that the high point of Tyler's literary afterlife comes, especially after 1840.

Wat Tyler appears several times in Chartist poetry, which was immensely important in the literature of Chartism. The leading Chartist newspaper of the day entitled *The Northern Star,* which began its publication in Leeds, regularly published poetry written by Chartist supporters. Research by Michael Sanders in *The Poetry of Chartism* (2009) has shown that between 1838 and 1852, *The Northern Star* printed a total of 1,482 poems in its columns.[21]

One such poem entitled *The Voice of Wat Tyler* appeared in *The Odd Fellow* in 1840. Wat Tyler's ghost urges his nineteenth-century countrymen to rise up and regain their rights:

> Rouse thee, Freedom! From thy grave –
> E'en from Custom's chartered cave,
> Wherein tyrants hide their prey,
> Murderers in a decent way.[22]

Tyler then calls upon the names of various radicals throughout history, such as Wycliffe and Cromwell, and tells his nineteenth-century counterparts that these early fighters for liberty are similarly urging them to fight on in the cause of 'divine equality'.[23] The use of Wat Tyler's ghost to speak to modern reformers is a recurring trope in other Chartist poems. Charles Cole, a little-known 'Labour-Mechanic Poet', authored *The Spirit of Wat Tyler*, which appeared in *The Northern Star* in 1848, and it uses the ghost of Tyler to admonish the nineteenth-century working classes for being duped by the establishment:

> 'God save the Queen';your dogs I see
> Have superseded donkeys;
> *Age of progressive industry!*
> *Of course you work [you're] monkeys!*
> God save the Queen! Still Britons slaves,
> In this land of bravery;
> Ye sing, 'Britannia rules the waves,'
> Yet bow to basest slavery.[24]

Other poems legitimise the Chartist cause by presenting their struggle as merely one in a long line of struggles for liberty throughout history. *A Song for the Next Rebellion* was written pseudonymously by a writer

who named himself Spartacus. The author's choice of pseudonym –
the tough Roman rebel leader who shook the entire Roman Empire
with his revolt – suggests that this particular writer held views that
were at the more extreme end of the Chartist political spectrum. The
names of historical rebels are invoked in order to spur the Chartists
into action:

> Up! Up! Ye English peasantry, for whom Wat Tyler bled;
> Up! Cited serfs, whose sturdy sires Cade and Archamber led;
> Up! Up! For equal rights and laws: your cause is all as good
> As when in the presence of the Smith a traitor monarch stood.[25]

Previous rebels such as Tyler, Cade, and Archamber may have failed,
but victory is sure to be theirs:

> Up! Up! If ye are Englishmen; be mindful of the day,
> When Cromwell strode o'er Worcester's fields, and scared a
> King away.
> Though Cade and Ket and Tyler failed, the 'crowning mercy'
> came: Hurrah for England's stalwart one! Your fortune be the
> same! …
>
> Up! Up! Ye toil-worn English slaves: if blood must needs be
> shed,
> Let it be England's tyrant lords, and not the famine-sped!
> Ay, hand-to-hand, and foot to foot, grapple with tyranny! –
> Our Saxon Thor is Lord again: Our England shall be free![26]

This is a call to action. The Chartists must emulate Tyler, Cade, and
Cromwell. Blood will need to be shed, and all freeborn Englishmen
should be prepared for this. The references to Cromwell and to 'scaring
a King away', however, does not mean that the Chartists were
disrespectful towards their own monarch. Absent in a lot of Chartist
literature are personal attacks against Queen Victoria. While Wat Tyler
poems often portray the medieval nobility and the nineteenth-century

upper classes as synonymous, none of them equate Richard II with the person of the Queen. Indeed, even the 'vicious republican' and Chartist activist, G.W.M. Reynolds (1814-79), never criticised Victoria personally. In his novel *The Mysteries of London* (1844-46), she is portrayed as being shielded from the woes of her subjects by corrupt government ministers. The result is that she is 'lamentably ignorant of the every-day incidents of life [...and] the Royal pair manifested a reluctance to believe in those melancholy occurrences which characterise the condition of the industrious millions.'[27] There is respect for the person of the Queen in Chartist literature, but often contempt for the institution of the monarchy.[28]

It will be recalled from the previous chapter that many radicals and reformers throughout the eighteenth and nineteenth centuries believed that history had been whitewashed in favour of the elites. Thus, the Chartists aimed to revise the 'official' history of the Peasants' Revolt. As we have seen, Wat Tyler's assassin, Walworth, was viewed positively prior to the late eighteenth century. In Chartist literature, however, Walworth becomes the man who *murdered* Wat Tyler. It is Wat Tyler, and not William Walworth, who was the patriot in 1381. It was Tyler's patriotic duty to strike the tax collector and lead the mob to London, for the medieval officials were causing harm to the nation by dividing it through onerous taxes. This is the view found in Charles Cole's *Sonnets After Reading a Part of History Relating to Wat Tyler* (1841).[29]

Moreover, in *The English Chartist Circular* it is said that although Wat Tyler did not have a noble title, he was of better moral standing than the upper-class Walworth (earlier radicals such as Bronterre had, of course, placed the assassin in the middle classes):

When the insurgent army marched into Southwark, Tyler ordered a number of Brothels, known by the name of the Bordello, or Stews, and situated on the Bankside, to be burnt. This may not appear to have been a very serious affair at first sight; but so it proved, for the proprietor of these dens of sensuality was no other than the 'famous Lord Mayor', Sir

William Walworth! In this disgraceful circumstance, there can be no doubt, originated the treacherous murder of Wat Tyler. This affords a valuable illustration of the morality of the higher classes at that time ... It is gratifying to know, and it speaks volumes for the purity of the feelings of the mass of people, that while the authorities were so base as to stoop to this infamous means of enriching themselves, they could find no instruments from among the English people to undertake the dirty work of renting these abodes of iniquity.[30]

This is clearly an attempt to impose an idea of Victorian sexual morality and respectability upon the character of the historic Tyler. The Victorians were almost obsessed with the idea of respectability which supposedly informed their conduct and morality in both public and private life. We have seen traces of this respectability superimposed onto Tyler's character before, with Bronterre's earlier description of him as a man who had 'a just sense of moral and manly decency'. Although a very middle-class ideology, respectability was open to the working classes, if they conducted themselves accordingly. And they were often divided by elite commentators in the press as either 'the respectable labouring poor' or 'the undeserving labouring poor'. And, of course, a respectable man viewed brothels with abhorrence: Wat Tyler burned down the brothels, not out of wickedness, but out of a just sense of moral decency (the historical Wat Tyler and his men did indeed burn down some of the brothels in Southwark, but there is little evidence to say that Walworth owned them). Therefore, the rehabilitation of Wat Tyler's character begun by Thomas Paine, was continued by the Chartist activists. Tyler is no longer admirable only because he fought for political representation, but because he was, to the Chartists at least, the medieval equivalent of a respectable Victorian gentleman. And of course, respectable men such as Chartist activists and their followers – the descendants of men such as Wat Tyler – deserved political representation in the House of Commons.

In addition, with the publication of Walter Scott's *Waverley, or, 'Tis*

Sixty Years Since (1814), the historical novel grew in popularity amongst the reading public. Scott himself would turn towards the medieval period with *Ivanhoe* (1819), a novel featuring Robin Hood and King Richard the Lionheart. Yet for the most part, these historical novels were expensive, published as they were in the three volume format. But there was a novelist whose works were inexpensive, who was sympathetic to the Chartists, and who was writing about Wat Tyler at the height of the second phase of the Chartist movement. The novel in question is *Wat Tyler, or, The Rebellion of 1381,* which was authored by Pierce Egan the Younger and published in 1841.

Pierce James Egan the Younger (1814-80) was the son of the famous Regency author, Pierce Egan (1772-1849). The younger Egan began life as an illustrator, and collaborated with his father on *The Pilgrims of the Thames in Search of the National* (1838) before turning his attention to fiction. His first novel *Quintin Matsys: The Blacksmith of Antwerp* (1839) gives a highly dramatic, fictionalised account of the life of the eponymous Flemish painter. Egan then turned his attention to Robin Hood with *Robin Hood and Little John, or, The Merry Men of Sherwood Forest* (1838-40). All of Egan's early novels express radical sentiments. This was recognised by one reviewer in *The London Journal*, a publication for which Egan served as editor between 1860 and his death in 1880. The commentator recognised that '[Egan] and the body of the people have sympathies in common.'[31] Thus, the eponymous painter in *Quintin Matsys* is depicted as a member of the working classes who leads an armed revolt against the nobles of the city of Antwerp.[32] In *Robin Hood and Little John,* although he is depicted as a nobleman, throughout all of his life the eponymous outlaw 'endeavoured to lift the wretched serfs out of the galling clutches of dire oppression'.[33] As a result of these novels, Egan became immensely popular. The scale of the popularity he enjoyed is evident in the remarks made in an article for *MacMillan's Magazine*:

> There is a mighty potentate in England whose name is Pierce Egan … Many among us fancy that they have a good general idea of what is English literature. They think of Tennyson and

Dickens as the most popular of our living authors. It is a fond delusion, from which they should be aroused. The works of Mr. Pierce Egan are sold by the half million. What living author can compare with him?[34]

All of Egan's works were penny bloods: they were published in weekly instalments and sold for a penny, and they were mainly read by people from the lower middle and working classes.[35]

Egan's diverse readership explains why his idea of 'the people' looks back to pre-1832 reform movements. To Egan the people comprise both the working and middle classes. To him, the events of 1381 were not a revolt simply by peasants, and Egan never calls the event 'the Peasants' Revolt'. The people in the novel who take part in the rebellion are drawn from various social classes. Faithful to the historical record, in the novel it is the townsfolk and tradesmen in the City of London who lower the drawbridge to allow Tyler and the rest of the rebels into the city.[36] When Tyler surveys the crowd that has gathered around him in London, he observes that, 'out of the whole assemblage, there was an immense number of better educated men, or rather whose position in life, as small tradespeople, had been more comfortable and higher in its relations than the serfs and villeins.'[37]

There was also a racial element to Egan's concept of 'the people'. The upper classes are represented by the Norman nobility, while the middle and working classes are composed of the Anglo-Saxons. The Saxons are described as 'the poorer class [who are] the true source of all power'. They need to rise up and form a council between themselves, 'so that they may not be, as they have been, trampled upon'.[38] One of Tyler's lower-class associates, named Leowulf (a name that obviously inspired by Beowulf), is described as

A Saxon, who prided himself on having no cross of Norman blood in his veins; nothing but the pure Saxon blood, and possessed the same unalloyed hatred to the Normans which his forefathers had borne towards them in the time of the first William.[39]

The idea of conflict between the Anglo-Saxons and the Normans is an idea straight out of Scott's *Ivanhoe* which opens with the following statement:

> A circumstance which greatly tended to enhance the tyranny of the nobility, and the sufferings of the inferior classes, arose as a consequence of the conquest by Duke William of Normandy. Four generations had not sufficed to blend the hostile blood of the Normans and Anglo-Saxons, or to unite, by common language and mutual interests, two hostile races, one of which still felt the elation of triumph, while the other groaned under all the consequences of defeat.[40]

There was some resistance to Norman rule in the immediate aftermath of the Conquest in 1066, but it had certainly disappeared by the 1190s when *Ivanhoe* is set, and was non-existent by the 1380s. In Egan's novel, then, Scott's vision of racial conflict is superimposed onto contemporary notions of class.

In the novel, Wat Tyler is a veteran of the Hundred Years War and he eventually marries his childhood sweetheart, Violet Evesham (after he has rescued her from ruffians, and thwarted one attempted rape in the forest at the beginning of the novel), and they have a daughter together. Meantime, the condition of England worsens. The Normans rule the Anglo-Saxons by terror. Yet Tyler and his fellow citizens are not law breakers, as he explains that the people 'did send petition after petition, but in vain – fresh taxes were imposed and rigorously exacted, and all their appeals and prayers were unheeded'.[41] Tyler and his fellow rebel leaders, Jack Straw and John Ball, seek the establishment of a 'code of laws', or a 'charter',[42] and included in this charter, for example, is 'the undoubted right to *elect* a sovereign' (emphasis added).[43] As Chris R. Vanden Bossche points out that the 'charter' that Tyler and his associates seek is highly reminiscent of the Chartist struggle.[44] Issues come to a head when a the poll tax is levied upon all people over the age of fifteen to pay for King Richard's foreign wars, and tax gatherers are sent out into the country to collect it. Still the people think that if they only appeal to the King, who will grant them their charter, then all of their grievances will be resolved. Tyler is only moved to lead the revolt after the incident with a Norman tax collector who visits Tyler's house. The tax collector finds Tyler's daughter at home alone and, 'full of strong drink',[45] attempts to rape her. At that instant, Tyler arrives home, seizes his hammer, and strikes the tax collector on the head, with the consequence that 'his brains were scattered about the place by one tremendous blow'.[46] This apocryphal event has almost become a fact in historical writing.[47] The attempted rape of his daughter, combined with the fact that the Saxons' political grievances are not being addressed, makes Tyler, Jack Straw, John Ball, and the people rise up and march on London.

Egan's Wat Tyler makes no attempt to conceal his contempt for royal authority:

'Thinkest thou, if thou hadst performed the duty for which the people placed thee on the throne ... would they have quitted their homes to assemble in a body and demand their rights? King, they placed thee on the throne.'

'I am the Lord's anointed,' exclaimed Richard haughtily; 'I received the Crown from God, not the people.'

'That is a juggle of priestcraft, which will only suit the weak minds of the superstitious,' said Wat.[48]

This exchange is unambiguous – the King's power emanates from the people, not from divine right, a notion which Tyler rubbishes. The only reason that a king should exist is 'to administer justice and attend to the common interest'.[49] Tyler further repudiates 'all idea of any right in the higher powers to oppress'.[50] In a further frank exchange with the King, Tyler demonstrates his disbelief of the notion that anybody is born higher than another when he asks him, 'in what are you better than us, that we should be sufferers by your whims and caprices?'[51] This is not to say that Egan detests all medieval royals. He would in 1850, after all, write *Edward, the Black Prince* in which the eponymous warrior is unambiguously portrayed as a hero. But Egan's admiration for this Prince stems from the fact that, as he writes in *Wat Tyler*, before the Prince's death the people 'looked up to him for everything in the shape of reform in the legislation'.[52] Nevertheless, when *Wat Tyler* was published in the midst of the second phase of the Chartist movement, Egan's talk of a 'Charter' and its egalitarian ideals, and the right to *elect* a sovereign cannot have failed to have resonance for many of his readers.

The Chartists were not generally republicans or revolutionaries. They simply wanted to build a fairer society through democratic means, in spite of the split between Physical and Moral Force Chartists. At the very end of the novel, however, Egan hints towards a republican solution to the problems facing both fourteenth- and nineteenth-century society by musing upon what might have happened had Tyler and the rebels succeeded:

> They might have tumbled the monarchy into dust, and from the grossest state of slavery and despotism, have sprung into an enlightened and popular form of government, which, if virtuously conducted, is as rightful and trustful in its relations as it is just in its principles.[53]

This is more than the great majority of Chartists ever wanted, but probably chimed with Egan's political sentiments at this stage of his literary career. According to a letter which Egan had published in *The Times*, his *Wat Tyler* actually began life as a novel about Oliver Cromwell, but he changed the setting due to the fact that another novel about Cromwell appeared while he was writing it.[54] It would have been interesting to see how far Egan would have carried his republican sentiments in his unfinished Cromwell novel.

Wat Tyler was well-received, and after its initial release in penny parts, it was bound together in volume form. A total of six editions appeared throughout the nineteenth century.[55] Egan was pleased with the sales, remarking in his preface to *Paul Jones, the Privateer* that 'the sale of "Robin Hood" (especially), and "Wat Tyler" &c. [have] been most extensive and highly flattering.'[56] Reviewers were also

pleased with the novel, with one reviewer remarking that 'the spirit
and animation which [Egan] throws into his tale place him higher in
the scale of merit than most of the contributors to the amusement of
the public in this class of publications.'[57] Another reviewer in *The Era*
was favourable also, expressing the wish that the whole work would
have been published immediately as a single volume rather than in
penny parts.[58] The novel was abridged and virtually plagiarised by an
anonymous author as *The Life and Adventures of Wat Tyler: The Good
and the Brave* (1851), where Tyler is described as 'the friend of the
poor, who supported their cause against the tyranny of their
oppressors'.[59] If popularity is measured in terms of reprints, or being
sold 'by the half million',[60] then Egan can lay claim to having been
one of the most popular authors of the nineteenth century.[61]

The Chartist Petitions of 1839 and 1842 were rejected by
Parliament. The Chartists simply redoubled their efforts, however,
and another glimmer of hope was felt in the fact that Fergus O'Connor
(1794-1855), one of the leading lights of the Chartist movement and
a proponent of 'Physical Force' Chartism, was elected as MP for
Nottingham in 1847. O'Connor organised a huge rally to be held on
10 April 1848. The event was well-attended and was to have been
followed by a procession to Parliament, but the authorities ruled this
illegal and so the peaceful demonstrators returned home after the main
event.[62] A fresh petition was launched and some sources say, perhaps
exaggerating, that this third petition was so large that the doors on
the House of Commons had to be taken down in order to get it inside.
O'Connor claimed that over five million signatures had been collected
on the petition. With such a huge amount of support for the petition,
and with revolutions sweeping the continent, surely parliament could
not now ignore the petition and risk public disorder?[63] Surely any
right-thinking politician would not risk a potential revolution in
England by denying the will of the people? But ignore it they did.
Only fifteen MPs supported the charter in Parliament. The
government argued that, while the Chartists claimed that five million
people had signed it, their own clerks had apparently managed to
examine the entire petition (in less than three days) and counted only

two million signatures. The government's bureaucrats must have accomplished this monumental task at faster than light speed! It is doubtful that the government's clerks could have examined the entire petition in this short time. Nevertheless, the Chartist cause had been discredited in the public arena. Chartism limped on until around 1852 when it effectively died as a political force. Besides, there was the emergence of an organised socialist movement in the second half of the century, and as we will see in the succeeding chapter, prominent socialists also appropriated the history of the 1381 rebellion. Despite its 'failure', governments of various shades throughout the course of the nineteenth and early twentieth centuries have gradually implemented all but one of the Chartists' demands. The property qualification for MPs was abolished in 1857, some working men got the vote in 1867 (it would not be until the twentieth century that the vote was extended to more men and women), secret ballots were introduced in 1872, salaries for MPs were introduced in 1911, and constituencies today are roughly of equal size. The demand for annual elections, decided upon by the Chartists as a means of preventing corruption (after all, what is the point in bribing an MP if he might not be in power in twelve months' time) would likely have been impracticable.

Given Britain's very gradual movement towards becoming a democratic society, would Wat Tyler be needed by the working classes after 1867? Might there even now be a process of gentrification taking hold upon Tyler's legend, similar to the one which occurred much earlier with the legend of Robin Hood after Anthony Munday's *The Downfall of Robert, Earle of Huntington* and *The Death of Robert, Earle of Huntingdon* (1597-98). Let us explore our hero's appearance in the nineteenth-century historical novel.

Notes

1 David Goodway, *London Chartism 1838-1848* (Cambridge: Cambridge University Press, 1982), p. 13.
2 On the Spa Fields Riots see John Stevenson, *Popular Disturbances in*

England 1700-1832 2nd Edn. (Abingdon: Routledge, 2013), pp. 243-4.

3 John Belchem, *Henry Hunt and the Evolution of the Mass Platform* (London: Longman, 1978).

4 John Belchem, 'Hunt, Henry [Orator Hunt] (1773–1835)' in *The Oxford Dictionary of National Biography* (Oxford: Oxford University Press, 2004; Online Edn. 2008) [Internet <www.oxforddnb.com/view/article/14193> Accessed 23 Oct 2016]

5 'Spa Fields Meeting', *The Morning Post* 3 December 1816, p. 2.

6 Scholarship on the Norman Yoke includes the following selected works: Christopher Hill, *Puritanism and Revolution* rev. ed. (Basingstoke: Palgrave, 1997); Marjorie Chibnall, *The Debate on the Norman Conquest* (Manchester: Manchester University Press, 1999); Clare A. Simmons, *Reversing the Conquest: Saxons and Normans in Nineteenth-Century British Literature* (New Brunswick, NJ: Rutgers University Press, 1990).

7 *And this is Wat's Son, 'All Tattered and Torn'* (London: J. Johnston, 1819) British Museum Archives, London 1865,1111.940. The 'all tattered and torn' is likely to be an allusion to William Hone's pamphlet published in the same year entitled *The Political House that Jack Built* (1819).

8 'The People', *Liverpool Mercury* 14 February 1817, p. 263.

9 'Poetry: Reformer and Leveller. Alter Idem', *The Morning Post* 8 January 1817, p. 3.

10 'Wat Tyler', *The Weekly Entertainer: or, Agreeable and Instructive Repository* 19 May 1817, pp. 390-2 (pp.390-1).

11 'Wat Tyler', p. 391.

12 On the Pentrich Rising see D.G. Wright, *Popular Radicalism: The Working Class Experience 1780-1880* 5th Edn. (Abingdon: Routledge, 2013), pp. 70-71.

13 *Account of the Life, Trial & Behaviour of Jeremiah Brandreth, William Turner and Isaac Ludlam: who were Executed on the New Drop, in front of the County Gaol, Derby, on Friday November 7, 1817, for High Treason* ([Derby]: Wilkins, printer, of whom the Trials may be had, [1817]) Harvard Library School of Law HOLLIS: 005938710.

14 'Smithfield Reform Meeting' *The Observer* 26 July 1819, p. 1.

15 Earl Grey, he of the tea.

16 On the history of workhouses see the following works: Norman Longmate, *The Workhouse: A Social History* rev. ed. (London: Pimlico, 2003); Simon Fowler, *The Workhouse: The People, the Places, the Life Behind Doors* (Barnsley: Pen & Sword, 2014); Peter Higginbotham, *Life in a Victorian Workhouse* (London: Pitkin, 2014).

17 Philo-Bronterre, 'Who Are Our Real Foes and Oppressors?', *Bronterre's National Reformer in Government, Law, Property, Religion, and Morals* 1: 5 (1837), pp. 37-8 (p.37).

18 *Ibid.*, p. 38.
19 Dobson, 'Interpretations of the Peasants' Revolt', p.356.
20 *Cassell's Illustrated History of England: A New and Revised Edition* 4 Vols. (London: Cassell, Petter & Galpin [n.d.]), 1: 413.
21 Michael Sanders, *The Poetry of Chartism: Aesthetics, Politics, History* (Cambridge: Cambridge University Press, 2009), p. 71.
22 'The Voice of Wat Tyler', *The Odd Fellow* 18 April 1840, p. 64.
23 *Ibid.*, p. 64.
24 Charles Cole, 'The Spirit of Wat Tyler', *The Northern Star and Trades Journal* 16 September 1848, p. 6.
25 'Hymns for the Unenfranchised: A Song for the Next Rebellion' *The Odd Fellow* 21 August 1841, p. 3.
26 *Ibid.*, p. 3.
27 G.W.M. Reynolds, *The Mysteries of London* ed. by Trefor Thomas (Keele: Keele University Press, 1996), p. 281.
28 John K. Walton, *Lancaster Pamphlets: Chartism* (New York: Routledge, 1999), p. 58-9; 'Republicanism remained a fringe creed within the Chartist movement, more a warning of the lengths to which frustration might lead than a serious part of the political agenda. In 1839 the Convention adjourned, with no serious opposition, to see the Queen open Parliament, and subsequently the Northern Star consistently brought its weight to bear against republican tendencies'.
29 Charles Cole, 'Sonnets After Reading a Part of History Relating to Wat Tyler', *Cleave's Penny Gazette of Variety and Amusement* 3 July 1841, p. 195.
30 'Historical Gleanings: The Murder of Wat Tyler', *The English Chartist Circular* [n.d.], p. 1.
31 Anon. 'The Merits of Mr. Pierce Egan as a Novelist', *The London Journal, and Weekly Record of Literature, Science, and Art* 17 October 1863, pp. 247-8 (p.248).
32 Quintin Matsys (c.1466-c.1530) was a Flemish painter of the Antwerp School. There is no evidence to suggest that he ever led a revolt against the nobles of Antwerp.
33 Pierce Egan, *Robin Hood and Little John; or, The Merry Men of Sherwood Forest* (London: W.S. Johnson [n.d]), p. 279.
34 'Penny Novels' *MacMillan's Magazine* June 1866, pp. 96-105 (p.96).
35 James C. Holt, *Robin Hood* 2nd Edn. (London: Thames and Hudson, 1989), p. 183; There has been a tendency among some historians to assume that their low price means that penny bloods were published either solely for the working classes or for children. The Robin Hood historian James C. Holt, for instance, says that Egan's Robin Hood 'was the first [Robin Hood] story deliberately written for children.' Knight, *Robin Hood: A Complete Study of*

the English Outlaw, p.186; However, Stephen Knight's contrasting assessment of Egan's audience is better as he argues that it was not children who read but adults. The reasons that Knight gives for this reasoning are that 'the novel is very closely printed, and is actually of three-decker length, running to nearly four hundred thousand words, beyond most children then and now.' *Wat Tyler* is of similar length to *Robin Hood*, and the edition of 1851 comprises, like *Robin Hood*, over five hundred pages of double-columned minute typeface. Egan's novels were first printed, furthermore, during the late 1830s and 1840s. This was a time when working-class adults were turning away from the literature of philanthropist organisations such as the Society for the Promotion of Christian Knowledge in favour of penny bloods, such as those written by Egan and his friend, the 'vicious republican' George William MacArthur Reynolds, the author of the biggest-selling novel of the Victorian era, *The Mysteries of London* (1844-45). Moreover, there is the purely practical fact that readers from the middle classes had pennies in much greater abundance than their working-class counterparts. Also, as it was pointed out in a previous chapter, even in the nineteenth century, the poorest families had to club together often to buy a broadside. And although the novels of Egan and Reynolds were penny publications, the form in which these novels survive is often the 'library editions' which were handsomely bound and priced accordingly. Clearly there was a market among affluent purchasers for this type of fiction. Thus, to use an anachronistic term, Egan's works would fall under the 'mass market' description, and the themes of democracy and egalitarianism which run throughout Egan's novels, as well as their violent words and imagery, suggest that these stories were primarily produced for an adult audience.

36 Pierce Egan, *Wat Tyler; or, The Rebellion of 1381* (London: G. Pierce, 1847), p. 844.
37 Egan, *Wat Tyler*, p.845.
38 Egan, *Wat Tyler*, p. 839.
39 Egan, *Wat Tyler*, p. 111.
40 Walter Scott, *Ivanhoe: A Romance* (Edinburgh: Adam & Charles Black, 1872), p. 22.
41 Egan, *Wat Tyler*, p. 795.
42 Egan, *Wat Tyler*, p. 835.
43 Egan, *Wat Tyler*, p. 799.
44 Chris R. Vanden Bossche, *Reform Acts: Chartism, Social Agency, and the Victorian Novel, 1832-1867* (Baltimore: Johns Hopkins University Press, 2014), p. 23.
45 Egan, *Wat Tyler*, p. 797.
46 Egan, *Wat Tyler*, p. 797.

47 Lister M. Matheson, 'The Peasants' Revolt through Five Centuries of Rumour and Reporting: Richard Fox, John Stow, and Their Successors', *Studies in Philology* 95: 2 (1998), pp. 121-51.

48 Egan, *Wat Tyler*, p. 861.

49 Egan, *Wat Tyler*, p. 839.

50 Egan, *Wat Tyler*, p. 838.

51 Egan, *Wat Tyler*, p. 862.

52 Egan, *Wat Tyler*, p. 794.

53 Egan, *Wat Tyler*, p. 868.

54 Pierce Egan, 'To the Editor of *The Times*', *The Times* 6 November 1841, p. 3. The Cromwell story that Egan is most likely referring to here is probably the anonymous serialised novel *Oliver Cromwell; or, Cavaliers and Roundheads* (1840-41).

55 *Wat Tyler* was reprinted several times: London: F. Hextall, 1841; F. Hextall, 1842; London, n.p. 1845; G. Pierce, 1846; London: G. Pierce, 1850; W.S. Johnson, 1851.

56 Pierce Egan, *Paul Jones, the Privateer* (London: F. Hextall, 1842), p. iii.

57 Anon. 'Wat Tyler. Parts II and III. By PIERCE EGAN the Younger. Hextall', *Satirist; or, the Censor of the Times* 7 February 1841, p. 42.

58 Anon. 'Literature and Art', *The Era* 20 December 1840, p. 1.

59 Anon. *The Life and Adventures of Wat Tyler: The Good and the Brave* (London: H.G. Collins, 1851), p. vii. Similarities to Egan's novel include, among other things, the representation of Tyler as a veteran returning from the Hundred Years War, the rescue of a village maiden, and Tyler dying in his bed at the end of the novel.

60 Anon. 'Penny Novels', p. 104.

61 Anon. 'Penny Novels', p. 104.

62 Estimates as to the number of attendees varied – some sources say 50,000 people were in attendance, the government said only about 15,000, while some sources say that over 150,000 people attended.

63 See Michael Rapport, *1848: Year of Revolution* (London: Abacus, 2009); the year witnessed a number of revolutions in places such as France, Germany, Italy, and it was also the year that Karl Marx and Friedrich Engels first published *The Communist Manifesto* (1848).

CHAPTER SIX

The Nineteenth-Century Historical Novel

[Wat Tyler] appears before us in history as the desperate insurgent,
drunk with success, and not desirous of peace.

William E. Heygate, *Alice of Fobbing* (1841)

In Essex they were on the point of rising, and word had gone how that
at St. Alban's they were well-nigh at blows with the Lord Abbot's
soldiers ... and that the valiant tiler of Dartford had smitten a poll-
groat bailiff to death with his lath-rending axe for mishandling a young
maid, his daughter; and that the men of Kent were on the move.

Once more I heard the voice of John Ball; 'Now, brother, I say farewell;
for now verily hath the Day of the Earth come ... I go to life and to
death, and leave thee; and scarce do I know whether to wish thee some
dream of the days beyond thine to tell what shall be.

William Morris, *A Dream of John Ball* (1888)

The rise of the novel in the English language began in the eighteenth century, with scholars usually taking either Defoe's *Robinson Crusoe* (1719) or Richardson's *Pamela* (1740) as the starting point for the emergence of the new genre. Prose romances had of course existed before the eighteenth century, but these were usually concerned with representing the lives of the nobility, acting in either farcical or fantastical settings. Novels, on the other hand, supposedly represented real life and manners. This is why many novels in the eighteenth-century depict members of the middling sorts on a journey to acquire status and wealth.[1] Indeed, the history of the novel is to a large extent intertwined with that of the rise of the middle classes. Its practitioners were, with some exceptions, drawn from the bourgeoisie, and it was those of middle-class status who formed the primary market for the genre. Additionally, the first novels written were usually set in the present, while unrealistic historical or Gothic tales, such as Horace Walpole's *The Castle of Otranto* (1764) were set in the medieval past.[2] It was only with the work of the aforementioned novelist, Walter Scott (1772-1831), that the realism of the novel was superimposed onto the historical romance. Unlike Robin Hood or King Arthur, Wat Tyler does not feature in many Victorian novels. Let us take a look, then, at the various Wat Tyler novels that appeared throughout the nineteenth century.

Wat Tyler's 'big break' in the historical novel came in a now little-known book entitled *The Bondman: A Story of the Times of Wat Tyler* (1833), which formed the fifth volume of Leith Ritchie's *Library of Romance* series (published in fifteen volumes between 1833 and 1835). It was written by a person known only as Mrs O'Neill, although some newspapers at the time wrongly attributed the novel to the series' editor, Ritchie.[3] Contemporary reviewers looked favourably upon the novel. *The Caledonian Mercury* stated that the novel 'contains much amusing and interesting matter, and commands the close and delighted attention of the reader from beginning to end'.[4] The praise is justified, for O'Neill's novel is an interesting and engaging tale. From the preface and the introductory chapter, it is evident that O'Neill's story is very well-researched as she has a clear understanding of the social and economic history of the period. The novel begins in August 1374 at Sudley Castle, where the local baron is receiving the homage of his vassals. At the ceremony, he grants freedom to one Stephen Holgrave, the bondman of the title, for having saved his life while on campaign in the French wars. Despite having been a bondman throughout the majority of his life, he has always harboured 'thoughts of freedom and independence'.[5] Once freed, Holgrave is industrious and grows rich from the fruits of his labour. His life is the epitome of nineteenth-century respectability: his wife, Margaret, and his mother, Edith, are proto-Victorian 'Angels of the House' who carry out their 'feminine occupations … at home'.[6] Holgrave eventually loses his freedom as a result of the wicked plots of the baron's servant, Thomas Calverley, who is secretly in love with Holgrave's wife. Wrongfully accused of a crime, Holgrave is told that he must submit to becoming a serf again. From that day forward he begins to resent the upper classes, asking himself, 'can it be that the lord of this castle and I are the sons of the same heavenly father?'[7] So Holgrave vows revenge on the lord of the manor. His vengeful feelings are further stoked by his brother-in-law, Father John, who assumes the name of John Ball when he is excommunicated from the Church. In Holgrave's village, there also resides a mysterious village blacksmith named Wat Tyler, whose firebrand revolutionary opinions find a willing listener in Holgrave.

We must pause here and remind ourselves of the context in which this novel was written. It was published early in 1833, so the author was likely working on it in 1832, the year of the Great Reform Act. While not overtly radical, the author's sympathies are definitely on the side of the rebels. O'Neill evidently admires Wat Tyler, calling him 'the worthy'.[8] And the novel is essentially a story of the growth of class consciousness amongst the medieval serfs. She speaks of bondmen, for instance, as 'the labouring class'.[9] The imposition of the poll tax in 1381 creates 'a coalition of the lower classes'.[10] As tax collectors up and down the country attempt to exact their dues, O'Neill speaks of strikes occurring throughout the land and 'a total suspension of labour'.[11] This is not simply a story of the peasants revolting against the government, however: O'Neill speaks of the revolt as being one carried out, not simply by bondmen, but also by freemen.[12] And the mob that eventually marches on London is not a mindless rabble, but a highly organised band of disenfranchised people, drawn from the working and middle classes, whose leaders have clear political goals. O'Neill, of course, does not portray the insurgents as saints, and shows them on occasion becoming inebriated, and being a little bit too brutal with some of the lords with whom they come into contact. Yet most of them, such as the 'worthy' Tyler, are essentially good, respectable people who simply find the government's treatment of them unbearable. The aristocracy and the Church are society's real villains. They treat the people with contempt. For example, the Archbishop of Canterbury calls the rebels 'the scum of the land'.[13] The King himself is depicted as treacherous, and grants the Charter of Liberties in the expectation that he will, immediately after the rebels have disbanded, simply revoke it. Tyler is then killed at Smithfield and with him the bondmen's hope of liberty is ended. Although the bondman of the title, Stephen Holgrave, is set at liberty towards the end of the novel, many of his comrades are still disenfranchised. Such scenes mirror the fact that the extension of the franchise in 1832 was found to be wanting by many members of the working classes, left behind by the newly-enfranchised middle classes (in the novel, one of the rebels' demands is 'general enfranchisement', although O'Neill does not state specifically what she means by this). If it was intended as a commentary on the events and political agitation of 1832, it certainly is not an optimistic narrative. At the end of the novel bondmen still exist, and the narrator holds out no hope of political enfranchisement for the working classes.

Egan's *Wat Tyler; or, the Rebellion of 1381* was the second Wat Tyler novel, but was discussed in the previous chapter. The third was William E. Heygate's *Alice of Fobbing; or, The Times of Jack Straw and Wat Tyler* (1860).[14] Wat Tyler is not the principal protagonist in the story. Instead it is the title character, Alice, who lives in Fobbing and is an eye-witness to some of the key events in the revolt. The novel opens with her and her lover sharing a romantic moment on the outskirts of the village when it is interrupted with Thomas de Bamptoun being chased out of the village by angry peasants armed with pikes and other assorted rustic weapons. Alice and her lover then get caught up in the events of the revolt against their will, meeting Tyler, Ball, and the rest along the way. It would be a mistake to assume that *Alice of Fobbing* was ever intended as a political or social commentary on contemporary events. Heygate evidently did his research, however, and his novel is replete with footnotes to various primary sources such as the works of Knighton and Froissart. Doubtless Heygate, as well as O'Neill, was trying to imitate Scott who pioneered the 'footnote novel'. Unlike O'Neill and Pierce Egan, Heygate has little sympathy for the rebels. This is Heygate's assessment of Wat Tyler's role in history after he has struck down the tax collector:

God be praised that the temptation has never been ours, that we have never been forced to either die for such an act as Wat Tyler's, or to head a rebellion. Whatever the provocation, whatever the justification, it is a fearful condition that is the state of rebellion. Henceforth we can no longer feel for poor Wat. He appears before us in history as the desperate insurgent, drunk with success, and not desirous of peace.[15]

As Alice and her husband survey what is essentially an English revolution, Heygate describes the revolt with little nuance. The rebels are bad, traitors to their king and to the established order. Little more need be said of this novel, for in the seventh chapter the revolt ends and Wat Tyler perishes. What follows is an unremarkable domestic romance between Alice and her husband, and neither Tyler nor any of the other leading rebels are mentioned after the events at Smithfield.

The fourth Wat Tyler novel came from the pen of one of the Victorian period's most popular historical novelists, William Harrison Ainsworth (1805-82). His name *should* be as famous as that of Charles Dickens today. In fact, some of Ainsworth's early novels such as *Rookwood* (1834) and *Jack Sheppard* (1839) outsold Dickens' *Oliver Twist* (1838) (Wat Tyler is also briefly mentioned by Dickens in *Bleak House*, published in 1853).[16] Ainsworth's family had taken part in the Peterloo protest in 1819, although this does not seem to have affected the young Ainsworth's politics. During his youth he adopted Tory principles and, amusingly, even declared himself for the Jacobite cause, despite the fact that the threat of a Stuart restoration effectively died in 1745.[17] Although his early works were phenomenally successful, his creative powers diminished later in his career, and it was in the latter stage of his career that Ainsworth published his Wat Tyler novel entitled *Merry England; or, Nobles and Serfs* (1874) which was originally serialised in the magazine *Bow Bells*.

Practically all of Ainsworth's works are historical novels, and to give Ainsworth credit they are rich in historical detail. He had usually authored novels set during the early modern period or the eighteenth century, and *Merry England*, 'the story of the conspiracy and insurrection of the serfs in 1381', is Ainsworth's only foray into the medieval period.[18] The novel begins in 1381 with Wat Tyler working in his shop, who is described in the following terms:

> Somewhat above middle height, and very powerfully built, he had a broad, manly visage, characterised by a stern expression … his dark locks were clipped close to his head, so as to reveal a massive brow, but his head was bushy and overgrown … the Smith's ordinary apparel was well-calculated to display his stalwart frame … Wat Tyler was in the prime of manhood.[19]

Ainsworth, like Egan before him, provides the reader with an entirely fictional backstory for Tyler. In fact, one might be forgiven for thinking he lifted Tyler's biography straight out of Egan's novel, for we are told that he is a veteran of the Hundred Years War, being 'an archer, who drew as strong a bow as a Sherwood forester'.[20] Originally, Wat Tyler had been nothing but a lowly serf, but having distinguished himself in the wars and attracting the notice and praise of Edward, the Black Prince, he was set free from villeinage.[21] The truth is that we know nothing of the historical Tyler's early life, although his having been a soldier is not totally out of the bounds of credibility. Pierce Egan used the same idea for his biography of Wat Tyler. Jack Straw, however, whose real name is said to be Guibald de Mauduit, is an outlaw who is so obviously based upon Robin Hood that it is to be wondered why Ainsworth does not simply insert Robin into the story.[22] Ainsworth's Jack Straw, like Robin Hood in many nineteenth- and twentieth-century portrayals, is first outlawed when he is caught killing one of the King's deer. Fleeing from the authorities, 'he was soon joined [in the forest] by several marauders, fugitives from justice like himself, and being superior to the rest of his lawless companions, was chosen as their leader.'[23] Other similarities to Robin Hood are described thus:

> Jack Straw and his band speedily became the terror of all travellers in Kent … but the robber chief modelled his conduct on that of another outlaw, Robin Hood; and while he despoiled the rich without scruple, he gave very liberally to the poor.[24]

Another similarity to Robin Hood is the fact that Straw dresses completely in green, and is also a nobleman.[25]

As Ainsworth's preface suggests, the novel is about the 'conspiracy' surrounding the events of 1381. Wat Tyler, Jack Straw, and John Ball are presented as revolutionary conspirators, in a manner reminiscent of Ainsworth's *Guy Fawkes, or, The Gunpowder Treason* (1841). Secret meetings take place between the three men where they discuss how best to incite a rebellion. Wat Tyler is the head of this radical organisation whose aims are 'a general partition of property and the abolition of ecclesiastical hierarchy'.[26] It is John Ball who spreads this message throughout the country, with the result that 'all who listened to the factious monk resolved to shake off their chains and be free.'[27]

The poll tax is soon levied upon all citizens over the age of sixteen. Ainsworth writes that 'the collectors set about their task with zeal; and everywhere complaints arose from the people of the brutal usage they experienced.'[28] Wat Tyler, Jack Straw, and John Ball hear the people's murmurs 'with a secret satisfaction'.[29] The disaffection in the country is perfect for the revolutionaries to incite people to rise up. Geoffrey Chaucer also makes an appearance, being one of the men involved in the planning of the insurrection. He is present when the tax collector assaults Tyler's daughter, Editha, and Chaucer accompanies the rebels on their march to London. However, towards the end of the novel, seeing that the tide is turning against the rebel leaders, Chaucer switches his allegiance to the King.

It is difficult to know who the reader is supposed to sympathise with in the novel. The aim of Tyler, Straw, and Ball is not simply social justice, but a complete overthrow of the existing order and the installation of themselves as lords and masters of the English people. They are motivated not from a firm belief in the rights of man, but by 'an intense *hatred* of the noble and rich, by a burning desire of vengeance upon the oppressors of the people' (emphasis added).[30] As Wat Tyler's army occupies London, he grows haughty and full of ambition.[31] The rebels leave a trail of death and destruction in their wake, as Ainsworth writes that 'houses, halls, and monasteries burnt and demolished met the eyes at every turn. Many of the small streets were encumbered with ruins or filled with goods that could not be carried off.'[32] Wat Tyler's own daughter, Editha, disapproves of his actions and eventually disowns him. And here is one of Ainsworth's more ridiculous subplots: Editha and Richard II are secretly in love, with Richard having 'never been touched so sensibly as by Editha's graces'.[33]

But the disparity of the lovers' social stations is of no consequence because it turns out that Editha was only Wat Tyler's adopted daughter and that she is, in fact, of noble descent. It is Editha who convinces Richard not to give into any of the rebels' demands at Mile End but to con the rebels by granting them their charters, which can easily be revoked after the revolt has passed.

After being stabbed by William Walworth, Wat Tyler's head is cut off and placed upon a spike in London for all to see. Jack Straw and John Ball are also beheaded. Editha never marries Richard II, despite his protestations, and instead joins a convent and lives the rest of her days in devotion to God. As with *Alice of Fobbing*, there is little evidence to suggest that the novel was ever intended as a commentary on contemporary issues, and there would be little point to argue that it was so. Indeed, rarely did any of Ainsworth's novels seek to make a political point. The reason for the novel's publication is likely to be the fact that, at this point in his career, Ainsworth needed the money. At this time he was even under contract to write works for the penny dreadful publisher, John Dicks, which is indicative of how much his reputation had declined since his heyday in the 1840s. *Merry England* was certainly not the best story for Ainsworth to attempt to recover his former glory, and the novel had a mixed reception. The most significant review of the work appeared in *The Saturday Review,* and it does not open promisingly:

> A story is told of a clergyman who in his old age always chose the same text and preached the same sermon. When his congregation, impatient at last at the sameness – for even Church congregations can grow impatient – let him know that they wished, like the men of Athens, to hear some new thing, on each following Sunday he gave out a new text indeed, but followed it up with the old sermon. Now, Mr. Harrison Ainsworth seems much to us the same thing. The texts that he takes are, if we may say so, the risings and rebellions of English history, but the tale he tells is always the same.[34]

According to the reviewer, *Merry England* was merely Ainsworth's *The Manchester Rebels of the Fatal '45: A Tale of the Good Old Times* (1874) rehashed and set during the medieval period, instead of eighteenth-century Lancashire. Victorian reviewers sometimes had their tongue firmly in their cheek when writing about new literary works. In the case of *Merry England*, the reviewer's main problem appears to be (and quite justifiably) the implausible love affair between Richard II and Tyler's daughter:

> The heroine of 'Merry England' should be, we suppose, Wat Tyler's daughter, or rather his supposed daughter, as she presently turns out to be. With her King Richard II falls madly in love a day or two after his tax gatherer had got knocked on the head for insulting her. As history here was too strong even for Mr. Ainsworth, there was nothing left for her, as she could not become Richard's wife, but an early grave.[35]

Other points of contention in the review are Ainsworth's use of faux medieval phrases:

> In what school of writers Mr. Ainsworth learnt his trade we have no means of knowing. He is ever hacking to pieces heroes and heroines, good men and miscreants, but his jointing is all done in one style and a very vulgar one. He has indeed a kind of antiquated mode of writing which in all his so-called historical novels he puts on whenever he happens to remember it ... 'Sdeath,' too, does not come amiss, for in [Richard's] oaths surely our author need not fear the reproach of anachronism [...but] he cruelly breaks the illusion by bringing in 'exalted personages,' 'nefarious characters,' and 'stalwart individuals.' ... At times, indeed, Mr. Ainsworth seems so well to assume an air of antiquity when it might be positively laid aside.[36]

One possible reason why Ainsworth had difficulty in recovering his former success is that by the time he was writing *Merry England*, the historical novel was increasingly perceived as a genre for children. This was partially due to the emergence of the flourishing children's literature industry in the second half of the century, which used historical settings and combined moralism with tales of adventure and derring-do. Even

Scott's *Ivanhoe*, for instance, while viewed as adult literature back in the 1820s, had become the preserve of children and young adults by the late Victorian period.

It is doubtful that parents would have purchased a three-volume novel such as Ainsworth's *Merry England* for their children. In fact, by the late Victorian period the three volume format for novels was dying.[37] In any case, Ainsworth never wrote his novels with children in mind. Older children may have purchased one of the many penny dreadfuls that were printed in large numbers. Penny dreadfuls, much like penny bloods, were cheaply printed magazines that were published weekly and sold, as their name suggests, for the price of one penny. Usually they recounted the tales of eighteenth-century highwaymen and women, such as *Black Bess, or, Knight of the Road* (c.1866) and *Jenny Diver, the Female Highwayman* (c.1850). Alternatively they might tell the stories of Victorian boy thieves, such as *The Wild Boys of London, or, the Children of the Night* (1864-66). Many of these penny dreadfuls, furthermore, were tales of medieval heroes such as George Emmett's *Robin Hood* (1869) and *The Sword of Freedom; or, The Boyhood Days of Jack Straw* (1890). In the latter novel, Tyler does not feature greatly, with the novel focusing, as its title implies, principally upon Straw's early life. The aforementioned examples were sold as standalone serials, much like comics are today. However, there were magazines such as *The Boys of England* and *The Young Englishman* that carried a number of stories in their columns. It is in *The Young Englishman* that the first Wat Tyler penny dreadful appeared in September 1867 entitled *Wat Tyler, or, The King and the Apprentice*. Egan's *Wat Tyler* was a penny blood, not a penny dreadful. The two genres, despite their similarities and their conflation in some popular history books and blogs, were not the same. Bloods were marketed towards adults, while dreadfuls were published primarily for children. Surprisingly, *Wat Tyler; or, The King and the Apprentice* seems to be wholly original and does not appear to have taken any inspiration at all from Egan's earlier novel (penny dreadful novelists often rehashed earlier tales by changing a few plotlines and inserting new characters). Even more refreshingly for a Victorian medievalist story, there is not a single hint in the novel of the by now tired theme of conflict between the Anglo-Saxons and the Normans. One drawback of *Wat Tyler; or, The King and the Apprentice*, however, is that like Ainsworth's *Merry England*, it uses faux-medieval language with its 'quoth' and 'forsooths'. Such words have a tendency to annoy the modern reader, and as we have seen in the case of Ainsworth's novel, they annoyed Victorian readers on occasion as well.

The novel begins when Tyler is fifteen years old, 'at a time when poor people were very heavily taxed, and the King and his government sought every day for fresh pretexes to impose fresh taxes upon, until at last the burden became intolerable'.[38] The young Tyler is an apprentice blacksmith. He is headstrong and gets into one or two fights with apprentices. This attitude leads the author to prophesy that the young Wat Tyler's attitude will one day 'likely involve him in trouble'.[39] Despite his brash attitude, he still has a good conscience and is devoted to his mother, 'for in his young heart there was a deep hidden spring of love and tenderness for his mother'.[40] Other typical boys' adventures follow: more scrapes with his fellows, getting arrested, and flirting with a childhood sweetheart.[41] Then he grows up and there is the familiar story of the tax collector, the revolt, and Wat Tyler's death.

Wat Tyler appears in another serial in *The Young Englishman* entitled *Bolingbroke; or, The Days of Chivalry* (1867). As a youth, Tyler rescues the young Henry Bolingbroke, and future King, from being murdered in the forest, and the two boys form an unlikely friendship. It is nevertheless a brief appearance, three chapters in total, and the rising is never alluded to. Another Wat Tyler story entitled *Gentle Deeds; or, Serfdom to Knighthood* appeared in *Our Young Folks' Paper* in 1886. The main protagonist is not Wat Tyler but a village boy named Simon. One day he happens to meet a stranger in his village, an adherent of the teachings of John Ball who tells him,

> 'Listen to what they said in old times: "When Adam delved and Eve span, who then was the gentleman?" Canst thou answer that question, good friend villein?'
> Simon coloured as the question was put to him. There was something in the kindly glance of the stranger that encouraged him to answer:
> 'The rhyme is one I never heard sir. But in those days it seems there were no gentlemen.'

The stranger laughed.

'Hast thou found the answer already? True, there were none. God made men equal, but men have made each other unequal. Even thou, a born serf and thrall, canst be gentle, if thou knowest the way.'[42]

Simon remains unconvinced. He grows up and joins the army, distinguishing himself fighting alongside the Black Prince, with the result that he is eventually rewarded with a knighthood. The novel bears some similarity to a Wat Tyler novel authored by G.A. Henty towards the end of the century.

Two characters named Wat Tyler appear in this novel, but only in the first few chapters. The influence of the Robin Hood legend can be seen in this serial, as the elder Wat Tyler is an outlawed yeoman who leads a band of outlaws called 'the Men in Green', who are defiant of all authority. Amongst the band is Wat Tyler the younger, the future leader of the rebellion. The outlaws are offered the chance of a pardon by the Black Prince if they will agree to fight in the war on the continent. Most of Tyler's men agree to go fight, but Tyler and his son refuse to become 'the slaves of noblemen'.[43] This is the last that is seen of the two Wat Tylers in the novel. The author, Frederick Whitaker, probably intended the narrative to carry on, with Simon returning home and helping to put down the Peasants' Revolt. But such was the cut-throat world of penny publishing that, if a story was flagging it was ended abruptly.[44] And *Gentle Deeds* does end in this manner with Simon rescuing a French noblewoman from a castle. After this episode there are no further adventures for Simon in succeeding issues of *Our Young Folk's Paper*.

There was a further serial named *Wat Tyler's Revenge* which appeared in *Boys of the Empire*. Wat Tyler is depicted as a good-natured working-class family man who 'slaves all day' to feed his family.[45] As expected, a tax gatherer comes to Tyler's house while he is out and attempts to find out the age of Tyler's daughter, Bertha:

Richard Varke [the tax collector], flushed with wine, had passed his arm round Bertha's waist, and was attempting to kiss her, while Dame Tyler, petrified with fright, sat in a corner, hugging her youngest child to her breast.[46]

Tyler comes home and is enraged:

> 'Ah! Dog!' cried Wat Tyler, snatching up a hammer. 'So I have caught thee, varlet, unhand my child ...'
> 'Oh, father!' Bertha cried, as she fled to him, 'do not let him harm me. He saith that it is within his power to claim me as his slave.'
> 'Then let him repeat his words in the depth of perdition,' Wat Tyler yelled. 'Richard Varke, take your last look on the world.'
> The hammer rose, and fell crashing into the brain of the tax gatherer, who, with one deep drawn groan, collapsed, and lay dead upon the forge.[47]

It is from that moment that the rebellion begins and the people of the village elect Tyler as their leader. The passage above is typical of many penny dreadfuls at the time, all of which contain just the right amount of killing and maiming to entertain young boys and satisfy their bloodlust. Indeed, brains are regularly pierced with arrows, as in *The Boyhood Days of Jack Straw; or, The Sword of Freedom*.[48] With violence graphically depicted, the stories in these magazines could be controversial. Individual stories were rarely cited in the press, but John Springhall has shown how, as a whole, the magazines which carried them were condemned by press commentators, who often set themselves up as the guardians of public morality. The main bone of contention appears to be that the magazines were 'pernicious' and were responsible for inducing young boys to commit crime.[49] The noted crime historian, Heather Shore, points to one example of a lad from 1852 who was convicted of stealing twenty-five pounds from a gentleman's pocket. He cites his heroes as being those found in juvenile penny literature.[50] Robert Kirkpatrick cites the case of 18-year-old Stephen Easton from Middlesex who found himself in the dock in 1877, having been indicted for burglary. According to reports of his trial, 'the prisoner said it was all owing to reading books – the *Boys of England, Young Men of Great Britain*, and others.'[51] Arthur and Hector Smith in 1868 assaulted a 65-year-old woman, and at their trial the court was told how 'there was no doubt that they had been for some time addicted to reading trashy publications.'[52] Among the publications named specifically in this case was *The Young Englishman* in which one of the aforementioned Wat Tyler stories appeared.[53] Whether reading these tales actually caused these youths – and there are many more besides the cases mentioned above – to commit crime is open to debate. Indeed, there are still debates about the impact of violent entertainment upon the minds of impressionable youths. It might be suspected that the offenders themselves played up to moralists' fears regarding violent literature in order to secure a more lenient sentence. The penny dreadful thus became a 'scapegoat' which Victorian moralists could blame for the rise of juvenile delinquency.[54]

Not every Victorian condemned the penny dreadfuls outright. Arthur Quiller-Couch, in an essay entitled *The Poor Little Penny Dreadful* (1896), commented that,

> Our friends have been occupied with the case of a half-witted boy who consumed penny dreadfuls and afterwards went and killed his mother. They infer that he killed his mother because he had read penny dreadfuls (post hoc ergo propter hoc), and they conclude very naturally that penny dreadfuls should be suppressed.[55]

But when Quiller-Couch read the stories for himself,

> I give you my word that I could find nothing peculiar about them. They were even rather ostentatiously on the side of virtue. As for the bloodshed in them, it would not compare with that in many of the five-shilling adventure stories at that time read so eagerly by boys of the middle and upper classes.[56]

Indeed, as John Springhall comments, 'if Victorian critics had taken the trouble to examine the publications … they would have discovered that, far from recommending the values of a criminal of oppositional subculture, their point of view was consistently aligned with support for the established order.'[57]

It is to one of the 'five-shilling' novels mentioned by Quiller-Couch that we must now turn as we examine G.A. Henty's *A March on London* (1897). Henty (1832-1902) was born in Cambridge, attended Westminster School and then Cambridge University. He worked as a journalist for the

Standard Newspaper, and the firm sent him abroad on a number of occasions to serve as a war correspondent. He had a firm and unshakeable belief in the civilising mission of the British Empire. This imperialist fundamentalism is heavily reflected in all of Henty's works, the publication of which coincided with the era of 'new' imperialism between 1884 and 1914, when European powers carved out the continent of Africa for themselves and imposed direct rule upon their respective territories.[58] The pro-imperial tone of his works can be gained by looking at the titles of just a few of the 122 works he put out in his lifetime: *A Final Reckoning: A Tale of Bush Life in Australia* (1887), *With Wolfe in Canada: The Winning of a Continent* (1887), *Maori and Settler: A Tale of the New Zealand War* (1891), *Under Wellington's Command: A Tale of the Peninsular War* (1899), and *With Buller in Natal: A Born Leader* (1901). Unsurprisingly, these works are filled with the rampant racial prejudices of the time that were connected to late Victorian imperial zeal. The result was that the 'heroic' deeds of the 'Great Men' of the British Empire in Henty's novels were often contrasted with the supposed racial inferiority of the natives who peopled British overseas territories.[59]

Henty only made a few forays into the medieval period, preferring, like Ainsworth, to set most of his stories in the early modern and modern periods. Although Henty was without doubt a patriot, he does have some sympathy with the fourteenth-century rebels. In the preface to *A March on London* he states that

> The uprising of the Commons, as they called themselves – that is to say, chiefly the folk who were still kept in a state of serfdom in the reign of Richard II – was in itself justifiable. Although serfdom in England was never carried to the extent that prevailed on the Continent, the serfs suffered from grievous disabilities. A certain portion of their time had to be devoted to the work of their feudal lord. They themselves were forbidden to buy or sell at public markets or fairs. They were bound to the soil, and could not, except under special circumstances, leave it.[60]

But this was not the only grievance that fourteenth-century commoners held against the authorities. According to Henty, the main grievance that the commons had is set down by him in the following terms: 'above all, they felt that they were not free men, and were not even deemed worthy to fight in the wars of their country.'[61] Ever the Empire's cheerleader, Henty is trying to fit the events of the historical rebellion to suit his own pro-imperial views: Tyler and his fellow rebels *above all* wanted to fight for their country, and the grievances about the poll tax were secondary. Whether Henty knew that, in actual fact, there were a lot of desertions in 1380 during the Hundred Years War is impossible to say.[62] Even if he did know, Henty would likely not have included this fact as it would not have fitted with his imperialist narrative.

It was primarily children from the middle and lower middle classes who read Henty's works, although his books were often given out as school prizes to working-class children, and the figure of the schoolboy hero was central to many of his works. His novel *With Clive in India: The Beginnings of an Empire* (1884), for example, tells the story of young Charlie Marryat who rises through the ranks of the East India Company and becomes one of Robert Clive's most trusted lieutenants. Wat Tyler is not the main protagonist of *A March on London*, and similar to Henty's other novels, a young boy named Edgar is its hero. Edgar's father takes him to London to complete his studies, and while he is there the revolt breaks out. Seeing a great multitude of people swarm into London, he makes clear his feelings towards the rebels when talking with his father, saying, 'I would rather charge them, sword in hand, with a band of stout fellows behind me.'[63] Edgar then softens his attitude somewhat:

'The exactions of the tax gatherers are indeed beyond all bearing, and if the people do but rise to demand fair treatment and their just rights as men, I should wish them success; but I fear that evil counsels will carry them far beyond this, and that they may attack the houses and castles of the gentry, although they be in no way the authors of their troubles.'[64]

He decides to visit the rebel camp at Dartford where he hears the inflammatory preaching of John Ball:

'Men of Kent!' one exclaimed, 'the day has come when you have to prove that you are men, and not mere beasts of burden, to be trodden under foot. You know how we are oppressed, how illegal exactions are demanded of us, and how, as soon as one is paid, some fresh tax is heaped upon us. What are we? Men without a voice, men whom the government regard as merely beings from whom money is wrung... 'tis not enough that our oppressors roll in wealth, may scatter it lavishly as they choose, and indulge in every luxury and every pleasure.'[65]

Henty's works were considered to be respectable reading for Victorian youths, in contrast to the penny dreadfuls which flourished at this period. Thus, Henty quickly neutralises any hope that young Edgar might join the rebels, as evident in the following exchange between Tyler and himself:

Such was the tenor of all the speeches, and they were everywhere received with loud cheers. As Edgar rode down the main street on his way home he heard shouting, and a brawny, powerful man came along, surrounded by a mob of cheering men. He looked at Edgar steadily, and stepped in front of his horse.

'You are the son of the man at St. Alwyth,' [said Wat Tyler], 'I have seen you in the streets before. What do you think of what we are doing?' ...

'I think that you have been cruelly wronged,' Edgar answered quietly, 'and that the four points that you demand are just and right. I wish you good fortune in obtaining them, and I trust that it will be done peacefully and without opposition.'

'Whether peacefully or not, we are determined that they shall be obtained. If it be needful, we will burn down London and kill every man of rank who falls into our hands, and force our way into the king's presence. We will have justice!'

'If you do so you will be wrong,' Edgar said.[66]

While Henty displays a grudging sympathy with the rebels' aims in his preface, there is no nuance in the main narrative. He makes sure to emphasise every negative aspect of the revolt:

'You must have seen scenes which must have made you almost ashamed of being an Englishman,' Sir Ralph said, angrily. 'This has been a disgraceful business. It was bad enough to destroy John of Gaunt's palace; for, although I love not Lancaster greatly, it was an ornament to London and full of costly treasures. For this, however, there was some sort of excuse, but not so for the burning of the Temple, still less for the destruction of the great house of the Knights of St. John, and also the manor-house of the prior of the order. I hear to-day that great numbers of Flemings have been slain, their houses pillaged, and in some cases burnt. Now comes the crowning disgrace. That the Tower of London, garrisoned by 1,200 men, and which ought to have defied for weeks the whole rabbledom of England, should have opened its gates without a blow being struck, and the garrison remained inert on the walls while the king's mother was being grossly insulted, and the two highest dignitaries of the state with others massacred is enough, by my faith, to make one forswear arms, put on a hermit's dress and take to the woods.'[67]

Edgar is present when Tyler meets Richard at Smithfield, and Tyler receives a very unflattering portrayal, being called 'an insolent varlet', while his confederates are called the 'rabbledom'.[68]

The events of the Revolt only take up the first half of the novel and Tyler dies in chapter nine (there are nineteen chapters altogether). The rest of the novel sees young Edgar entering the army to go and defend England's possessions in France. No doubt Henty imagined this last plotline to be the medieval equivalent of serving the nineteenth-century British Empire. The message to Henty's young readers is clear: be loyal to your King, and defend your country's overseas possessions, like Edgar does in the novel. The consequences of following such a course of life will enable young men to rise through the ranks. At the end of the novel, Edgar is knighted for his services to the Crown.

Another arch-imperialist, Henry Newbolt, adapted Froissart's chronicles in a children's book entitled *Froissart in Britain* (1902). This is the man who, in one of his poems, glorified war and exhorted young men to enlist and serve the British Empire, or in his words, 'play up, play up, and play the game'.[69] In the preface to *Froissart in Britain*, Newbolt states that reading the deeds of heroic Englishmen from history should inspire 'pride, to see our own likeness in the mirror of the past, and to know the greatness of the race from which we come'.[70] This reference to race, specifically the so-called 'British race', draws upon contemporary ideas of the supposed racial superiority of those of Anglo-Saxon descent. It was an idea propagated by imperialist statesmen such as Joseph Chamberlain (1836-1914). These thinkers reasoned that, given the existence of the British Empire, and of course the powerful influence of other European powers across the globe, it was self-evident that Europeans, especially those of Anglo-Saxon descent, had a God-given right to rule over supposedly inferior peoples.[71] Although Newbolt is generally disapproving of Wat Tyler and the rebels, and denounces them as 'ungracious people … enraged and mad',[72] Englishmen could still take pride in their example. Newbolt writes that the revolt was the first time that 'the "Commons of England" [made] their first great claim for their birth right of freedom and equality before the law'.[73] Obviously, the ideas freedom and equality before the law that Newbolt writes of in that passage were not to be extended to the subject peoples of the British Empire.

Thus far, none of the novels discussed here could possibly be counted as 'high' literature. O'Neill's *The Bondman* was easily forgotten, it seems, and only went through two editions. Ainsworth's *Merry England*, written at a time when he needed money, is poorly executed, as are the numerous penny dreadfuls featuring Wat Tyler and Jack Straw. Only Egan's *Wat Tyler*, earlier in the nineteenth century, gave the eponymous hero the epic literary treatment that he deserved, but it was still a penny publication. After Egan's novel, for a quality literary depiction of the events of 1381, readers would need to wait until William Morris (1834-96) turned his pen to the subject in the late nineteenth century. Although it does not feature Wat Tyler except in passing, Morris's *A Dream of John Ball* (1888) warrants special attention because it is a major work in the post-medieval literary history of the 1381 rebellion. In the words of *The Oxford Dictionary of National Biography*, Morris was 'a designer, author, and visionary socialist'.[74] To that we can add that Morris was a medievalist, because from an early age, he loved reading tales of medieval times. When he grew up he was involved with the Pre-Raphaelites, a group of painters who were heavily influenced by the medieval period. By the late 1870s and 1880s, having previously avoided publicly speaking out upon political matters, he was increasingly attracted to socialism. In 1883 he joined the Democratic Federation (soon to be renamed the Social Democratic Federation). While socialism is usually perceived of as a workers' movement, the associations that were founded during the late Victorian period in Britain were predominantly middle-class.[75] After joining the Democratic Federation, Morris began reading Karl Marx's *Das Capital* (1867). Having come to the conclusion that 'the contrasts of rich and poor are unendurable and ought not to be endured by either rich or poor,'[76] Morris became active in the socialist movement and a number of writings for socialist periodicals followed. Still retaining his love of the medieval period which had developed in his youth, in *A Dream of John Ball,* Morris looks to the medieval period to find evidence of prototypical socialist thought.[77] The novel thus represents a fusion of medievalism and socialist ideals.

A Dream of John Ball first appeared in the 13 November 1886 issue of *The Commonweal.* Let us briefly examine the social and political context at the time that Morris's novel was being serialised. During the 1880s, the industrialised world was in the midst of an economic depression. This caused much harm to the British economy which was already losing its pre-eminence as *the* major industrial power to competitor nations such as the United States and Germany.[78] British exports were falling, the agricultural sector was hit, threatening famine in Ireland, and trade unionism was on the rise. Workers' wages had also stagnated, and many working people lost their jobs. As is usually the case, it was the poorest who suffered the brunt of these problems. For much of the nineteenth century, it was assumed by many thinkers, politicians, and even some workers that it was impossible for socio-economic factors to be responsible for a man being out of work. If a man did not have a job, this was usually viewed as a moral failing on his part. But in the 1880s, statesmen, the press, and the public began speaking of a new phenomenon: unemployment. This word entered common parlance at this point in time and leading economists began to argue that it was not always possible for a person to find work due to failings in the economy.[79] If they could not find employment, it did not necessarily follow that a person was being idle. Nevertheless, it would take time for older attitudes towards the supposedly 'undeserving poor' to die out, and to some extent Victorian ideas towards unemployment are still with us today in some parts of the right-wing press, when those without a steady occupation are often denounced as 'lazy', 'feckless', or as 'scroungers'.

A series of workers' protests, organised by the Social Democratic Federation and the Irish National League were held at Trafalgar Square, London, between 1886 and 1887. The people at these meetings were protesting against unemployment, as well as the British government's suspension of civil rights in Ireland in response to protests there. On 8 November the London Police Commissioner banned further public meetings taking place there. This did not deter the workers, however, and the most significant mass meeting was held on 13 November 1887. Over a thousand policemen were sent to patrol the vicinity that day, in addition to the Life Guards and Grenadier Guards, and they clashed violently with the protestors. In scenes reminiscent of Peterloo, with their truncheons the police injured approximately two hundred people, and three of the protestors were killed. Morris and other leading lights of the socialist movement were spectators on the day, dubbed 'Bloody Sunday' at the time.[80]

To Morris and his like-minded friends, socialism was able to provide the answers to society's socio-economic problems. However, they were in a minority in thinking this, and socialism was a relatively new ideology, imported from the continent. In England, at least, it needed a sense of historical legitimacy, which is why Morris sees in John Ball's teachings the beginnings of English socialism.

In the novel, a modern traveller falls into a deep sleep and awakens in a fourteenth-century village. As he moves about the village he hears tidings of 'the valiant tiler of Dartford [who] had smitten a poll-groat bailiff to death with his lath-rending axe for mishandling a young maid, his daughter; and that the men of Kent were on the move.'[81] The villagers become excitable as they learn that the priest, John Ball, is about to speak to them in the village square. He talks to the peasants about their dire position in society, but reminds them of their duty to the fellowship. The idea of fellowship was important to Morris, who argued that it promoted happiness in work, and bound working men to each other.[82] It was 'a moral ideal of brotherhood',[83] which would make work truly pleasurable because

> Men would follow knowledge and the creation of beauty for their own sakes, and not for the enslavement of their fellows, and they would be rewarded by finding their most necessary work grow interesting and beautiful under their hands without their being conscious of it.[84]

Morris conceived of the impending battle between capital and labour, the end of the struggle between the bourgeoisie and the workers, as being one of mastership against fellowship.[85] The traveller eventually manages to speak alone with John Ball. Perceiving the traveller to be from the future, John Ball begins to ask him many questions, inquiring particularly as to how the revolt of the Essex men will fare. Ball also expresses his hope for the future, saying that he foresees a time without kings and lords, a time when,

> those that labour become strong and stronger, and so soon shall it come about that all men shall work and none make to work, and so none shall be robbed, and at last shall all men labour and live and be happy, and have the goods of the earth without money and without price.[86]

But it is the traveller's responsibility to tell John Ball that, even in the nineteenth century, 'there shall be Kings and Lords and Knights and Squires still, with servants to do their bidding, and make honest men afraid.'[87] Moreover, the working man 'shall sell himself, that is the labour that is in him, to the master who suffers him to work'.[8] Furthermore,

> there shall ever be more workers than the masters may set to work, so that men shall strive eagerly for leave to work; and when one says, I will sell my hours at such and such a price, then another will say, and I for so much less; so that never shall the Lords lack slaves willing to work, but often the slaves shall lack Lords to buy them.[89]

To apply an anachronistic term here, Morris is arguing that wages in the nineteenth century have become a 'race to the bottom' as workers attempt to undercut each other. Yet although the socio-economic position of the working classes is dire, both in John Ball's day as much as it is in Morris's era, the traveller does hold out the hope of a better future:

> John Ball, be of good cheer, for once more thou knowest, as I know, that the fellowship of Men shall endure, however many tribulations it may have to wear through ... Men shall be determined to be free; yea, free as thou wouldst have them, when thine hope rises the highest, and thou art thinking not of the King's uncles, and poll-groat bailiffs, and the villeinage of Essex, but of the end of all, when men shall have the fruits of the earth and the fruits of their toil thereon, without money and without price.[90]

John Ball and Wat Tyler would be defeated at Smithfield. Nineteenth-century workers might be defeated in their own struggles. But these defeats, according to Morris, are a necessary marking point on the road to building a socialist utopia.[91]

After its serialisation during 1886 and 1887, Morris's novella was then published in one volume by the publishers Reeves and Turner in 1888, accompanied with a beautiful engraving for its frontispiece by Edward Burne-Jones depicting the Biblical figures, Adam and Eve. Eve looks on as Adam 'delves', and underneath in bold letters is John Ball's famous slogan: 'When Adam delved and Eve span, who was then the gentleman?'[92] It was reprinted dozens of times by various publishers during the late 1880s and early 1890s, often without the frontispiece. Morris's private Kelmscott Press published an illustrated edition of the work in 1892, complete with the frontispiece as well as detailed engravings bordering every page.

If John Ball's teachings in *A Dream of John Ball* represented the beginnings of English socialism, Morris's follow-up work entitled *News from Nowhere* (1890) depicts life in a future socialist utopia. *News from Nowhere* was originally serialised, as *A Dream of John Ball* was, in *The Commonweal*, and revised by Morris and reprinted in volume form thereafter.[93] In the novel, a man in the nineteenth century is travelling home one evening 'using the means of travelling which civilisation has forced upon us like habit … that vapour-bath of hurried and discontented humanity, a carriage of the underground railway'.[94] (Evidently, a journey on the London Underground in the Victorian era was as hot and unpleasant as many people find it today.) The hour is late, for the traveller has attended an evening lecture at the Socialist League upon the subject of 'what would happen on the morrow of the [socialist] revolution'.[95] As he travels home, he muses to himself, 'if I could but see a day of it … if I could but see it'.[96] When home, he goes to bed and awakens in the future in London, at some time after the year 2003. It is a time when workers are no longer slaves to industrial capitalism. Instead, men take pleasure in their work, existing in true fellowship, for 'each man is free to exercise his faculty to the utmost, and everyone encourages him in so doing'.[97] The traveller finds that all private property has been abolished in this utopia. In consequence of this, all civil and criminal law has also been abolished, for the root cause of all these crimes was private property and the acquisition of wealth. Thus, *News from Nowhere* depicts a time in the future when 'mastery has changed into fellowship'.[98] The much-anticipated idyllic world in which men lived together in fellowship, which Morris and his fellow socialists yearned for, could only come about as the result of a long series of struggles between workers and masters, capitalists and labourers, which began with John Ball and 'the valiant tiler of Dartford'.

In the late Victorian period, some historians presented the history of the Peasans' Revolt in terms of class struggle. This can be seen in Charles Edmund Maurice's *Lives of English Popular Leaders in the Middle Ages: Tyler, Ball, and Oldcastle* (1875). Maurice was both a barrister and lecturer in history, as well as brother-in-law to the noted social reformer, Octavia Hill (1838-1912). His work is an early example of social history, or, 'history from below', similar to J.R. Green's *A Short History of the English People* (1875), which purports to be 'a history, not of English Kings or English Conquests, but of the English People'.[99] Maurice feels a great deal of affinity with the rebels, and even calls Wat Tyler his 'fellow worker'.[100] He goes into a thorough analysis of 'the class struggle in Richard II's Reign'.[101] Maurice is also aware of the diverse social makeup of the rebel crowd, which includes bondmen, freemen, apprentices, and townsmen.[102]

Class-based analyses of the revolt filtered through into minor works of fiction published for children, such as Henriette Burch's *Dick Delver: A Story of the Peasant Revolt of the Fourteenth Century* (1889). It was published by the Religious Tract Society, and although one might expect such a work to emphasise religion, it is instead, according to Miriam E. Burstein, filled with politics and references to 'capitalists' and 'labourers'. However, although the novel uses the language of class struggle, the same scholar points out that its main concern is to present Wat Tyler's rebellion as the forerunner of a more Whiggish struggle for liberty, which began with the Reformation and was continued through to the Glorious Revolution.[103]

Written in the same dream-like prose as Morris's *A Dream of John Ball* is the novel by Florence Converse entitled *Long Will: A Romance of the Days of Piers Plowman* (1903). Converse was born in America in 1871, and led a life that certainly challenged American gender norms. From 1919 to 1954, she was in a relationship with another woman, an academic named Vida Dutton Scudder (1861-1954).[104] As its title suggests, *Long Will* is a prose romance based upon William Langland's fourteenth-century poem *Piers Plowman*. The novel opens with Langland, the Long Will of the title, laying on a hill in the Malverns, singing to himself,

'In a summer season when soft was the sun,
I set me in a shepherd's coat as I a shepherd were;
In the habit of a hermit, yet unholy of works,
Wandered I wide in this world wonders to hear.
But in a May morning on Malvern Hills
There befell me a wonder, wonderful me thought it;
I was weary of wandering and went me to rest
Under a broad bank by a burn side,
And as I lay and leaned and looked on the waters,
I slumbered in a sleep.'[105]

(Readers familiar with Langland will know that those lines are taken straight out of his fourteenth-century masterpiece.) Will's reverie is rudely interrupted by a young boy who laughs at him because his poet's words are unlike anything heard at the Court. But the boy asks him to sing more words, and to tell his tale. What follows is an overview of fourteenth-century life, in which an 'all-star cast' appears, including Richard II, John Ball, Wat Tyler, Jack Straw, John Wycliffe, and Geoffrey Chaucer. A significant portion of the latter half of the novel is taken up with the events of 1381 which is told from Will's perspective, even though Langland's original poem, written c.1377, does not reference the rising. The revolt begins in Fobbing when the men of the village chase the tax collector from their midst, and then, 'the people began to rise little by little, as it were a fire creeping in the grass.'[106] Although he associates with the rebels, Will is reluctant to give his whole-hearted support to the cause, being a man who preaches love and fellowship, and one of Tyler's messengers has a hard job convincing Will to participate in the revolt:

> Thus saith Wat Tyler to him men call Long Will, 'Thou hast a daughter. What wilt thou do if she be mishandled?' Will thrust Jack Straw from him that he fell on his knees by the wall. 'What wilt thou do?' cried the runner. 'Wilt not thou – even thou – slay the man? And what shall Wat Tyler do that is no clerk, but one itching for war? And I have a daughter', saith Wat Tyler, 'but she is avenged. The man is slain. This man came to gather the tax, – and I heard my daughter cry out. – Prate no more of love. I have slain the man. I have given the sign.' This is the word of Wat Tyler.[107]

Although this does not entirely convince Will, he still agrees to copy out John Ball's letters so they can be distributed amongst Wat Tyler's army.[108] While the rebel leaders are depicted as well organised and intelligent, they often have a hard time controlling the mob, whose passions are inflamed very easily on several occasions. For example, when the rebel army see that Sudbury and Hales are in Richard's barge, they become enraged, crying, 'Traitors! – Give up the traitors! – The Chancellor! – The Chancellor! – Poll Tax is his! – 'Tis Simon Sudbury taxed us! – They will be slain!'[109] This outburst prompts Stephen, one of Tyler's lieutenants, to exclaim, 'How shall these jack fools be hushed … they spoil all!'[110] Converse depicts Richard II as honourable and heroic after Wat Tyler's death. Although his evil advisors wish to put the remaining members of the mob to the sword, Richard cries out against this, saying, 'I will not betray my people [...for] these are my children! Mine! Mine! Let not a hair of their heads be harmed!'[111] After the revolt, Langland lives until an old age, and dies under the care of a monk at Malvern Priory, under the shadow of the hills where his adventures first began.

As we have seen thus far, the story of the Great Revolt inspired several novelists throughout the nineteenth century. What is surprising is that, although the term 'Peasants' Revolt' originated during the Victorian era, very rarely did any novelist or historian conceive of the revolt in such simplistic terms. All of the novelists studied here are aware that the rebels were drawn from a diverse range of social classes. The novels work best when they are commentaries upon contemporary political and social issues. During the early-to-mid twentieth century, there are very few novels which feature Wat Tyler. Indeed, the twentieth century, with some exceptions, was a quiet century for the rebel hero. Unlike Robin Hood and King Arthur, the Wat Tyler story was never made into a movie. There were also few new literary works published during the next century. As far as reprints of Victorian novels are concerned, only William Morris's *A Dream of John Ball* was republished on a regular basis, and continues to be today. In the final chapter, we will, therefore, be taking a look at representations of Wat Tyler in the succeeding century.

Notes

1 John Richetti, 'Introduction', in *The Cambridge Companion to the Eighteenth-Century Novel* ed. by John Richetti (Cambridge: University Press, 1996), pp. 1-8 (p.7).
2 Horace Walpole's *The Castle of Otranto* (1764) is indeed a very funny but truly ridiculous read: at the beginning of the novel, a large stone helmet falls from the sky, crushing a young boy who is on his way to get married. Seeing that his son is dead, the boy's father resolves to cast off his own wife and marry the dead boy's fiancée. Understandably perturbed, the newly-widowed bride to be runs off into the vaults of the castle, while the father and his retainers chase her through the vaults. Meantime, a large army approaches the castle, carrying a very large sword which requires upwards of a hundred men to bring it into the castle. Finally at the end of the novel a large statue rises out of the ground, picks up the sword and the aforementioned helmet, and flies to heaven.

3 'Literary Notices', *Caledonian Mercury* 11 May 1833, p. 3.

4 'Literary Notices', p. 3.

5 O'Neill, *The Bondman: An Historical Narrative of the Times of Wat Tyler* (London: Smith & Elder, 1833; repr. 1837), p.12.

6 *Ibid.*, p. 11.

7 *Ibid.*, p. 139.

8 *Ibid.*, p. 274.

9 *Ibid.*, p. 249.

10 *Ibid.*, p. 244.

11 *Ibid.*, p. 259.

12 *Ibid.*, p. 260.

13 *Ibid.*, p. 309.

14 There is no scholarly biography of Heygate to refer to thus far, although a very informative journal article can be found here: George Herring, 'W.E. Heygate: Tractarian Clerical Novelist', *Studies in Church History* Vol. 48 (2012), pp. 259-70.

15 William E. Heygate, *Alice of Fobbing; or, The Times of Jack Straw and Wat Tyler* (London: John Henry & James Parker, 1860), p. 24.

16 William Harrison Ainsworth, *Jack Sheppard: A Romance* 3 Vols. (London: Richard Bentley, 1839); Ainsworth's most successful and most notorious literary work. The violence in it apparently induced a servant named Benjamin Courvoisier to murder his master, Lord William Russell, MP. There was a huge outcry in the press as moralists grew concerned about the effects of violent entertainment upon the minds of youths. Jack Sheppard also spawned several cheap 'penny dreadful' imitations throughout the century. On Dickens's references to Wat Tyler in Bleak House see the following article: Harvey P. Sucksmith, 'Sir Leicester Dedlock, Wat Tyler, and the Chartists: The Role of the Iron-Master in *Bleak House*', *Dickens Studies Annual* Vol. 4 (1975), pp. 113-31.

17 For a detailed biography of Ainsworth see Stephen J. Carver, *The Life and Works of the Lancashire Novelist William Harrison Ainsworth 1805–1882* (New York: Edwin Mellen, 2003).

18 William Harrison Ainsworth, *Merry England, or, Nobles and Serfs* 3 Vols. (London: Tinsley Brothers, 1874), 1: iii.

19 *Ibid.*, 1: 3-5.

20 *Ibid.*, 1: 5.

21 *Ibid.*, 1: 5-6.

22 Although readers today are used to seeing the story of Robin Hood set during the 1190s, the time of Richard I and 'bad' King John, it was not unusual for Victorian writers to set Robin in different time periods: both George Emmett in *Robin Hood and the Archers of Merrie Sherwood* (1869)

and G.P.R. James in *Forest Days* (1843) situate the legend of the outlaw during the time of Simon de Montfort's rebellion.

23 Ainsworth, *Merry England, or, Nobles and Serfs*, 1: 13.

24 *Ibid.*, 1: 14.

25 *Ibid.*, 1: 15-16.

26 *Ibid.*, 1: 10.

27 *Ibid.*, 1: 11.

28 *Ibid.*, 1: 19.

29 *Ibid.*, 1: 19.

30 *Ibid.*, 1: 7.

31 *Ibid.*, 3: 175.

32 *Ibid.*, 3: 237.

33 *Ibid.*, 3: 22.

34 'Ainsworth's Merry England', *Saturday Review of Politics, Literature, Science and Art* 3 October 1874, p. 448.

35 *Ibid.*, p. 449.

36 *Ibid.*, p. 448.

37 Yaffa C. Draznin, *Victorian London's Middle-Class Housewife: What She Did All Day* (Westport, CT: Praeger, 2000), p. 151.

38 'Wat Tyler; or, the King and the Apprentice', *The Young Englishman's Journal Devoted to the Youth of England, Ireland, Scotland and Wales* No. 22 (1867), p. 337.

39 *Ibid.*, p. 338.

40 *Ibid.*, p. 339.

41. Wat Tyler; or, the King and the Apprentice', *The Young Englishman's Journal Devoted to the Youth of England, Ireland, Scotland and Wales* No. 24 (1867), p. 374.

42 Frederick Whitaker, 'Gentle Deeds; or, Serfdom to Knighthood', *Our Young Folks' Paper* 8 May 1886, p. 298.

43 Frederick Whitaker, 'Gentle Deeds; or, Serfdom to Knighthood', *Our Young Folks' Paper* 29 May 1886, p. 343.

44 *The New Newgate Calendar* 1: 1 (1863), p. 16; one story in this periodical literally ends mid-sentence.

45 'Wat Tyler's Revenge', *Boys of the Empire* 3: 52 (1889), pp. 15-16 (p.15).

46 *Ibid.*, p. 16.

47 *Ibid.*, p. 16.

48 *The Boyhood Days of Jack Straw; or, The Sword of Freedom* (London: [n.pub.] [n.d.]), p. 155.

49 John Springhall, 'Pernicious Reading? The Penny Dreadful as Scapegoat for Late-Victorian Juvenile Crime' *Victorian Periodicals Review* 27: 4 (1994), pp. 326-49.

50 Heather Shore, *Artful Dodgers: Youth and Crime in Early 19th-Century London* (Woodbridge: Boydell, 1999), p. 128.

51 *Reynolds's Newspaper* 28 October 1877 cited in Robert Kirkpatrick, *Wild Boys in the Dock: Victorian Juvenile Literature and Juvenile Crime – Children's Books History Society Occasional Paper XI* (London: Children's Books History Society, 2013), p. 10.

52 Kirkpatrick, *Wild Boys in the Dock*, p. 17.

53 *Ibid.* p. 17.

54 Springhall, 'Pernicious Reading', p. 326.

55 Arthur Quiller-Couch, *Adventures in Criticism* (London: Cassell, 1896) cited in Kirkpatrick, *Wild Boys in the Dock*, p. 28.

56 *Ibid.*, p. 28.

57 Springhall, 'Pernicious Reading', p. 328.

58 In 1884 representatives of European powers met at Berlin and carved out territories for themselves on the African continent. While the British had had an empire prior to the 1880s, for the most part, they were content to let private corporations undertake imperial expansion. For the subcontinent there was the East India Company, the Hudson Bay Company carried out its operations in North America, and the Van Dieman's Land Company had ventures in Tasmania. It was only after the Indian Rebellion in 1857 that the British government gradually assumed direct rule over India. The need for direct rule over many of Britain's colonies in the late nineteenth century became more pressing when a newly-unified Germany, as well as the United States, were acquiring colonies for themselves and challenging Britain's position as the top industrial and economic power. Some private companies were still operating in the colonies even after this, however, such as the Royal Niger Company which received its charter in 1886, and the British Royal South Africa Company, led by the arch-imperialist Cecil Rhodes, which became a chartered company in 1889.

59 Chris Bongie, *Friends and Enemies: The Scribal Politics of Post/Colonial Literature* (Liverpool: Liverpool University Press, 2008), p. 140.

60 G.A. Henty, *A March on London; Being a Story of Wat Tyler's Insurrection* (London: Blackie, 1898), p. v.

61 *Ibid.*, p. v.

62 'Desertion from the English Army', in *The Peasants' Revolt of 1381* ed. by R.B. Dobson (London: MacMillan, 1970), pp. 94-5.

63 Henty, *A March on London*, p. 51.

64 *Ibid.*, p. 51.

65 *Ibid.*, p. 53.

66 *Ibid.*, p. 55.

67 *Ibid.*, pp. 150-151.

68 *Ibid.*, pp. 160-161.

69 Henry Newbolt, *Vitaï Lampada* [Internet <www.poemhunter.com/poem/vita-lampada/> Accessed 21 March 2017]. The memorials to the war dead at Charterhouse College similarly list those alumni who 'played up, played up, and played the game'. Sadly, imperial warfare was not a game.

70 Henry Newbolt, *Froissart in Britain* (London: J. Nisbet, 1902), p. xviii.

71 Niall Ferguson, *How Britain Made the Modern World* 2nd Edn. (London: Penguin, 2004), p. 262. See also Gregory Claeys, 'The "Survival of the Fittest" and the Origins of Social Darwinism', *Journal of the History of Ideas* 61: 2 (2000), pp. 223-40.

72 Newbolt, *Froissart in Britain*, p. 108.

73 Newbolt, *Froissart in Britain*, p. xxii.

74 Fiona MacCarthy, 'Morris, William (1834–1896)', in *The Oxford Dictionary of National Biography* (Oxford: Oxford University Press, 2004; Online Edn. 2009) [Internet <www.oxforddnb.com/view/article/19322> Accessed 30 Jan 2017].

75 Mark Bevir, *The Making of British Socialism* (Princeton, NJ, Princeton University Press, 2011), p. 37.

76 William Morris, 'Letter to C.E. Maurice, 1883', cited in Charles Harvey and Jon Press, *William Morris: Design and Enterprise in Victorian Britain* (Manchester: Manchester University Press, 1991), p. 159.

77 Nicholas Salmon, 'A Reassessment of A Dream of John Ball', *Journal of William Morris Studies* 14: 2 (2001), pp. 29-38 (p.30).

78 The Unification of Germany occurred in 1871.

79 Ian Gazeley and Pat Thane, 'Patterns of Visibility: Unemployment in Britain during the Nineteenth and Twentieth Centuries', in *Forming Nation, Framing Welfare* ed. by Gail Lewis (London: Routledge, 1998), pp. 181-226 (p.184).

80 John Charlton, 'London, 13 November 1886', *Socialist Review* No. 224 (1998) [Internet <pubs.socialistreviewindex.org.uk/sr224/charlton.htm> Accessed 5 February 2017].

81 William Morris, *A Dream of John Ball and a King's Lesson* (London: Longman, 1912), p. 18.

82 Ruth Kinna, 'William Morris and the Problem of Englishness', *European Journal of Political Theory* 5: 1 (2006), pp. 85-99

83 Bevir, *The Making of British Socialism*, p. 245.

84 William Morris, 'The Society of the Future', cited in Florence Boos & William Boos, 'The Utopian Communism of William Morris', *History of Political Thought* 7: 3 (1986), pp. 489-510 (p.495).

85 Ruth Kinna, 'Socialist Fellowship and the Woman Question', in *Writing on*

the Image: Reading William Morris ed. by David Latham (Toronto: University of Toronto Press, 2007), pp. 183-196 (p.188).

86 Morris, *A Dream of John Ball and a King's Lesson*, p. 116.

87 *Ibid.*, p. 117.

88 *Ibid.*, p. 120.

89 *Ibid.*, p. 125.

90 *Ibid.*, pp. 146-7.

91 Taylor, *London's Burning*, pp. 25-6.

92 Morris, *A Dream of John Ball and a King's Lesson*, p. i.

93 J. Alex Macdonald, 'The Revision of *News from Nowhere*', *Journal of William Morris Studies* 3: 2 (1976), pp. 8-15.

94 William Morris, *News from Nowhere* (London: Longman, 1918), p. 2.

95 *Ibid.*, p. 2.

96 *Ibid.*, p. 2.

97 *Ibid.*, p. 95.

98 *Ibid.*, p. 247.

99 J.R. Green, *A Short History of the English People* (London, 1874; repr. London: Macmillan, 1902), p. xxiv.

100 Charles Edmund Maurice, *Lives of English Popular Leaders in the Middle Ages* (London: Henry S. King, 1875), p. i.

101 Maurice, *Lives of English Popular Leaders in the Middle Ages*, p. 128.

102 *Ibid.*, p. 163.

103 Burstein, *op cit.*

104 Lillian Faderman, *Odd Girls and Twilight Lovers, A History of Lesbian Life in Twentieth-Century America* (London: Penguin, 1991), pp. 23-4.

105 Florence Converse, *Long Will: A Romance of the Days of Piers Plowman* (New York: Dutton, 1929), pp. 7-8.

106 *Ibid.*, p. 265.

107 *Ibid.*, pp. 267-8.

108 *Ibid.*, p. 268.

109 *Ibid.*, p. 273.

110 *Ibid.*, p. 273.

111 *Ibid.*, p. 333.

CHAPTER SEVEN

'Let's Finish the Job'

He was a great leader, a King among men.

J.C. Hardwick, *Master and Man* (1924)

*I don't remember hearing anything about God making Barons on
the morning of the seventh day, and serfs in the afternoon.*

Christopher Logue, *Medieval England* (1969)

Wat Tyler, John Ball, and Jack Straw can justifiably be called the first
English revolutionaries. Yes, there had been riots and rebellions before
1381, but it was Tyler and his comrades who mounted the first serious
challenge to the established order. And the memory of these men lived
on, especially that of Wat Tyler and John Ball. As we have seen, Wat
Tyler's name has been invoked by various authors many times
throughout the early modern and modern periods. It is usually at times
of social and political upheaval that his 'spectre' appears. With the
exception of a play and a ballad, Tyler's post-medieval literary afterlife
effectively begins in the seventeenth century with the English
Revolution (1642-51). Tyler was appropriated in this early period by
Royalists. They compare Oliver Cromwell (1599-1658) to Wat Tyler,
and use the story of Tyler's life and death to highlight what they saw
as the inevitable consequences of mounting a rebellion against an
anointed king. Oddly, and certainly surprisingly, Wat Tyler's memory
was never appropriated by Cromwell or the Parliamentarians. Perhaps
Tyler was too radical for someone such as Cromwell, who, in the words
of even his own son, wished to set himself up as Lord Paramount over
the people of England, Scotland, and Ireland. Wat Tyler's name

continued to be used as a symbol of wanton riot and rebellion throughout the eighteenth century. It was only at the end of the eighteenth century, when Thomas Paine and Robert Southey depicted Tyler as man who fought for political rights and liberty against a tyrannical government, that he became a symbol of hope to successive reformers and radicals. As we have seen, after Paine and Southey, reformers such as Henry Hunt, as well as the Chartists during the mid-nineteenth century, legitimised their cause by invoking the spirit of Wat Tyler. Socialists would do the same at the end of the Victorian period. Studying Tyler's post-medieval literary representations, therefore, serves as a window through which the cultural historian can examine changing reactions to riot, rebellion, and revolution.

The twentieth century did not witness any major reinterpretations of Wat Tyler's story. There was J.C. Hardwick's *Master and Man: A Tale of the Peasants' Revolt of 1381* (1924), which gives the following favourable assessment of John Ball's life and deeds:

> And Ball, the priest? Alas! as you know, they put him to death. He, indeed, as I think, was a martyr; he died for others, for the poor, the ignorant, and the oppressed. Cheerful, brave, generous, he fought his fight and lost; and then, very patiently, he died ... He was a great leader, a King among men. Yet it is not always the best men who succeed. But, perhaps, there is a defeat which is more noble than victory, and very precious in the sight of the Lord is the death of His saints.[1]

Hardwick's novel only went through one edition, and the early-to-mid twentieth century was a quiet time for Wat Tyler. I have not been able to locate any new Wat Tyler stories or plays written during the Second World War (1939-45). The reason for this may be a patriotic one, for no one wanted to celebrate the life of a man who fought against his king at a moment in history when the whole nation needed to come together to fight a common enemy. After the war Wat Tyler almost disappears from popular culture. As to why this is, we can only speculate, although I suspect that one possible reason might be because it was the era of the first strong Labour government.[2] Under Clement Attlee (1883-1967), they enacted a number of far-reaching social and economic reforms that were designed to benefit the common man. Attlee's administration delivered on their promises of operating a centrally planned economy run along Keynesian economic principles. Within their policies were measures such as a commitment to full employment, with the full cooperation of trade unions, as well as healthcare that was to be free at the point of need, in the form of the National Health Service. This cooperation between government and unions, combined with a welfare state and a centrally planned economy, is known as the post-war consensus. The consensus model of government lasted into the next decade. All of Labour's measures were subsequently carried on by the Conservative governments of Anthony Eden (1897-1977) and Harold Macmillan (1894-1986). In fact, it was the latter who, at a Tory rally in 1957, proclaimed that under his premiership most Britons 'had never had it so good'. Thus, there were fewer reasons for the radical ghost of Tyler to emerge during the mid-twentieth century.

While there have been many well-produced television documentaries, there have been, to my knowledge, no cinematic portrayals of the events of 1381. An interesting American educational film entitled *Medieval England: The Peasants' Revolt of 1381* appeared in 1969. The role of Wat Tyler was played by none other than the famous Anthony Hopkins. Shot in black and white, the thirty-five minute movie is dark and atmospheric. The film opens with John Ball on horseback, played by Christopher Logue (1926-2011), preaching to the assembled peasants on a bitterly cold, windy English field:

In the beginning, God made the world, and it was good, and he made man, and man was good. But I don't remember hearing anything about God making barons on the morning of the seventh day, and serfs in the afternoon. The only difference I ever heard of was that some of us are women, for which, much thanks. No – when Adam delved, and Eve span, who was then the gentleman? God made the fields and the trees, but he didn't say: I make this field for Lord Muck, and I make this tree for his lady wife.[3]

The scene then switches to the villagers of Fobbing. While the good peasants plead with Thomas de Bamptoun that they have already paid the poll tax, and that they cannot bear to pay any more, Bamptoun cruelly exhorts them to 'work harder'.[4] Bamptoun then takes a liking to a village girl of tender age, at which point Thomas Baker stabs him. Swiftly skipping over events in the interval, we next meet Tyler in the streets of London at nightfall. Hopkins portrays Tyler as a dark, brooding revolutionary firebrand. He is described as having been formerly a soldier, and he approaches the camera with a torch. Breaking the fourth wall he says, 'let me show you how you repeal a law or two'.[5] He then sets his torch to a pile of legal parchments. Then, heroically turning to the assembled peasants, he declares, 'now hear this! If might, have right, let the people speak!'[6] And in speaking with the King's messenger before the meeting at Mile End, Tyler says, 'Tell him [the King] that if he doesn't come tomorrow, I'll burn London.'[7]

The film is heavily indebted to Marxist historiography, the dominant mode of historical analysis in the academy during the 1960s. The revolt is described as one of the first great clashes 'between capital and labour'.[8] Wat Tyler at one point refers to his fellow revolutionaries as 'Comrades'.[9] At another point, Tyler even has the cheek to address the King as his comrade. Although the historian who advised the filmmaker in the production is not credited, it is similar in its standpoint to much of the work that the neo-Marxist historian Rodney Hilton was carrying out at the time.[10] Certainly John Ball's preaching that everything should be held in common, and the film's talk of capital versus labour, and Tyler saluting his fellow rebels as 'comrade', was an anomaly in a period when American educational films usually were produced from a white, conservative, capitalist and Christian perspective.[11]

I suggested above that perhaps there was no new reinterpretation of the Wat Tyler story during the 1950s and 1960s because it was the 'never had it so good' era. We then see Wat Tyler reappear when the post-war consensus breaks down in Britain.[12] Intermittent strikes plagued both Labour and Conservative governments during the 1970s, and Britain's working week was reduced to just three days in 1974 (it is not my intention here to go into the rights or wrongs of the strikes). While

Conservative Prime Minister Edward Heath (1916-2005) largely sought reconciliation with the unions, preferring to adhere to the consensus model of governing, a junior member of his cabinet, the Education Secretary Margaret Thatcher (1925-2013), had other ideas, especially after the Conservative government was defeated in a snap election in 1974. Instead of being a disciple of the economic theories of John Maynard Keynes (1883-1946), she was a follower of the radical ecenomic theorist, Friedrich A. Hayek (1899-1992). His book, entitled *The Road to Serfdom* (1944), argues against government intervention in the economy. The central thesis of Hayek's work is that state capitalism, or centralised economic planning, is undemocratic and inevitably leads to the subjugation of the people, as had happened in certain Communist communities. Furthermore, when governments control the economy, individual freedom is curtailed. For citizens to enjoy the fruits of freedom and democracy, the free market must reign supreme. These doctrines convinced Thatcher and some of her like-minded colleagues in the Conservative Party to commit to a policy of the privatisation of some key industries.[13]

Thatcher was eventually elected as leader of the Conservative Party, and her government came to power in 1979. In 1981, it happened to be the 600th Anniversary of the Great Revolt. Prominent left-wing activists composed mostly of representatives from the Labour Party and the trade unions, as well as some members of the British Communist Party, organised a mass meeting at Blackheath to be held on 4 May. The week before, Rodney Hilton had given a public lecture on the historical context of the revolt. Badges were given to attendees that read, 'Peasants' Revolt, 1381-1981: Let's Finish the Job.'[14] Despite this big show of left-wing militancy, however, the decade proved to be a dire one for the Labour Party and the left in general. The Conservatives under Thatcher got elected three times, but ultimately she overreached herself. Thomas Paine's words, 'poll taxes have always been odious', are applicable as much to the 1980s and they are to the 1380s.[15] The British people's anger towards another such 'odious' tax was raised when Thatcher's government introduced a flat-rate per capita 'Community Charge'. The charge was intended to overhaul the existing system of local government funding, which relied on taxes based upon local property values. It was piloted in Scotland in 1989, and introduced in England and Wales in 1990. Despite its fancy name, it soon acquired the nickname of 'poll tax', even on the government's official information leaflet entitled *The Community Charge (or, the So-Called 'Poll Tax')* (1990). Despite widespread opposition to the tax (an All-Britain Anti-Poll Tax Federation was swiftly formed), and widespread evasion, the government pressed ahead with the charge (ironically, in Exeter, the address of the Community Charge/Poll Tax Registration Office was based at Wat Tyler House, King William Street).[16] Another striking coincidence with the events of 1989-90 and 1381 is the fact that the first MP to speak out against the planned introduction of the Poll Tax was named Jack Straw, something which amused one or two commentators in the press.[17] Like his medieval namesake, Jack Straw (the MP) called in Parliament for a 'People's Rebellion'.[18] It was not only the Left that condemned the Poll Tax, but also the Church of England, and even some Tory-controlled city councils.[19]

In such a context, it should not surprise anyone that Wat Tyler's name was invoked once more, especially by those on the left of the political spectrum. One amusing appropriation of Tyler's name during the 1980s was brought to my attention by a friend of mine who worked in Leeds City Council Finance Office in 1990. He told me that he received a letter which, in polite terms, told the city council to 'shove your poll tax'. The letter was signed 'Wat Tyler'. He says that his boss was 'livid', and ordered him to track down the man responsible so that he could be taken to court. My friend resisted the urge to sarcastically tell his manager that they were six hundred years too late in tracking down Wat Tyler – probably for the best.[20] As well as non-payment, a series of protests against the poll tax occurred throughout 1989 and 1990. Tory newspapers and magazines criticised such protests, like Michael Trend did in an article for *The Spectator*, who thought that they would amount to nothing.[21] However, we know that the most serious protest against the Thatcher government occurred one year later, in Trafalgar Square, on 31 March 1990, in addition to the numerous protests that had already occurred throughout the country. It was at Trafalgar Square that some protestors marched against the government with slogans emblazoned with the words 'AVENGE WAT TYLER'.[22] The events of the day did much to contribute towards the downfall of Thatcher, who resigned in November of the same year. Her successor, John Major, quickly announced that the tax would be abolished. Clearly, when it comes to taxation, as the events of both 1381 and 1989-90 illustrate, the British people can only be pushed so far before they snap.

In spite of the dearth of Wat Tyler novels during the twentieth century, there has been a novel published very recently: Melvyn Bragg's *Now is the Time* (2015). His work has received favourable reviews from many quarters, including Juliet Barker.[23] I would also like to echo Barker's sentiments, for Bragg's tale is a well-researched and gripping novel which is hard to put down. Of course, it is not my purpose to review Bragg's story here as a critic would, but merely to make a few remarks upon his portrayal of Wat Tyler and the events of 1381. We first meet Wat Tyler in Bragg's novel hunting down outlaws in the forest, which actually bears some resemblance to the first encounter with Wat Tyler in Pierce Egan's 1841 novel. In Bragg's story, Tyler and the rebels look back to the Anglo-Saxon era as an idyllic time when there were no bondmen, and they seek the re-establishment of Saxon laws.[24] Thus, Bragg draws upon the idea of the Norman Yoke, as many Georgian and Victorian writers did. Of Tyler's character, Bragg tells us that he had a sense of fair play and was locally revered by his fellow villagers as a good man.[25] While the historical rebels had always counted themselves as loyal subjects of the King, in Bragg's novel, shortly before the fateful meeting at Smithfield, John Ball realises that the King and his attendants are planning something wicked, and that the young royal cannot be trusted.[26] Yet Tyler is willing to give the young king the benefit of the doubt. The boy, surely, could not be plotting anything against him, and his cold reception must be down to nerves. He is uneasy about the sheer number of Tyler's armed followers facing him.[27] John Ball, of course, is right not to trust the King, and at Smithfield, the King's men slowly surround Tyler. Walworth then delivers that fatal blow.

So what is next for Tyler's legacy? On the one hand, it does not look good; the events of 1381 are not on the mandatory history syllabus for either primary or secondary schoolchildren. Instead, schoolchildren are often saturated with Tudors, Stuarts, and the First and Second World Wars. The sad truth is that pupils today know more about Henry VIII's six wives than they do of Wat Tyler or other radical leaders from history. On the other hand, Tyler's story and the events of 1381 continue to be retold by historians and novelists. Juliet Barker's excellent history has already been mentioned, but there is also Dan Jones's best-selling account of the event entitled *Summer of Blood: The Peasants' Revolt of 1381* (2009). There may indeed come a time like 1381 again, when the English people hold a mass protest so as to give a quick reminder to their government as to who in the nation really holds power. When, or if that happens, I have no doubt that we will once again see Wat Tyler's name reappear.

Notes

1 J.C. Hardwick, *Master and Man: A Tale of the Peasants' Revolt of 1381* (London: The Sheldon Press [n.d.]), p.154.

2 I say that Clement Attlee's Labour government was the first strong Labour government, because we can hardly credit the early twentieth-century Ramsey MacDonald Labour administration with having done anything ground-breaking.

3 *Medieval England: The Peasants' Revolt* (dir, John Irvin, 1969).

4 *Ibid.*

5 *Ibid.*

6 *Ibid.*

7 *Ibid.*

8 *Ibid.*

9 *Ibid.*

10 Richard J. Wurtz, 'Medieval England: The Peasant's Revolt (Review)', *Film & History: An Interdisciplinary Journal of Film and Television Studies* 2: 1 (1972), p. 25; this review indicates that a study guide was published along with this film which might have shed more light upon who the historians were behind it. However, I have been unable to locate a copy of this.

11 Geoff Alexander, *Films You Saw in School: A Critical Review of 1,153*

Classroom Educational (1958-1985) in 74 Categories (Jefferson, NC: MacFarland, 2014), p. 81.

12 Ashton, *London Underground: A Cultural Geography*, p. 147.

13 The first moves towards privatisation were taken when the Conservatives were in opposition, when Nicholas Ridley produced his Report on the Nationalised Industries in 1977.

14 Stephen Williams, 'Radical Objects: The Peasants' Revolt Badge', *History Workshop* 19 April 2017 [Internet <www.historyworkshop.org> Accessed 19 April 2017].

15 Paine, 'The Rights of Man', p. 327.

16 Dorothy Wood, 'The Community Charge' *The Times* 27 June 1989, p. 15.

17 Auberon Waugh, 'Another Voice: Perhaps poll tax will once again prove the last Straw' *The Spectator* 10 July 1987, p.7.

18 Waugh, 'Another Voice', p. 17.

19 'End of an era as poll tax signals Maggie's downfall', *The Northern Echo* 9 April 2013 [Internet <www.thenorthernecho.co.uk/news/10342279. End_of_an_era_as_poll_tax_ signals_Maggie___s_downfall/> Accessed 25 March 2017].

20 This amusing incident was communicated to me by Mark Dobson. He now serves as the Independent City Councillor for the Garforth area of Leeds, West Yorkshire.

21 Michael Trend, 'From Tyler to Thatcher: The Failure of the Great "Poll Tax" Protest' *The Spectator* 9 June 1989, p. 16.

22 Several historians have pointed out that many protestors had this slogan on their placards: Barker, *England Arise*, p. 418; Taylor, *London's Burning*, p. 23;

23 Juliet Barker, 'Now Is the Time by Melvyn Bragg review – fictionalising the peasants' revolt' *The Guardian* 1 October 2015 [Internet <www.theguardian.com/books/2015/oct/01/now-is-the-time-melvyn-bragg-peasants-revolt-history> Accessed 25 March 2017].

24 Melvyn Bragg, *Now is the Time* (London: Sceptre, 2015), pp. 298-9.

25 *Ibid.*, p. 43.

26 *Ibid.*, p. 276.

27 *Ibid.*, p. 298.

APPENDIX

Wat Tyler
Poems, Songs and Ballads

The Rebellion of Wat Tyler, Jack Straw and Others Against King Richard the Second; how Sir William Walworth, lord Mayor of London, stabbed Tyler in Smithfield, for which the King knighted Sir William, with Five Aldermen More, Causing a Dagger to be Added in the Shield of the City Arms

Wat Tyler is from Dartford gone,
And with him many proper men,
And he a captain is become,
Marching in field with fife and drum.

Jack Straw another in like case,
From Essex flocks a mighty pace:
Hob Carter with his straggling train,
Jack Shepherd comes with him amain;

So doth Tom Miller in like sort,
As if he meant to take some sort:
With bows and bills, with spear and shield,
On Black-heath they have picht their field.

An hundred thousand men in all,
Whose force is not accounted small:
And for King Richard did they send,
Much evil to him they did intend,

For the war which our noble King
Upon the commons them did bring:
And now because his royal grace
Denied to come with their chase

They spoiled Southwark round about,
And took the marshall's prisoners out:
All those that in the King's-bench lay,
And liberty they set that day,

And then they marched with one consent
Through London with a rude intent;
And to fulfil their leud desire,
They set the Savoy all on fire:

And for the hate they did bear
Unto the Duke of Lancashire,
Therefore his house they burned quite,
Through envy, malice and despite.

Then to the Temple did they turn,
The lawyers books eke did they burn,
And spoil'd their lodgings one by one,
And all they laid their hands upon.

Then unto Smithfield did they hie,
To St. John's place that stands thereby,
And set the same on fire flat,
Which burned seven days after that.

Unto the Tower of London then,
Fast trooped these rebellious men,
And having entered soon the same,
With divers cries and mickle shame;

The grave lord chancellor then they took,
Amaz'd with fearful piteous look.
The lord high treasurer likewise they
Took from that place the present day;

And with their hooting loud and shrill,
Cut off their heads on Tower Hill.
Into the city came they then,
Like leud disordered frantick men.

They rob'd the churches every where,
And put the priests in deadly fear.
Into the counters then they get,
Where men in prison lay for debt;

They broke the doors, and let them out,
And threw the counter books about,
Tearing and spoiling them each one,
And records all they light upon.

The doors of Newgate broke they down,
That prisoners ran about the town,
Forcing all the smiths they meet
To knock the irons from their feet:

And then like villains void of awe,
Followed Wat Tyler and Jack Straw.
Although this outrage was not small,
The king gave pardon to them all,

So they would part home quietly:
But they his pardon did defie.
And being in Smithfield then,
Even threescore thousand fighting men,

APPENDIX

Which there Wat Tyler then did bring
Of purpose for to meet the king.
And therewithal his royal grace,
Sent Sir John Newton to that place,

Unto Wat Tyler willing him
To come and speak with our royal king.
But the proud rebel in despight,
Did pick a quarrel with the knight.

The mayor of London being by,
When he beheld this villainy,
Unto Wat Tyler he rode then,
Being in th' midst of all his men:

Saying, traytor yield 'tis best,
In the King's name I thee arrest,
And therewith to his dagger start,
He thrust the rebel to the heart,

Who falling dead upon the ground,
The same did all the host confound:
So down they threw their weapons all,
And humbly they for mercy call:
Thus did the proud rebellion cease,
And after followed joyful peace.

Thomas Evans (ed.), *Old Ballads, Historical and Narrative* 2 Vols. (London: T. Evans, 1777)

The Chartist Song
by Thomas Cooper
To the Tune of the *Brave Old Oak*

A Song for the Free — the brave and the free —
Who feareth no tyrant's frown:
Who scorneth to bow, in obeisance low,
To mitre or to crown:
Who owneth no lord with crosier or sword.
And bendeth to Right alone;
Where'er he may dwell, his worth men shall tell,
When a thousand years are gone!

For Tyler of old, a heart-chorus bold
Let Labour's children sing!
For the smith with the soul that disdain'd base control.
Nor trembled before a king;
For the heart that was brave, though pierced by a knave
Ere victory for Right was won —
Then tell his fair fame, and cheer his blythe name.
When a thousand years are gone!

For the high foe of Wrong, great Hampden, a song —
The fearless and the sage!
Who, at king-craft's frown, the gauntlet threw down,
And dared the tyrant's rage;
Who away the scabbard threw, when the battle blade he drew.
And with gallant heart led on!
How he bravely fell, our children shall tell.
When a thousand years are gone!

For the mountain child of Scotia wild —
For noble Wallace a strain!
O'er the Border ground let the chaunt resound :
It will not be heard in vain.

176

APPENDIX

For the Scot will awake, and the theme uptake
Of deeds by the patriot done:-?-
They hold his name dear, nor refuse it a tear,
When a thousand years are gone!

An anthem will swell for bold William Tell,
The peasant of soul so grand!
Who fearlessly broke haughty Gesler's yoke,
And set free his fatherland:
His deeds shall be sung, with blythesome tongue,
By maiden, sire, and son,
Where the eagles climb o'er the Alps sublime.
When a thousand years are gone!

For our Charter a song! It tarrieth long —
But we will not despair;
For, though Death's dark doom upon us all may come,
Ere we the blessing share,—
Our happy children they shall see the happy day
When Freedom's boon is won;
And our Charter shall be the boast of the Free,
When a thousand years are gone!

The Poetical Works of Thomas Cooper
(London: Hodder & Stoughton, 1877)

The Spirit of Wat Tyler
by Charles Cole

Taxation burthens ev'rything
By art of nature given;
The sick man's rushlight, twinkling,
The glorious beam of Heaven –
Out all of wear and all we eat,
To glut the scheming spoiler;
There wants to make our list complete
But a Poll Tax, and a TYLER.

'A Tyler,' murmured from the grave
A voice the sound repelling –
'Peace! Would-be Briton! Dastard! Slave!
And from his earthly dwelling
The shade of Tyler stood confess'd:
His back was gored and riven;
But not a mark was on his breast
By Walworth's dagger given.

The same they hailed immortal steel!
Renowned in civic story!
Satanic badge of servile zeal,
Converting shame to glory!
'Dost mark the wound,' the spirit said,
'Neath which slaves saw me stagger
From horse to earth, 'tis well repaid,
For London wears the dagger!

Now to the purpose – I am He,
Who not for fame competed,
But would have seen my country free
And have her foes defeated:
Mine was a deed the good desired,

APPENDIX

The shackled chain was round us;
We rose at once like men inspired,
And burst the links that bound us!

But what avail'd it? Soon the youth
Whose Kingly craft entrapp'd them,
To trust his honour and his truth,
Again his chains enwrapp'd them.
And still ye cowards ye are bound,
As 'twere a serpent coiling
Its dreadful weary length around
Your limbs, all faint and toiling!

Long, long ye proudly bore the load,
Lift up your laurell'd casement,
But now the burthen brings the goad,
Reward of self-abasement!
Mark! Man that would be – Peterloo,
Wexford in slaughter sharing –
Merthyr and Newtonberry too,
And think of Cook and *Baring*!

While locomotives move by steam,
(Earth shudders at the story)
Your waggon boasts a *human* team,
And *this* is England's glory!
And this is Britain! Worms like these
Upon its surface creeping –
The tyrant of the Portuguese
Had none in viler keeping.

'God save the Queen;' your dogs I see
Have superseded donkeys;
Age of progressive industry!
Of course you work your monkeys!

179

God save the Queen! Still Britons slaves,-
In this land of bravery;
Ye sing, 'Britannia rules the waves,'
Yet bow to basest slavery.

A shadow called REFORM I see
Exulting o'er the nation;
Though Cade was slain ingloriously,
For seeking *reformation*!
Muir and his fellow martyrs brave,
Their mem'ries unrespected;
You scarce can trace Fitzgerald's grave,
And Emmet lies neglected;

The world contains the graves of men,
All trait of whom hath vanished;
Their spirit must revive again,
Or freedom's ever banished.
And who said'st, to be complete,
Your list requires a Poll Tax;
Dog! That can'st lick a tyrant's feet,
Out, thou would'st pay a *soul-tax*.

The spirit passed in bitter wrath,
With eye indignant blazing;
And wailing Walworth track'd his path,
Still on his death wound gazing.
My kindred spirits still survive,
To rouse for coming glory,
Till not a Britain but will strive,
To profit from his story.

Charles Cole, 'The Spirit of Wat Tyler',
The Northern Star 16 September 1848

APPENDIX

The Man Who Slew Wat Tyler
by Spartacus

The people's leader faced the King,
The Commons right he pleaded;
A scurvy knave broke through the ring,
And stab'd him basely he did.
Here, Fishmonger! A word with you;
Now, man! Don't burst your biler,
But own a gallows was the due
Of him who slew Wat Tyler.

Let's hope your fishmongrel Co.
Have other ground of glory;
For Walworth was a coward blow:-
Read e'en Hume's courtly story.
You Yankee Nigger-driver, you
Just harken to a riler;
And conscience flog you not a few:
Your fellow slew Wat Tyler.

Let honest freemen scorn the slave,
Why stabb'd the people's leader;
But double loathing brand the knave,
Who plays assassin's pleader!
When slavering lies can damn the True,
And Vile be saved by Viler,
Then, Yankee snob! We'll praise, with you,
The man who slew Wat Tyler.

The Star of Freedom 5 June 1852

A Song for the Next Rebellion
by W.J. Linton
(To the Tune of *The Fine Old English Gentleman*)

Up! Up! Ye English peasantry, for whom Wat Tyler bled;
Up! Cited serfs, whose sturdy sires Cade and Archamber led;
Up! Up! For equal rights and laws: your cause is all as good
As when in the presence of a Smith a traitor monarch stood.
Then up for equal rights and laws, like the Men of the olden time.

Up! Up! – your sires were Englishmen who fought at Hampden's side
Bethink you how the Hampden lived, and how the Hampden died!
The Hampden spirit liveth yet – let Privilege beware! –
The echo of his battle-song shall fill our English air.
Then up, ye noble Englishmen, true sons of the olden time.

Up! Up! – If ye are Englishmen, be mindful of that day
When Cromwell strode o'er Worcester-Field and scared a king away.
Tough Cade and Ket and Tyler fail'd, the 'crowning mercy' came: -
Hurrah for England's Stalwart One! Your fortune be the same!
Hurrah for England's Stalwart One, the Man of the olden time!

Remember how the noble life of Eliot was entomb'd!
How Sydney and how Russell bled! – be ye not prison doom'd!
Better to die as Hampden died than on the gallows-tree:
Meet we our death in the open field, as best becomes the free!
Ay, live or die like Englishmen, the Brave of the olden time!

Up! Up! Ye toil-worn English slaves: if blood must needs be shed,
Let it be England's tyrant lords', and not the famine-sped! –
Ay, hand to hand, and foot to foot, close fast with Tyranny:-
Our Saxon Thor is lord again: our England shall be free!
Ay, freer than it ever was in the best of the olden time.

The English Republic (1853)

182

Ballads from English History: Wat Tyler; or, the Servile War by G. S. O.

About five hundred years ago,
And at the time when Cowslips blow,
The men of Kent, enraged by wrong,
Rose up in arms – a mighty throng.

It was at Maidstone some one said,
'We'll have Wat Tyler for our head;'
'Ay, ay,' ten thousand lips replied,
'We could not have a better guide.'

Out of his prison came John Ball,
To be a preacher to them all;
John was a priest of evil fame,
Whose words had set the world aflame.

'All men must work,' this preacher said,
'Their equal work for equal bread;
For never was there gentleman
When Adam delved and Eve span.'

Woe then to him who did not *trudge*,
But went on horseback – were he judge,
Bishop or lord, or merchant, who
Could go and not bemire his shoe.

Woe to the rich who drank the wine,
And ate the meat and manchets fine;
Woe to the great men's homes of state,
Filled with soft raiment, gems, and plate.'

Intent on all the preacher spoke,
To lawless deeds the mob awoke,
Weaponed with cudgels, scythes, and flails,
They slew the jailors and sacked the jails.

With drunken shouts and savage joy
They fired the palace of Savoy,
They burned St. John's in Clerkenwell,
Altar and vestment, book and bell.

The rebels then more daring grew,
And bade the Tower its gates undo:
And though twelve hundred manned that place,
They trembled so at Tyler's face,

And feared so much a broken skin,
They let him and his forces in,
Who swarmed across the lowered bridge,
And filled the Tower from base to ridge.

There half in anger, half in mirth,
They vexed the game they'd run to earth;
They caught and kissed the Princess Joan
(Mother of Richard on the throne).

They dragged the Archbishop Simon out
With many a curse and bitter flout;
They had no pity for his prayers,
His sacred rank nor silver hairs.

To death they doomed him that same hour,
Within a bowshot of the Tower:
The doom was doomed, the murder done,
Before all London and the sun.

APPENDIX

The King is to the Abbey gone,
To say his early orison;
Before the holy altar there,
Ere now monarchs bent in prayer,

And found deliverance from their woes.
And he might be as one of those;
Heaven help thee, boyish King, we say,
For thou wilt need it much this day!

When prayer was ended he arose
And sallied out to front his foes,
And many held their breath in pain,
To see him with so small a train

Speed to his mark, for woe or weal,
With face of flint and nerve of steel;
Yet why was Richard made a king,
If not to do a Kingly thing?

A king should cheerful risk his life,
To stay the storms of murderous strife,
To pacify rebellious men,
And send them happy home again.

And well that day he paid the debt,
A slight young prince, *not fifteen yet*;
His father's mantle had, in truth,
Fallen upon the royal youth.

No axe he swung, nor mail he wore,
Like his great namesake long before;
But clad in robes of peace he rode
Fresh from the quiet house of God.

'In Smithfield,' it was told the King,
'there is a monster gathering;'
To Smithfield, then, the King will ride
With Lord Mayor Walworth at his side.

At length before the Abbey gate,
Richard drew bridle. 'Here I wait;
And from this spot will ever ride,
Till these poor serfs are pacified!'

When from his place Wat Tyler saw
The lilies bloom, the lion's paw,
Cried he, 'The King himself is there,
And now's my time to do and dare!

Move not, my men, I'll go alone,
And beard that youngster on the throne;
Yes, horse to horse, and face to face,
I'll set the truth before his grace.'

'King!' said the Tyler, drawing nigh,
'Seest thou those men?' 'Yea, true, and why
Dost ask me such a simple thing?'
'Because,' said Wat, 'I am their King:

And every man has sworn to-day
To do my bidding.' Here, they say,
The rebel with his dagger played;
When Walworth, for his king afraid,

Strode up and struck him. Turned he then,
Bleeding and gashed, to join his men;
But reached them not, for, lo, a squire
Smote the fierce Tyler in the mire,

APPENDIX

With thrust of death. The rebels cried,
'They've killed our captain and our guide!
Now, men, your arrows to the string,
And shoot him dead, this traitor king!'

The fate of king and kingdom hung
Upon his eye, his hand, his tongue;
A thousand bows on him were bent,
A twang, and his frail life was spent,

When, lo, his pluck the danger quelled,
Its boldness never yet excelled;
Into the rebel ranks he sped,
All wrathful they for Tyler dead.

'My men,' he cried, 'what do ye do?
Your chief was false to me and you.
I am your king – come, follow me
To plenty and to liberty!'

The end had come. Some slunk away,
Some thought it wiser to obey,
And in the field were not a few
Who stood, scarce knowing what to do.

The war was done – in that same hour
King Mob was rifled of his power,
And once again his wilful jaws
Felt the strong bridle of the laws.

Chatterbox 14 April 1888

Wat Tyler: Murdered 16th June, 1381
by Leonard Wells

Mark how the conflict still doth wage
Where Labour grapples with its foe;
The watchwords thrill adown our age
As thro' the years long ago.

Hark how the cheers ring loud and long
As some tired leader hurries by –
Some chief who 'mid the battle-throng
Has bravely held our banner high.

Yet comrades, as ye gladly greet
The heroes of our later day,
Forget not those who dared defeat
In many a bitter old-world fray.

'Twas in the leafy month of June
Wat Tyler strove for liberty,
And died in struggling for the boon,
A victim of foul treachery.

Do we not well to guard the fame
Of him who scorned to crouch or yield?
Our tyrants flaunt their bloody shame –
Gaze on the City's tainted shield.

See! There they proudly vaunt the guilt
That laid our dauntless hero low!
Shall we forget the blood they spilt
In those sad days of long ago?

APPENDIX

The mists that brood about the past
Surround him with a clinging haze
Yet still Wat Tyler's form looms vast,
Lit by the light of vanished days.

And in these times of stress and strife,
When labour once more dares to claim
An easier lot, a nobler life,
Again our lips invoke his name.

Oh! People's leader, at the sound
Once more the old stern scenes appear;
We see the peasants gather round
A chieftain void of doubt or fear.

And hope thrills many a saddened face,
And resolution lights each eye,
As on by lane or marketplace
They forward sweep, to do or die.

Mark how the barons' boasted might
Quails 'neath the outraged people's frown,
As in the holy cause of Right
They boldly camp in London town.

Alas! When victory seemed secure,
Trusting a treacherous monarch's word,
The dauntless chieftain of the poor
Fell 'neath a hireling courtier's sword.

Yet shall the tale of how he fell
Ring o'er the tumult of the years,
And thro' the stirring music swell
When Labour's triumph-day appears.

Comrades! The self-same strife we wage
That brave Wat Tyler waged of old;
And, as we dare the tyrants' rage,
His name shall bid our hearts grow bold.

Aye! Still the memory of the brave
Who fought and died for truth and right
Shall thrill us when the war-flags wave,
And nerve us thro' the din of fight!

Reynolds's Newspaper 17 June 1888

Bibliography

Primary Sources

Account of the Life, Trial & Behaviour of Jeremiah Brandreth, William Turner and Isaac Ludlam: who were Executed on the New Drop, in front of the County Gaol, Derby, on Friday November 7, 1817, for High Treason ([Derby]: Wilkins, printer, of whom the Trials may be had, [1817]) Harvard Library School of Law HOLLIS: 005938710

Addison, Joseph and Steele, Richard, *The Spectator* ed. by Morley, Henry (London: G. Routledge [n.d.])

Ainsworth, William Harrison, *Merry England; or, Nobles and Serfs* 3 Vols. (London: Tinsley, 1874)

– *The Manchester Rebels of the Fatal '45* (London: Routledge, 1880)

– *Old Saint Paul's* 3 Vols. (London: Hugh Cunningham, 1841)

– *Guy Fawkes* 3 Vols. (London: Richard Bentley, 1841)

– *Rookwood: A Romance* 3 Vols. (London: Richard Bentley, 1834)

– *Jack Sheppard: A Romance* 3 Vols. (London: Richard Bentley, 1839)

– *The South Sea Bubble* (London: J. Dicks [n.d.]).

And this is Wat's Son, 'All Tattered and Torn' (London: J. Johnston, 1819) British Museum Archives, London 1865,1111.940

Burke, Edmund, *An Appeal from the New to the Old Whigs* 3rd Edn. (London: J. Dodsley, 1791)

Arthur, C.J., *Marx's 'Capital': A Students' Edition* (London: Lawrence & Wishart, 1993)

Black Bess; or, Knight of the Road (London: E. Harrison, c.1866)

Blake, William, 'Wat Tyler and the Tax-Gatherer (after Henry Fuseli)'. Print. In Allen, Charles, *A New and Improved History of England: From the Invasion of Julius Caesar to the End of the Thirty-seventh Year of the Reign of King George the Third* (London: J. Johnson, 1798)

Boucher, Jonathan, *A View of the Causes and Consequences of the American Revolution* (London, 1797)

Boys of the Empire 1889

Bragg, Melvyn, *Now is the Time* (London: Sceptre, 2015)

British Mercury 1714

The Briton 1762

Bronterre's National Reformer in Government, Law, Property, Religion, and Morals 1837

Burke, Edmund, *An Appeal from the New to the Old Whigs* 3rd Edn. (London: J. Dodsley, 1791)

Reflections on the Revolution in France (London: J. Dodsley, 1790)

The Bury and Norwich Post: Or, Suffolk, Norfolk, Essex, Cambridge, and Ely Advertiser 1817

Burch, Henrietta, *Dick Delver: A Story of the Peasant Revolt of the Fourteenth Century* (London: Religious Tract Society, 1889)

Caledonian Mercury 1833

Cassell's Illustrated History of England: A New and Revised Edition 4 Vols. (London: Cassell, Petter & Galpin [n.d.])

The Character of a Leading Petitioner (London: W. Davis, 1681)

Cleave's Penny Gazette of Variety and Amusement 1841

Cleveland, John, *The Idol of the Clovvnes, or, Insurrection of Wat the Tyler with his Priests Baal and Straw together with his Fellow Kings of the Commons against the English Church, the King, the Laws, Nobility and Royal Family and Gentry, in the Fourth Year of King Richard the 2d, An. 1381* (London: [n.pub.] 1653)

– *The rebellion of the rude multitude under Wat Tyler and his priests Baal and Straw, in the dayes of King Richard the IId, Anno. 1381. Parallel'd with the late rebellion in 1640, against King Charles I of ever blessed memory. / By a lover of his King and country* (London: Printed and sold by J.R. and in Westminster Hall, and at the New Exchange, Fleetstreet, and St. Pauls Church-Yard, [1660])

– *The Rustick Rampant or Rurall Anarchy Affronting Monarchy in the Insurrection of VVat Tiler* (London: Printed for F.C. and are to be sold at Westminster-Hall and the Royall Exchange, 1658).

Commonweal 1886-89

The Community Charge (or, the So-Called 'Poll Tax') (London: Dept. for the Environment, 1990)

The Constitution of the United States of America and Selected Writings of the Founding Fathers (New York: Barnes & Noble, 2012)

Converse, Florence, *Long Will: A Romance of the Days of Piers Plowman* (New York: Dutton, 1929)

Cruikshank, George, *A Free Born Englishman! The Admiration of the World!!! And the Envy of Surrounding Nations!!!!!* (London [n.pub.] 1819) London, British Museum BM Satires 1865,1111.2136

Cumberland, Richard, *Richard the Second* (London, 1792)

– *The Memoirs of Richard Cumberland Written by Himself* (London: Lackington, 1806)

Dean, James M. (ed.), *Medieval English Political Writings* (Kalamazoo, MI: Medieval Institute Publications, 1996)

Defoe, Daniel, *The Shortest Way with Dissenters* (London: [n.pub.], 1702)

A Dialogue between Wat Tyler, Mischievous Tom, and an English Farmer (London: J. Stockdale, 1793)

Dickens, Charles, *Oliver Twist* (London: Bentley, 1838; repr. London: Odhams, 1936)

– *Bleak House* ed. by Roberts, Doreen (London: Wordsworth, 1993)

Dobson, R.B. (ed.), *The Peasants' Revolt of 1381* (London: Macmillan, 1970)

Dryden, John, *King Arthur; or, The British Worthy. A Dramatick Opera* (London: Tonson, 1691; repr. London: Tonson, 1731)

Fables Ancient and Modern (London: Tonson, 1700)

Egan, Pierce, *The Pilgrims of the Thames in Search of the National* (London: W. Strange, 1838)

Egan, Pierce James, *Wat Tyler; or, The Rebellion of 1381* (London: G. Pierce, 1847)

– *Wat Tyler; or, The Rebellion of 1381* (London: F. Hextall, 1841)

– *Wat Tyler; or, The Rebellion of 1381* (London: F. Hextall, 1842)

– *Wat Tyler; or, The Rebellion of 1381* (London: [n.pub.], 1845)

– *Wat Tyler; or, The Rebellion of 1381* (London: G. Pierce, 1846)

– *Wat Tyler; or, The Rebellion of 1381* (London: G. Pierce, 1850)

– *Wat Tyler; or, The Rebellion of 1381* (London: W.S. Johnson, 1851)

– *Paul Jones, the Privateer* (London: F. Hextall, 1842)

– *Edward, the Black Prince* (London: W.S. Johnson, 1851)

– *Robin Hood and Little John; or, The Merry Men of Sherwood Forest* (London: W.S. Johnson, 1851)

– *Quintin Matsys: The Blacksmith of Antwerp* (London: F. Hextall, 1839)

Elliot, Charles W. (ed.), *The Harvard Classics: Chronicle and Romance – Froissart, Malory, Holinshead. With Introductions, Notes, and Illustrations* (New York: Collier, 1910)

Emmett, George, *Robin Hood and the Archers of Merrie Sherwood* (London, 1869)

The English Chartist Circular [n.d.]

The Era 1840

Evans, Thomas, *Old Ballads, Historical and Narrative, with Some of Modern Date, Now First Collected and Reprinted from Rare Copies with Notes* (2 Vols. London: Thomas Evans, 1777; repr. 4 Vols. London: Printed for R.H. Evans in The Strand, 1810)

Fielding, Henry, *Joseph Andrews and Shamela* ed. by Keymer, Thomas (Oxford: Oxford University Press, 2008)

Gardiner, Samuel R. (ed.), *Constitutional Documents of the Puritan Revolution* 2nd Edn. (Oxford: Clarendon Press, 1899)

Gay, John, *The Beggar's Opera* 3rd Edn. (London: John Watts, 1729)

The Gazetteer and New Daily Advertiser 1780

The Gentleman's Magazine and Historical Chronicle 1817

Glover, Halcott, *Wat Tyler: A Play in Three Acts* (London: Bloomsbury, 1927)

Goldsmith, Oliver *The History of England, From the Earliest Times to the Death of George II* (4 Vols. London: T. Davies, 1771; repr. 2 Vols. Boston: Chester Stebbins, 1814)

Green, J.R., *A Short History of the English People* (London, 1874; repr. London: MacMillan, 1902)

Guardian 2015

Hardwick, J.C., *Master and Man: A Tale of the Peasants' Revolt of 1381* (London: The Sheldon Press [n.d.])

Harris, Nicholas (ed.), *The Letters of Joseph Ritson, Esq. Edited Chiefly from Originals in the Possession of his Nephew* 2 Vols. (London: William Pickering, 1833)

Henty, G.A., *A March on London; Being a Story of Wat Tyler's Insurrection* (London: Blackie, 1898)
– *With Clive in India: The Beginnings of an Empire* (London, 1884)
– *With Wolfe in Canada: The Winning of a Continent* (London, 1887)
– *A Final Reckoning: A Tale of Bush Life in Australia* (London, 1887)
– *Maori and Settler: A Tale of the New Zealand War* (London, 1891)
– *Under Wellington's Command: A Tale of the Peninsular War* (London, 1899)
– *With Buller in Natal: A Born Leader* (London, 1901)
Here begynneth a lytell geste of Robyn Hode (London: Wynken de Worde [n.d.]) Cambridge University Library Shelfmark: Sel.5.18. English Experience Reprints.
Heygate, William E., *Alice of Fobbing; or, The Times of Jack Straw and Wat Tyler* (London: John Henry & James Parker, 1860)
The History of all the Mobs, Tumults, and Insurrections in Great Britain, from William the Conqueror to the Present Time. To Which is Added, The Act of Parliament and Proclamation Lately Publish'd for Punishing Rioters (London: Printed for J. Moore near St. Paul's, 1715)
The History of Wat Tyler and Jack Straw (London: [n. pub.], 1788)
The History of Wat Tyler and Jack Straw. Being a Relation of their Notorious Rebellion, Which Begun in the Fourth Year of King Richard the Second's Reign, how it was Carried on and Ended in the Death of Wat Tyler, who was Slain by Sir Will. Walworth, Lord Mayor of London, in West Smithfield: with their Villainous Mad Pranks they Plaid and the Mischief they did before they were Dispersed (London: Printed and Sold by Edw. Midwinter, at the Star in Pye Corner, near West Smithfield [n.d.])
Hone, William, *The Political House that Jack Built* (London: Printed for W. Hone, 1819)
Howard, Robert, *The Life and Reign of King Richard the Second by a Person of Quality* (London: Printed for M.L. and L.C. and sold by Langly Curtis, 1681)
Hughes, P.L. and Larkin, J.F. (eds.), *Tudor Royal Proclamations* 3 Vols. (New Haven: Yale University Press, 1969)
Irvin, John (dir.), *Medieval England: The Peasants' Revolt* (1969)
The Iust Reward of Rebels; or, The Life and Death of Iack Straw, and

Wat Tyler, who for their Rebellion and Disobedience to their King and Country, were Suddenly Slaine, and all their Tumultuous Rout Overcome and Put to Flight. Whereunto is added the Ghost of Iack Straw, as he lately appeared to the Rebels in Ireland, wishing them to Forbeare and Repent of their Divellish and Inhumane Actions against their lawful King and Country (London: Printed for F. Couls, I. Wright, T. Banks, and T. Bates, 1642)

James, G.P.R., *Forest Days: A Romance of Old Times* 3 Vols. (London: Saunders & Otley, 1843)

Jenny Diver; or, The Female Highwayman (London: [n.pub.] [n.d.])

Johnson, Charles, *A General and True History of the Lives and Robberies of the Most Notorious Pyrates* ed. by Heyward, Arthur (London: Routledge, 1927)

– *Lives of the Most Remarkable Criminals* ed. by Heyward, Arthur (London: Routledge, 1927)

Johnson, Samuel (ed.), *The Works of the English Poets, with Prefaces, Biographical and Critical* 75 Vols. (London: A. Strachan, 1790)

Keltie, J.S. (ed.), *The Works of Daniel Defoe* (Edinburgh: W.P. Nimmo, 1869)

Kinney, A.F. (ed.), *Rogues, Vagabonds and Sturdy Beggars: A New Gallery of Tudor and Early Stuart Rogue Literature* (Amherst: University of Massachusetts Press, 1990)

Langland, William, *The Vision of Piers Plowman* ed. by Schmidt, A.V.C. (London: Everyman, 1995)

A Letter to Lieutenant Collonel John Lilburne, Now Prisoner in the Tower (London: Henry Hills, 1653)

The Life and Adventures of Wat Tyler: The Good and the Brave (London: H.G. Collins, 1851)

The Life and Death of Iacke Strawe, A Notable Rebel in England: Who was Kild in Smithfield by the Lord Maior of London (Printed at London by Iohn Danter, and are to be Solde by William Barley at his Shop in Gratious-Street ouer against Leaden-Hall, 1593)

Liverpool Mercury 1817

The London Journal 1863

BIBLIOGRAPHY

Luard, Henry Richards, *Flores Historiarum* 3 Vols. (London: Eyre & Spottiswoode, 1890)

MacMillan's Magazine 1866

Maurice, Charles Edmund, *Lives of English Popular Leaders in the Middle Ages: Tyler, Ball, and Oldcastle* (London: Henry S. King, 1875)

Mayhew, Henry *London Labour and the London Poor* ed. by Douglas-Fairhurst, Robert (Oxford: Oxford University Press, 2010)

Memoirs of Oliver Cromwell and His Children 3 Vols. (London: Chapple, 1816)

The Mirror of Literature, Amusement, and Instruction 1824

The Monthly Review, or, Literary Journal 1817

Morris, William, *A Dream of John Ball and a King's Lesson* (London: Longman, 1912)

– *A Dream of John Ball and a King's Lesson* (London: Kelmscott, 1892)

– *News from Nowhere* (London: Longman, 1918)

Morley, Henry *Memoirs of Bartholomew Fair* (London: Chapman & Hall, 1859)

The Morning Post 1817

Munday, Anthony, *The Downfall of Robert, Earle of Huntington* (W. Leake, 1601). Malone Society Reprints.

– *The Death of Robert, Earle of Huntington* (W. Leake, 1601). Malone Society Reprints.

O'Neill, *The Bondman: An Historical Narrative of the Times of Wat Tyler* 2nd Edn. (London: Smith & Elder, 1837)

Newbolt, Henry, *Froissart in Britain* (London: James Nisbet, 1902)

– Newbolt, *Vitaï Lampada* [Internet <www.poemhunter.com/poem/vita-lampada/> Accessed 21 March 2017]

The Northern Echo 2013

The Northern Star 1848

Northcote, James, *The Death of Wat Tyler*, engraved by J.R. Rogers. Print. [n.d.]

Nuttall, P.A. (ed.), *The History of the Worthies of England by Thomas Fuller, D.D.* 3 Vols. (London: T. Tegg, 1840)

The Observer 1819

The Odd Fellow 1840–1841

Oliver Cromwell; or, Cavaliers and Roundheads: A Tale of the Civil Wars (London: W. Strange, 1841)

Our Young Folks' Paper 1886

Paine, Thomas, *The Rights of Man* ed. by G. Vale (New York: G. Vale, 1848)

Parker, Martin, *The Wandering Jew's Chronicle: or, The Old Historian, His Brief Declaration, Made in a Mad Fashion, of each Coronation, that Past in this Nation, Since William's Invasion, For no Great Occasion, But Meer Recreation, To Put Off Vexation* ([n.p.] [n.pub.] [n.d.]) Bodleian Library Broadside Ballads Wood 401(121) RoudV13587

Peacock, Thomas Love, *Maid Marian and Crotchet Castle* ed. by Saintsbury, George (London: Macmillan, 1895)

Percy, Thomas (ed.), *Reliques of Ancient English Poetry* 3 Vols. (London: J. Dodsley, 1765)

Peterson, Joseph H., *The Lesser Key of Solomon: Lemegeton Clavicula Salomonis* (York Beach, ME: Weiser Books, 2001)

A Pleasant Commodie Called Looke About You (London: Wm. Ferbrand, 1600)

Pyle, Howard, *The Merry Adventures of Robin Hood* (New York: Scribner, 1883)

The Quarterly Review 1817

Raymond, G.F. *A New, Universal, and Impartial History of England, From the Earliest Authentic Records, and Most Genuine Historical Evidence, to the End of the Present Year. Containing an Authentic, Candid, and Circumstantial Account of Every Memorable Transaction, Interesting Event, and Remarkable Occurrence, Recorded in the Annals of Great Britain* (London: C. Cooke, 1790)

Reynolds, George William MacArthur, *The Mysteries of London* ed. by Thomas, Trefor (Keele: Keele University Press, 1996)

Reynolds's Newspaper 1869

Richardson, Samuel, *Pamela* ed. by Keymer, Thomas (Oxford: Oxford University Press, 2008)

BIBLIOGRAPHY

Rigaud, J.F. *Wat Tyler Killing the Tax Collector* (1798), engraved by J. Rogers (London: J. & F. Tallis [n.d.])

Ritson, Joseph (ed.), *Robin Hood: A Collection of all the Ancient Poems, Songs, and Ballads, Now Extant, Relative to that Celebrated English Outlaw* 2 Vols. (London: T. Egerton, 1795)

Sala, George Augustus, *Wat Tyler, MP: An Operatic Extravaganza* (London, 1869)

Satirist; or, the Censor of the Times 1841

Saturday Review 1874

Scott, Walter, *Ivanhoe: A Romance* 3 Vols. (Edinburgh: Adam & Charles Black, 1872)

– *Waverley, or, 'Tis Sixty Years Since* 3 Vols. (Edinburgh: Constable, 1814)

Smith, Alexander, *A Complete History of the Lives and Robberies of the Most Notorious Highwaymen, Footpads, Shoplifts and Cheats* ed. by Arthur Heyward (London: G. Routledge, 1933)

Southey, Robert, *Wat Tyler; a Dramatic Poem in Three Acts* (London: W. Hone, 1817)

– 'Wat Tyler; A Dramatic Poem in Three Acts', *Sherwin's Weekly Political Register* (London: T. Sherwin, 1817)

– 'Harold; or, The Castle of Morford' Bodleian MS. Eng. Misc. e. 21 (Summary Catalogue 31777)

The Spectator 1988

Stow, John, *A Summarie of English Chronicles: Containing the Race of Kings Since Brutus the First of this Realm* (London: T. Marshe, 1566)

The Sword of Freedom; or, The Boyhood Days of Jack Straw (London: Boys of England Office [n.d])

Sue, Eugene, *The Wandering Jew* (London: Appleyard, 1845)

Timbs, John *The Romance of London: Strange Stories, Scenes, and Remarkable Persons of the Great Town* 2 Vols. (London: F. Warne [n.d.])

The Times 1787-1989

Walpole, Horace, *The Castle of Otranto* ed. by Lewis, W.S. (Oxford: Oxford University Press, 2008)

Wat Tyler and Jack Straw; or, The Mob Reformers. A Dramatick

Entertainment as it is Performed at Pinkethman's and Gifford's Great Theatrical Booth in Bartholomew Fair (London: J. Roberts, 1730)

The Weekly Magazine, or, Edinburgh Amusement 1769

The Weekly Entertainer: or, Agreeable and Instructive Repository 1817

The Wild Boys of London, or, the Children of the Night 2 Vols. (London: [n.pub] 1866)

Wilson, John Laird, *John Wycliffe, Patriot and Reformer: The Morning Star of the Reformation* (London: Wagnalls, 1884)

The Young Englishman 1867

Secondary Sources

Anderson, Benedict, *Imagined Communities: Reflections on the Origin and Spread of Nationalism* 3rd Edn. (London: Verso, 2006)

Archer, Ian W., *The Pursuit of Stability: Social Relations in Elizabethan London* (Cambridge: Cambridge University Press, 1991)

Arnold, G., *Held fast for England: G.A. Henty, Imperialist Boys' Writer* (London: Hamilton, 1980)

Ashford, David, *London Underground: A Cultural Geography* (Liverpool: Liverpool University Press, 2013)

Ashley, L.R., *Authorship and Evidence: A Study of Attribution and the Renaissance Drama Illustrated by the Case of George Peele (1556-1596)* (Geneva: Libraire Droz, 1968)

Aston, Margaret, 'Corpus Christi and Corpus Regni: Heresy and the Peasants' Revolt', *Past & Present* No. 143 (1994), pp. 3-47

Bakhtin, M. *Rabelais and His World* Trans. by Helene Iswolsky (Bloomington: Indiana University Press, 1984)

Barroll, J.L., *Politics, Plague, and Shakespeare's Theater: The Stuart Years* (Ithaca: Cornell University Press, 1991)

Basdeo, Stephen 'Robin Hood the Brute: Representations of the Outlaw in Eighteenth-Century Criminal Biography' *Law, Crime and History* 6: 2 (2016), pp. 54-70

– 'Radical Medievalism: Pierce Egan the Younger's Robin Hood, Wat Tyler, and Adam Bell' in *Leeds Working Papers in Victorian Studies Volume 15: Imagining the Victorians* ed. by Stephen Basdeo and Lauren Padgett (Leeds: LCVS, 2016), pp. 48-64

BIBLIOGRAPHY

– 'Dying Speeches, Daring Robbers, and Demon Barbers: The Forms and Functions of Nineteenth-Century Crime Literature, c.1800-c.1868' (Unpublished MA Thesis, Leeds Metropolitan University, 2014)

Begiato, Joanne, 'Between Poise and Power: Embodied Manliness in Eighteenth- and Nineteenth-Century British Culture' *Transactions of the Royal Historical Society* Vol. 26 (2016), pp. 125-147

– 'Manly Bodies in Eighteenth- and Nineteenth-Century England' Royal Historical Society Conference: Masculinity and the Body in England, 1500-1900. University of Northampton, July 2015 [Internet <royalhistsoc.org/joanne-bailey-manly-bodies-in-eighteenth-and-nineteenth-century-england/> Accessed 11 November 2016]

Belchem, John, *Henry Hunt and the Evolution of the Mass Platform* (London: Longman, 1978)

Bell, Ian, *Literature and Crime in Augustan England* (Abingdon: Routledge, 1991)

Benedictow, Ole J., 'The Black Death: The Greatest Catastrophe Ever' *History Today* 55: 3 (2005) [Internet <www.historytoday.com/ole-j-benedictow/black-death-greatest-catastrophe-ever> Accessed 17 February 2017].

Beningfield, Thomas J., *London, 1900–1964: Armorial Bearings and Regalia of the London County Council, the Corporation of London and the Metropolitan Boroughs* (London: J Burrow & Co., 1964)

Bevington, David, *Shakespeare* (Oxford: Blackwell, 2002)

Bevir, Mark, *The Making of British Socialism* (Princeton, NJ, Princeton University Press, 2011)

Black, J.B. *The Reign of Elizabeth: 1558–1603* 2nd. Edn. (Oxford: Clarendon Press, 1958)

Bongie, Chris, *Friends and Enemies: The Scribal Politics of Post/Colonial Literature* (Liverpool: Liverpool University Press, 2008)

Boos, Florence and Boos, William 'The Utopian Communism of William Morris', *History of Political Thought* 7: 3 (1986), pp. 489-510

Boulukos, George, 'How the Novel Became Middle Class: A History of Histories of the Novel', *Novel* 42: 2 (2009), pp. 245-252

Bradley, A.C. *Shakespearean Tragedy: Lectures on Hamlet, Othello, King Lear and Macbeth* (London: Penguin, 1991)

Breight, Curtis C., *Surveillance, Militarism and Drama in the Elizabethan Era* (Basingstoke: Palgrave MacMillan, 1996)

Brewer, John, *The Pleasures of the Imagination: English Culture in the Eighteenth Century* 2nd Edn. (Abingdon: Routledge, 2013)

Brooks, Chris, *The Gothic Revival* (London: Phaidon, 1999)

Buick, Adam, 'William Morris and Incomplete Communism: A Critique of Paul Meier's Thesis', *Journal of William Morris Studies* 3: 2 (1976)

Buick, Adam, 'A Revolutionary Socialist', *Journal of William Morris Studies* 6: 1 (1984), pp. 18-28

Burke, Peter, *Popular Culture in Early Modern Europe* 3rd Edn. (Farnham: Ashgate, 2009)

Burns, Arthur and Innes, Joanna (eds.), *Rethinking the Age of Reform: Britain 1780-1850* (Cambridge: Cambridge University Press, 2003)

Burstein, Miriam E., 'On a slightly different literary note: *Dick Delver*' *The Little Professor: Things Victorian and Academic* 24 November 2004 [Internet <littleprofessor.typepad.com/the_little_professor/ 2004/11/on_a_slightly_d.html> Accessed 23 March 2017]

Burwick, Frederick, *The Encyclopaedia of Romantic Literature* 3 Vols. (Chichester: John Wiley & Sons, 2012)

Carver, Stephen J., *The Life and Works of the Lancashire Novelist William Harrison Ainsworth 1805-1882* (New York: Edwin Mellen, 2003)

Cavendish, Richard, 'London's Last Bartholomew Fair', *History Today* 55: 9 (2005) [Internet <www.historytoday.com/richard-cavendish/ londons-last-bartholomew-fair> Accessed 26 November 2016]

Charlton, John, 'London, 13 November 1886', *Socialist Review* No. 224 (1998) [Internet <pubs.socialistreviewindex.org.uk/sr224/ charlton.htm> Accessed 5 February 2017]

Chibnall, Marjorie, *The Debate on the Norman Conquest* (Manchester: Manchester University Press, 1999)

Claeys, Gregory, 'The "Survival of the Fittest" and the Origins of Social Darwinism', *Journal of the History of Ideas* 61: 2 (2000), pp. 223-240

BIBLIOGRAPHY

Cone, Carl B., *The English Jacobins: Reformers in Late 18th Century England* (New Brunswick: Transaction, 1968)

Coote, Stephen, *Samuel Pepys: A Life* (London: Hodder & Stoughton, 2000)

Couch, Arthur Q., *Adventures in Criticism* (London: Cassell, 1896)

Dias, Rosie, 'Loyal Subjects? Exhibiting the Hero of James Northcote's Death of Wat Tyler' *Visual Culture in Britain* 8: 2 (2007), pp. 21-43

Dobson, R.B. and Taylor, J. (eds.), *Rymes of Robyn Hode: An Introduction to the English Outlaw* 2nd Edn. (Stroud: Sutton Publishing, 1997)

Draznin, Yaffa C., *Victorian London's Middle-Class Housewife: What She Did All Day* (Westport, CT: Praeger, 2000)

Duggan, Christopher, *A Concise History of Italy* (Cambridge: Cambridge University Press, 1994)

Dunn, Alistair 'The Many Roles of Wat Tyler', *History Today* June 2001, pp. 28-9

Dyer, Christopher, *Everyday Life in Medieval England* (London: Hambledon, 2000)

Evans, Eric J., *Britain before the Reform Act: Politics and Society 1815-1832* 2nd Edn. (Abingdon: Routledge, 2008)

– *The Great Reform Act of 1832* 6th Edn. (New York: Routledge, 2000)

Faderman, Lillian, *Odd Girls and Twilight Lovers, A History of Lesbian Life in Twentieth-Century America* (London: Penguin, 1991)

Faller, L.B. *Turned to Account: The Forms and Functions of Criminal Biography in Late Seventeenth- and Early Eighteenth-Century England* (Cambridge: Cambridge University Press, 1987)

Faulkner, Peter, *William Morris and the Idea of England* (London: William Morris Society, 1992)

Ferguson, Niall, *How Britain Made the Modern World* 2nd Edn. (London: Penguin, 2004)

Fowler, Simon, *The Workhouse: The People, the Places, the Life Behind Doors* (Barnsley: Pen & Sword, 2014)

Gazeley, Ian and Thane, Pat, 'Patterns of Visibility: Unemployment in Britain during the Nineteenth and Twentieth Centuries', in

Forming Nation, Framing Welfare ed. by Gail Lewis (London: Routledge, 1998), pp. 181-226

George, Dorothy, *Grub Street: Studies in a Subculture* (London: Methuen, 1972; repr. Abingdon: Routledge, 2014)

Gibson, N.H., *The Shakespeare Claimants: A Critical Survey of the Four Principal Theories Concerning the Authorship of the Shakespearean Plays* (Abingdon: Routledge, 2005)

Gilvary, Kevin (ed.), *Dating Shakespeare's Plays: A Critical Review of the Evidence* (Tunbridge Wells: Parapress, 2010)

Given-Wilson, Chris, *The English Nobility in the Late Middle Ages* (Abingdon: Routledge, 1996)

Gladfelder, Hal, *Criminality and Narrative in Eighteenth-Century England: Beyond the Law* (Baltimore: John Hopkins University Press, 2001)

Goldstein, Leba M., 'The Pepys Ballads' *The Library* 21: 4 (1966), pp. 282-292

Goodway, David, *London Chartism 1838-1848* (Cambridge: Cambridge University Press, 1982)

Gransden, Antonia, *Historical Writing in England: c.1307 to the Early Sixteenth Century* (London: Routledge, 1996)

Gribling, Barbara, *Negotiating the Late Medieval Past: the Image of Edward the Black Prince in Georgian and Victorian England* (Woodbridge: Boydell, 2016)

Griffin, Dustin, *Patriotism and Poetry in Eighteenth-Century Britain* (Cambridge: Cambridge University Press, 2002)

Groom, N., *The Making of Percy's Reliques* (Oxford: Oxford University Press, 1999)

– 'The Purest English: Ballads and the English Literary Dialect' *The Eighteenth Century* 47: 2/3 (2006), pp. 179-202

Hardwick, Paul, '"Lo, Here is Felawshipe": Morris, Medievalism, and Christian Socialism in America', in *Worldwide Pre-Raphaelitism* ed. by J. Tobin (New York: SUNY, 2005), pp. 235-251

– '"Biddeth Piers Ploughman go to his Werk": Appropriation of Piers Plowman in the Nineteenth and Twentieth Centuries', in *Studies in Medievalism XII: Film and Fiction: Reviewing the Middle Ages* ed.

by Shippey, T.A. and Arnold, M. (Cambridge: Brewer, 2003), pp. 171-195

Harvey, Charles, and Press, Jon, *William Morris: Design and Enterprise in Victorian Britain* (Manchester: Manchester University Press, 1991)

Von Hayek, F., *The Road to Serfdom* 2nd Edn. (Abingdon: Routledge, 2001)

Herring, George, 'W.E. Heygate: Tractarian Clerical Novelist', *Studies in Church History* Vol. 48 (2012), pp. 259-270

Heywood, I. and Seed, J. *The Gordon Riots: Politics, Culture and Insurrection in Late Eighteenth-Century Britain* (Cambridge: Cambridge University Press, 2012)

Hibbert, Christopher, *King Mob: The Story of Lord George Gordon and the Riots of 1780* (Dorchester: Dorset Press, 1990)

Higginbotham, Peter, *Life in a Victorian Workhouse* (London: Pitkin, 2014).

Hill, Christopher, *The World Turned Upside Down: Radical Ideas during the English Revolution* 4th Edn. (London: Penguin, 1991)

– *Puritanism and Revolution* rev. ed. (Basingstoke: Palgrave, 1997)

Hill, Matthew and Fraistat, Neil, *Romantic Circles: A Refereed Scholarly Website Devoted to the Study of Romantic-Period Literature and Culture*, University of Maryland [www.rc.umd.edu/editions/wattyler/]

Hill, Tracey, *Anthony Munday and Civic Culture* (Manchester: Manchester University Press, 2004)

Hilton, Rodney *Bond Men Made Free: Medieval English Peasant Movements and the English Rising of 1381* (New York: Viking, 1973)

– *The Change Beyond the Change: A Dream of John Ball* (London: William Morris Society, 1990)

– and Ashton, T.H. (eds.), *The English Rising of 1381* (Cambridge: Cambridge University Press, 1984)

Hobsbawm, Eric, *Uncommon People: Resistance, Rebellion, and Jazz* (London: Abacus, 1998)

Holt, James C., *Robin Hood* 2nd Edn. (London: Thames and Hudson, 1989)

Honan, Park, *Christopher Marlowe Poet and Spy* (Oxford: Oxford University Press, 2005)

Hughes, Ann, *The Causes of the English Civil War* (New York: St. Martin's, 1991)

Jacobus, L.A., *John Cleveland* (Boston: Twayne, 1975)

Jefferson, D.W., *Walter Scott: An Introductory Essay* (Edinburgh: University of Dunedin Press, 2002)

Jones, Dan, *Summer of Blood* (London: Harper, 2010)

– 'The Peasants' Revolt' *History Today* June 2009, pp. 33-9

Kaufman, Alexander, *The Historical Literature of the Jack Cade Rebellion* (Abingdon: Routledge, 2009)

Kingstone, Helen, *Victorian Narratives of the Recent Past: Memory, History, Fiction* (Basingstoke: Palgrave, 2017)

Kinna, Ruth, *William Morris: The Art of Socialism* (Cardiff: University of Wales Press, 2000)

– 'Socialist Fellowship and the Woman Question' in *Writing on the Image: Reading William Morris* ed. by David Latham (Toronto: University of Toronto Press, 2007), pp. 183-196

– 'William Morris and the Problem of Englishness' *European Journal of Political Theory* 5: 1 (2006), pp. 85-99

Kirkpatrick, Robert, *Wild Boys in the Dock: Victorian Juvenile Literature and Juvenile Crime – Children's Books History Society Occasional Paper XI* (London: Children's Books History Society, 2013)

Knight, Stephen, *Reading Robin Hood: Content, Form and Reception in the Outlaw Myth* (Manchester: Manchester University Press, 2015)

– *Robin Hood: A Mythic Biography* (Ithaca: Cornell University Press, 2003)

– *Robin Hood: A Complete Study of the English Outlaw* (Oxford: Blackwell, 1994)

Knoppers, L.L., *Constructing Cromwell: Ceremony, Portrait, and Print 1645-1661* (Cambridge: Cambridge University Press, 2000)

Kuriyama, Constance, *Christopher Marlowe: A Renaissance Life* (Ithaca: Cornell University Press, 2002)

Lamson, Roy, 'English Broadside Ballad Tunes of the 16th and 17th Centuries', *Papers Read by Members of the American Musicological Society at the Annual Meeting* (September 11th to 16th, 1939), pp. 112-121

Lawrence, W.J., *Pre-Restoration Stage Studies* (Cambridge, MA: Harvard University Press, 1927)

Levin, Carole, *The Reign of Elizabeth I* (Basingstoke: Palgrave Macmillan, 2002)

– *'The Heart and Stomach of a King': Elizabeth I and the Politics of Sex and Power* (Philadelphia: Penn State University Press, 1994)

Levine, J.M., 'Why Neoclassicism? Politics and Culture in Eighteenth-Century England', *Journal for Eighteenth-Century Studies* 25: 1 (2002), pp. 75-101

Lincoln, Andrew, *Walter Scott and Modernity* (Edinburgh: Edinburgh University Press, 2007)

Lindsay, Jack, *Nine Days' Hero: Wat Tyler* (London: D. Dobson, 1964)

Longmate, Norman, *The Workhouse: A Social History* rev. ed. (London: Pimlico, 2003)

LoPatin, Nancy D., *Political Unions, Popular Politics and the Great Reform Act of 1832* (Basingstoke: MacMillan, 1999)

Macdonald, J.A., 'The Revision of *News from Nowhere*', *Journal of William Morris Studies* 3: 2 (1976), pp. 8-15

Matheson, Lister M., 'The Peasants' Revolt through Five Centuries of Rumour and Reporting: Richard Fox, John Stow, and Their Successors', *Studies in Philology* 95: 2 (1998), pp. 121-151

McElligot, Jason, *Royalism, Print and Censorship in Revolutionary England* (Woodbridge: Boydell, 2007)

McKeon, M., *The Origins of the English Novel, 1600-1747* (Baltimore: Johns Hopkins University Press, 1987)

Mentz, Steve and Dionne, Craig (eds.), *Rogues and Early Modern English Culture* (Michigan: University of Michigan Press, 2006)

Millgate, Jane, *Walter Scott: The Making of a Novelist* (Toronto: University of Toronto Press, 1984)

Mitchell, Rosemary, *Picturing the Past: English History in Text and Image, 1830-1870* (Oxford: Oxford University Press, 2000)

Muir, Edward, *Ritual in Early Modern Europe* (Cambridge: Cambridge University Press, 1997)

Myrone, Martin, *Bodybuilding: Reforming Masculinities in British Art 1750-1810* (New Haven: Yale University Press, 2005)

Neuberg, Victor E., *Popular Literature: A History and Guide* (London: Routledge, 1977)

Newbolt, Peter, *G.A. Henty (1832–1902): A Bibliographical Study* (Aldershot: Scolar Press, 1996)

Nicholson, Helen, 'The Hospitallers and the "Peasants' Revolt" of 1381 Revisited' in *The Military Orders Volume 3: History and Heritage* ed. by Victor Mallia Milanes (Aldershot: Ashgate, 2007), pp. 225-233

Oakley-Brown, Liz, 'Framing Robin Hood: Textuality and Temporality in Anthony Munday's Huntingdon Plays', in *Robin Hood: Medieval and Post Medieval* ed. by Helen Phillips (Dublin: Four Courts Press, 2005), pp. 113-128

Oman, Charles, *The Great Revolt of 1381* (Oxford: Clarendon, 1906)

Ormrod, W.M., 'The Peasants' Revolt and the Government of England', *Journal of British Studies* 29: 1 (1990), pp. 1-30

The Oxford Dictionary of National Biography (Oxford: Oxford University Press, 2004; Online Edn. 2008) [www.oxforddnb.com]

The Oxford English Dictionary (Oxford: Oxford University Press, 2017) [www.oxforddictionaries.com]

Pakenham, Thomas, *The Scramble for Africa* (London: Abacus, 1991)

Palliser, D.M., *The Age of Elizabeth: England under the Later Tudors, 1547–1603* 2nd Edn. (London: Longman, 1992)

'The Pepys Collection' *English Broadside Ballad Archive* (University of Santa Barbara, California) [ebba.english.ucsb.edu/page/pepys]

Plummer, Alfred, 'The Place of Bronterre O'Brien in the Working-Class Movement' Economic History Review 2: 1 (1929), pp. 61-80

Poklad, Josh, 'Signs and Blunders: A Critique of the Current State of Victorian Consumption Studies' in *Leeds Working Papers in Victorian Studies Volume 15: Imagining the Victorians* ed. by Stephen Basdeo and Lauren Padgett (Leeds: LCVS, 2016), pp. 165-179

Prescott, Andrew, 'Writing about Rebellion: Using the Records of the

Peasants' Revolt of 1381', *History Workshop Journal*, No. 45 (1998), pp. 1-27.

Raimond, Jean, 'Southey's Early Writings and the Revolution' *The Yearbook of English Studies: The French Revolution in English* Vol. 19 (1989), pp. 181-196

Rapport, Michael, *1848: Year of Revolution* (London: Abacus, 2009)

Ribner, Irving, *The English History Play in the Age of Shakespeare* (Princeton, NJ: Princeton University Press, 1957; repr. Abingdon: Routledge, 2005)

Richetti, John (ed.), *The Cambridge Companion to the Eighteenth-Century Novel* (Cambridge: University Press, 1996)

Rogers, Nicholas, *Crowds, Culture and Politics in Georgian Britain* (Oxford: Clarendon Press, 1998)

Rowse, A.L., *The England of Elizabeth: The Structure of Society* (Madison: University of Wisconsin Press, 2003)

Rubenstein, W.D., 'The End of Old Corruption in Britain, 1780-1860' *Past and Present*, No. 101 (1983), pp. 55-86

Rudé, George, *The Gordon Riots in Paris and London in the Eighteenth Century* (London: Fontana/Collins, 1974)

Russell, Conrad, *The Fall of the British Monarchies, 1637–42* (Oxford: Oxford University Press, 1991)

Russell, J.S., 'Is London Burning? A Chaucerian Allusion to the Rising of 1381', *The Chaucer Review* 30: 1 (1995), pp. 107-9

Salmon, Nicholas, 'A Reassessment of A Dream of John Ball' *Journal of William Morris Studies* 14: 2 (2001), pp. 29-38

– 'The Revision of *A Dream of John Ball*' *Journal of William Morris Studies* 10: 2 (1993), pp. 15-17

Sanders, Michael, *The Poetry of Chartism: Aesthetics, Politics, History* (Cambridge: Cambridge University Press, 2009)

Santini, Monica, *The Impetus of Amateur Scholarship: Discussing and Editing Medieval Romances in Late-Eighteenth and Nineteenth-Century Britain* (Bern: Peter Lang, 2009)

Saunders, Robert, *Democracy and the Vote in British Politics, 1848-1867: The Making of the Second Reform Act* (Farnham: Ashgate, 2013)

Schillinger, Stephen, 'Begging at the Gate: Jack Straw and the Acting Out of Popular Rebellion' *Medieval & Renaissance Drama in England* 21 (2008), pp. 87-127

Shapiro, James, *1599: A Year in the Life of William Shakespeare* (London: Faber and Faber, 2005)

Sharp, Cecil J., *English Folk Song: Some Conclusions* (London: Simpkin & Novello, 1907)

Shepherd, Leslie *The History of Street Literature* (Newton Abbot: David & Charles, 1973)

Shoemaker, Robert, 'The London 'Mob' in the Early Eighteenth Century', *Journal of British Studies* 26: 3 (1987), pp. 273-304

Shore, Heather, *Artful Dodgers: Youth and Crime in Early 19th-Century London* (Woodbridge: Boydell, 1999)

Simmons, Clare A., *Popular Medievalism in Romantic-Era Britain* (New York: Palgrave, 2011)

– *Reversing the Conquest: History and Myth in Nineteenth-Century British Literature* (New Brunswick, NJ: Rutgers University Press, 1990)

Skelly, Colin, 'An "Impossibilist" Socialist? William Morris and the Politics of Socialist Revolution versus Social Reform' *Journal of William Morris Studies* 15: 2 (2003), pp. 35-51

Springhall, John, 'Pernicious Reading? The Penny Dreadful as Scapegoat for Late-Victorian Juvenile Crime' *Victorian Periodicals Review* 27: 4 (1994), pp. 326-349

Stevenson, John, *Popular Disturbances in England 1700-1832* 2nd Edn. (Abingdon: Routledge, 2013)

Stone, Lawrence, *The Causes of the English Revolution, 1529–1642* (London: Routledge, 1972)

Sucksmith, Harvey P., 'Sir Leicester Dedlock, Wat Tyler, and the Chartists: The Role of the Iron-Master in *Bleak House*', *Dickens Studies Annual* Vol. 4 (1975), pp. 113-31

Suzuki, Mihoko, 'The London Apprentice Riots of the 1590s and the Fiction of Thomas Deloney' *Criticism* 38: 2 (1996), pp. 181-217

Swingen, Abigail L., *Competing Visions of Empire: Labor, Slavery, and the Origins of the British Atlantic Empire* (New Haven: Yale University Press, 2015)

Taylor, Antony, *London's Burning: Pulp Fiction, the Politics of Terrorism and the Destruction of the Capital in British Popular Culture, 1840-2005* (London: Bloomsbury, 2012)

Thompson, Edward Palmer, *William Morris: Romantic to Revolutionary* (Pontypool: Merlin Press, 2011)

Thompson, F.M.L., *The Rise of Respectable Society: A Social History of Victorian Britain, 1830-1900* (Cambridge, MA: Harvard University Press, 1988)

Tomalin, Claire, *Samuel Pepys: The Unequalled Self* (London: Penguin, 2012)

Turner, Michael J., *Independent Radicalism in Early Victorian Britain* (Westport, CT: Praeger, 2004)

Vanden Bossche, Chris R., *Reform Acts: Chartism, Social Agency, and the Victorian Novel, 1832-1867* (Baltimore: John Hopkins University Press, 2014)

Villalon, L.J. Andrew & Kagay, Donald J., *The Hundred Years War: a Wider Focus* (Leiden: Brill, 2005)

Walton, J.K., *Lancaster Pamphlets: Chartism* (New York: Routledge, 1999)

Watt, Ian, *The Rise of the Novel: Studies in Defoe, Richardson and Fielding* (London: Chatto & Windus, 1957)

Williams, E.N., *The Eighteenth-Century Constitution, 1688-1815* (Cambridge: Cambridge University Press, 1960)

Williams, Stephen, 'Radical Objects: The Peasants' Revolt Badge', *History Workshop* 19 April 2017 [Internet <www.historyworkshop.org> Accessed 19 April 2017].

Wilson, Ben, *Decency & Disorder, 1789-1837* (London: Faber, 2007)

Wraight, A.D. and Stern, Virginia F., *In Search of Christopher Marlowe: A Pictorial Biography* (London: Macdonald, 1965)

Wright, D.G., *Popular Radicalism: The Working Class Experience 1780-1880* 5th Edn. (Abingdon: Routledge, 2013)

Wurtz, Richard J., 'Medieval England: The Peasant's Revolt (Review)', *Film & History: An Interdisciplinary Journal of Film and Television Studies* 2: 1 (1972), p. 25

Würzbach, Natascha, *The Rise of the English Street Ballad 1550-1650* Trans. Gayna Walls (Cambridge: Cambridge University Press, 1990)

Zemon-Davis, Natalie, *Society and Culture in Early Modern France* (Palo Alto, CA: Stanford University Press, 1965)

Ziegler, Philip, *The Black Death* (London: Folio Society, 1997)

Image Credits
(Images taken from the author's collection, unless otherwise stated)

Ainsworth, William Harrison, *Jack Sheppard: A Romance* 3 Vols. (London: Bentley, 1839)

Converse, Florence, *Long Will: A Romance of the Days of Piers Plowman* (London: J.M. Dent, 1929)

Egan, Pierce, *Wat Tyler; or, The Rebellion of 1381* (London: W.S. Johnson, 1851)

Evans, Thomas, *Old Ballads, Historical and Narrative* (London: T. Evans, 1784)

Morris, William, *A Dream of John Ball and a King's Lesson* (London: Longman, 1912)

Newbolt, Henry, *Froissart in Britain* (London: J. Nisbett, 1902)

Northcote, James, *The Death of Wat Tyler*. Engraving (London: J. Rogers [n.d.])

O'Neill, *The Bondman* (London: Smith & Elder, 1837)

Raymond, G.F. 'The Burning of St. John's Monastery in Smithfield by Wat Tyler and the Rabble', engraving in *Raymond's History of England* (London: J. Cooke [n.d.])

'Richard II appeases the Rebels on the Death of Wat Tyler', engraving in *Spencer's New History of England* (London: Alexander Hogg, 1793)

Rigaud, J. *Wat Tyler Killing the Poll Tax Collector*. Engraving (London: J.F. Tallis [n.d.])

Southey, Robert, *Robert Southey's Poetical Works* (Paris: A. & W. Galignani, 1828)

Index